GW00578624

EAST HAM PALACE

Manager : HARRY LOSS   Box Office open from 10 a.m.   Telephone : GRA.

| 6-30 | MONDAY. NOV. 15TH. 1948 | 8- |

THE VOICE OF THE WHISTLER

★ RONALDE ★

Direct from His Sensational Triumph at Radio City, New York

TOMMY FIELDS
LONDON'S LANCASHIRE COMEDIAN

CONTINENTAL NOVELTY A

RUBY SAGA & C

★ VAL SETZ
THE TALKING JUGGLER

DON COLLII
MUSICAL NOVELTY ACT

JACQUELINE BOYER
THE ORIGINAL MIDGET ELIZABETH

LUCILLE BENSTEAD
"CHLOE"

FR PREST
CLEA

FINS ECLIPSE THEATRE

Chairman PRINCE LITTLER   Man. Director VAL PARNELL   Props. MOSS' EMPIRES, Ltd.   Phone CANONBURY 2345   Manager DAVID W. WEBSTER

| 6.25 | Week of MONDAY, FEBRUARY 4th | 8.40 |

THE VOICE OF VARIETY

RONNIE RONALDE

COLUMBIA'S GREAT RECORDING STAR

GOLD AND CORDELL   JOHN & SUMA LAMONTE
DISTINCTIVE DANCERS

JOYCE   MAGIC AT ITS BEST ROBERT

MAURICE AND MAY GODFREY

HIPPODROM

"ST. GILES" NORWICH
An F.J.B. THEATRE   Resident Manager - DENNY
Direction - F. J. BUTTERWORTH   TELEPHONE - NORWI

| 6.10 ★ | MONDAY, FEB. 8th | ★ 8. |
| | MATINEE: SATURDAY at 2.30 | |

COLUMBIA'S GREAT RECORDING ST

RONNIE RONALDE

BRITAIN'S FAMILY FAVOURITE

ORCHESTRA UNDER THE DIRECTION OF STEFFA

TERRY O'NEILL
WITH PEGGY HAIG
SMILE AWHILE

LES TRAVERSOS
ARTISTRY IN DANCE

LES & LEN ROGERS
STRIKING THE RIGHT NOTE

TONY & RUBY
SENSATION IN MID-AIR

THE ACROBATS EXTRAORD

REXAN0
THE COMFORTABLE COMED

NAT HOP

TRUBE BROS. LTD., London & St. Albans

Theatre Royal
PORTSMOUTH

IN THE HEART OF THE CITY
Chairman & Managing Director: E. H. SPERRING   Manager: C. A. PAICE   In conjunction with MOSS' EMPIRES, Ltd.   BOX OFFICE OPEN 10 a.m. to 8 p.m.   Telephone: 73328

| 6.15 | WEEK COMMENCING MONDAY, JULY 13th | 8.30 |

BRITAIN'S FAMILY FAVOURITE

RONNIE RONALDE

COLUMBIA'S GREAT RECORDING STAR

THE RICHARD SISTERS
DANCING STORY

DICKIE HENDERSON
THE DEBONAIR ENTERTAINER

KRISTA & KRISTEL
OUTSTANDING TWIN TRAPEZISTS

WALTHON & DORRAINE
BALANCING ON THE ROLLER

HACKFORD & DOYLE
Wood & Wind Mostly Wind

WOODS & JARRETT
TWO DARK GENTLEMEN

TRUBE BROS. LTD., London & St. Albans

FOREWORD

BOYS ON THE STARRY WAY TO SUCCESS

by *Arturo Steffani*
who created and presented the '21 Silver Songsters' Boys Choir and Ronnie Ronalde.
This foreword was discovered in his personal papers after his death in 1974 in Guernsey,
Channel Islands.

I have always endeavoured to regard myself as a teacher of stagecraft and boy vocalism
and not in any way as a 'Talent Scout'. It does not need a clever person to realize
whether a boy has a voice or not, and for me to claim 'discovery' of a boy singer serves
no useful purpose whatsoever. It is the polishing and careful guidance of
a voice that becomes the important factor and therein lays the kernel of my work.

Master Ronnie Ronalde, was doubly gifted, not only possessing a fine soprano voice
but could also whistle extremely well. Ronalde had already made one or two radio
broadcasts when Paul Beverley brought him to me. It was his voice that interested me
most, but the possibilities of the inclusion of his whistling abilities at some future date
did not altogether escape me; in fact he was very soon given a number to whistle which
he performed in a manner to which I had no claim, knowing whatsoever about whistling,
although being a countryman I was able to point out and name the common types of
English songbirds, whereupon the lad would proceed to imitate them to an amazing
degree of perfection.

Exasperating hours were spent at the piano, where Ronalde learned to whistle in
perfect tune and tone. This ambitious lad was determined, that his whistling melodies
should not consist of meaningless 'chirps' and 'non-harmonic cadences' but must be
the true melody, perfectly in tune and melodious to the ear. A unique performer.

I have no hesitation in using the words of Oliver Goldsmith about Ronalde:

THE PINK OF PERFECTION

First edition published 1998 (December) by
Blackbird Publications Ltd.
PO Box 328, Silverdale
Auckland, New Zealand
e-mail rronalde@ihug.com.nz

ISBN 0-473-05692-5
Typeset in Times New Roman

Cover concept by Blackbird Publications Ltd.
Design and layout by Blackbird Publications Ltd.

Printed in New Zealand by KB Print Ltd.
PO Box 100 108 NSMC
Telephone: 09-415 6734

Grateful acknowledgement to all whose pictures have been used to enhance my stories.

4

AROUND THE WORLD ON A WHISTLE

By **RONNIE RONALDE**

A life of a poor London boy who whistled up a fortune around the world, starting to earn pennies whistling in the streets as a six year old to become one of the highest paid international entertainers.

MARTIN BELL

HOUSE OF COMMONS
LONDON SW1A OAA

In the fickle and ephemeral world of show business there are few enduring talents. Performers are like butterflies. They flourish briefly and brilliantly, vanish as mysteriously as they appeared and then are quickly forgotten. Today's celebrities are tomorrow's nonentities.

Ronnie Ronalde does not belong in that company. Incredibly, he has completed sixty years of singing and whistling his way into the hearts of millions all over the world. His notes are as perfect, with a birdlike perfection, and his gifts as shining bright as they ever were. Now he has added to them a talent for writing - in his own account of those extraordinary years.

My father Adrian Bell would have loved that, had he lived long enough to read it. He was himself a writer of rare quality. We were neighbours of Ronnie's in Beccles in the East of England at the height of his early fame. Our gardens sloped side by side down to the River Waveny. We could hear Ronnie practising. We were proud of him - not for his renown but for his whistling and singing which were quite unlike anything we had ever heard. He certainly outsang and outwhistled the local birds. We went to his performances at the theatre on the end of the pier at Great Yarmouth, and were flattered to go backstage. My father, who was not an impressionable man, was deeply impressed by Ronnie.

And now, all those years later... My own life has changed quite radically. I have switched almost accidentally from being a war reporter to being an M.P., which is almost as dangerous. I never intended it. It just happened. My father sadly is no longer with us. But the essential Ronnie Ronalde has never changed. He has matured and prospered and conquered another world, the one 'down under'. He is still doing what he always did and doing it better than anyone, with a matchless talent entirely his own. Here's wishing him all the luck he deserves in his seventh decade in show business.

With very best wishes to you both

Martin

Monterey
Roman Ride
Crowthorne
Berks
RG11 6BU

AROUND THE WORLD ON A WHISTLE

When I first saw Ronnie Ronalde, not only did he impress me, but made a sensational impact on the audience.

Whenever I went to see a prospective recording artiste for Columbia Records, I used to pay great attention to the audience. On this occasion the audience went wild even though Ronnie was a new artiste at the time. Things soon altered and from his first record he was always in the charts. His individual brilliant style and his unique presentation deserved the success he became, and the worldwide stardom he still enjoys.

I can't believe Ronnie is celebrating 60 years and still going strong.
His recordings will live forever.

Norman Newell
Ronnie's Recording Manager
for Columbia Records

I dedicate this book
to my
Mother

to my dear wife
Rosemarie

And to my grandchildren

Samuel and Nathan

Stephanie, Richard and Matthew

and
Christopher

So they know what their Pop was all about

Contents

OVERTURE

You whistle when you are happy but you don't whistle when you are sad.

BBC's Terry Wogan, always happy over the radio remarked where have all the whistler's gone? the postman? the paperboy? come back Ronnie Ronalde, all is forgiven!

Neil Finn called his album 'Try whistling This'; Andrew Lloyd Weber's show is 'Whistle down the Wind'.

Jim Bolger and Bob Dole are talented whistlers and so was Hitler, always in perfect tune whistling the complete 'Meistersinger' in a weird sounding penetrating vibrato.

Historically the first musical sound could have been a whistle blown through a hollow bamboo cane.

In the twelfths century a sheep bone whistle was unearthed in Dublin.

The Medieval European Church frowned on whistling it was said to arouse woman's sexual instincts; the American Indian believed in its powers too. The English Church thought whistling was evil and Captain Cook's sailors called whistling the music of the devil, believing it could invite a storm.

Samuel Pepy's Diaries refer to 'streetboys' whistling.

Hudson of Birmingham patented a whistle in 1880 claiming it could be heard 1 1/2 miles away.

The police started to use a whistle in 1885, later one was attached to all Life Saving Equipment.

American Lecturer Charles Hutchen instructed his students to learn to pucker their lips for whistling is an art and Lauren Bacall told Humphrey Bogart, 'just pucker your lips and blow' and when he died and still couldn't whistle Bacall put a gold whistle in his urn inscribed: 'if you want anything just whistle'.

BEGINNERS PLEASE

FIRST HALF

I learned whistling from boys in the streets of London after my uncle Alf, a London taxi driver, said he'd give me a shilling if I could whistle for a taxi which proves there is nothing unusual to be able to whistle but what is unusual is to make a living out of it.

Act One

WHISTLING FOR PENNIES

'Where did you get all that money?' asked my mother.

I had just come in from school, very pleased and excited, holding out two hands full of pennies.

'I earned it with my whistling, Mum!'

I told her about a gang of workmen who, while repairing the road, were interrupted in their toils by my whistling and imitating of 'Songbirds'. Looking up from their hole in the road they realized that it was little me, whistling.

'Go on lad, let's have some more warbling!' said one.

'Just like my blinking canary!' said another.

'I'll give you a penny if you give us another tune!' called a third.

'Well, Mum, you know I like to whistle.'

So I continued to trill away and soon a small crowd had gathered, and at the end of my little Concert the workman who had offered a penny pulled off his cap, dropping his penny into it. He proceeded taking his cap around, reminding onlookers that good talent was worth a few pence.

My mother stood looking at me, tears running down her dear face.

'Here, Mum, it's all for you!'

I knew she was out of housekeeping money, because that very morning before breakfast I'd been sent on an errand to Farrington's Bakery for a loaf of bread 'on tick'.

'Don't cry, Mum, I'll make you lots of money.'

I was thinking that I could always whistle in the street or to the theatre queues and send my brother Alfred, who was three years younger than me, around with a hat.

My parents met and married in Islington, London, where I was born. My grandfather, Charles John Waldron, came from Scotland. He could not write, but signed his name with a cross, and my grandmother, Sarah O'Connor from Ireland most likely did the same, because my father, another Charles found, when he was in his forties, that his birth date had been recorded incorrectly at Somerset House.

My birth date was, I believe, recorded correctly, but it has always been vague to me, because I altered it after a North of England impresario, Jack Taylor, contracting me for his Blackpool *South Pier* Summer Show, told me, that at my young age, I was earning far to much money. This prompted me at once to up my age a few years. This in turn helped me when I was taking my fist steps into Theatre Production, Presentation and Management. It seemed to earn me more help and respect. Not like it was when aged seventeen I told comedian Dickie Henderson's father, Dick Henderson (Tip Toe through the Tulips) to keep to his time. He called me a 'cheeky young sod' and nearly threw his only stage prop, his Bowler hat, at me, but I think he thought better of it as I might have jumped on it.

I believe that my Irish and Scots ancestry has been beneficial in my career as an entertainer, and I must also include the Welsh, who influenced the early part of my life, starting, so I am told, when a Welsh midwife smacked my bottom at the crucial moment. This happened in our Islington flat, which consisted of two and a half rooms and a landing on the top floor of a tenement house. Our sole form of lighting came from fixed gas brackets with mantles on each side of the fireplace. The mantles often broke with us three children playing about and because Mother could not always afford the replacement cost of a penny, we would end up with just a jet of gaslight.

The cooking, also with gas, was done on the landing. For warmth we had an open coal fire in one room. Water was obtained by going down a flight of stairs to a small corner sink with one cold water tap, which would often freeze during the winter months. The Islington Council Water Board would then open a mains tap in the road so that we could collect water in buckets, carry them to our flats and, among other much needed uses, start to clear the by then overfilling lavatories. Our house had one lavatory, down three flights of stairs from our flat, and there was a second lavatory in the backyard, down a further two flights of stairs. These two lavatories served four families and so a chamber pot under the bed was a real necessity, as was the slop bucket on the landing. My father was often forced to use the downstairs sink as his urinal, especially on pub nights, when the two lavatories were continuously occupied.

Off the landing was a short, narrow staircase, leading to a small attic with a lookout window, which I'd use to practice my birdcalls on the neighbours working in their back gardens. They would look up, trying to see the little robin or blackbird, not realizing that it was me, little Ronnie, skylarking. My bird-whistles would gradually slide into the melody of that favourite army march, 'Colonel Bogey', which would really confuse the gardeners.

None of the doors in the flat had keys. The only key used by all four families was the one for opening the street door. This was tied to a piece of string, which could be pulled through the letterbox in the door.

I came into this world when the 'Bisto Kids' were on the adverts and ailments were treated in old-fashioned ways by equally old-fashioned antidotes. The linseed poultice was used for everything from septic wounds to congestion of the lungs and syrup of figs made its way down our throats once a week. My brother, sister and I stood gathered around Mother, who, with spoon in hand, carefully administered a measured dose to each one of us. With our outstretched necks and gaping mouths we must have looked like a nest of newly born thrushes, waiting to receive a share of the communal worm.

When sometimes ill in bed I would listen to the tradesmen down in the street, calling and selling their wares. I was fascinated by their different sounds. The milkman's sounded like a split yodel, 'Yel-up, yel-up', and the coalmen's was 'Coal-er-manner'. I admired these coalmen with their black faces. They would put a hundredweight sack of coal on their shoulder and carry it right up the four flights of stairs to our flat, never complaining.

Often, when there was no money, we would have to go without coal and I would look around for a substitute, such as the tar blocks the Islington Council used to relay the roads. All the boys in the street and me with my little self-made cart followed the road workers, fighting fiercely for a share of the old blocks as the workmen hooked them out to replace them with new. One of those sticky black tar blocks would last a full night in our fireplace, keeping us warm. I used to love watching the dancing flames and the glow these burning blocks radiated, and even grew to enjoy the smell of the blazing tar, which today would horrify the cancer conscious medical world.

As a child I always seemed to be nursing some scars. Once, playing Tarzan on our bed with its old jagged metal bedposts, I sustained a deep long cut from my wrist right down to the tip of the middle finger. I was covered in blood. Mother poured iodine over this horrendous wound, wrapped it tight with some towelling and put me to bed. We couldn't afford to run to the doctor every time something happened.

As head monitor of my class I had the job of distributing books to each desk. For speed I would jump from seat to seat, but one day, unfortunately, I missed one step and hit my nose on the back of an iron-framed bench. Again I was covered in blood, but this time I was rushed to hospital by the master and received seven stitches on my nose. Then, during a fight in the schoolyard, I slipped on the wet asphalt, missed my opponent with my intended right-hand punch but hit the wall instead, severely damaging my hand. To add insult to injury, I then fell onto the other boy's clenched fist and ended up with a huge black eye as well. I really did have my full share of mishaps but my father would say sympathetically: 'You're going to be lucky one day, son, don't worry.' I couldn't quite understand the 'lucky' bit.

I started school at the age of five and vividly remember, due to our usual cold and damp British climate, many children having colds. They would have their handkerchiefs or, more often than not, pieces of rag, fastened with a safety pin to their shirts or jerseys to wipe their forever running noses. I also remember boys walking past me, barefoot, from nearby Hoxton, the birthplace of the notorious Kraye Brothers, making me feel quite sad, especially when it was raining or during the cold winter months. Now, living in New Zealand, I see many children and adults, who enjoy walking barefoot, but then the weather is kinder.

During the thirties was much unemployment and my father had his spell of being out of work. To increase our family income, my mother would go out, singing and playing the piano in clubs and pubs, where she was always in great demand. My mother was also a dressmaker and so could earn some extra money. Normally, when my father was in work, he would take out two pounds every Friday from his weekly wage packet and give it to my mother for her week's housekeeping. There were five of us to feed, a Chow dog and a cat. The rent alone was 10 shillings and with food, coal, gas and clothes to purchase, my mother was always short of money. There were many times when my father could not go to the local Pub for a beer, which was purgatory for him - and for the family. After finishing work in the evenings he would get off the bus and his steps seemed to be programmed towards the pub, although he was not a drunkard, he just liked to be out, especially on weekends.

Pocket money was in short supply so I was driven to earn my own at an early age. I would run errands for neighbours, collect empty jam jars and sell them, or collect the horse-manure from the streets and sell it to keen garden-lovers. Another moneymaker was the 5th of November, Guy Fawkes Night. We would create a guy out of some old clothes, top the painted face with a hat and put the figure into a cart. Then we sought out the best position in the street, such as the bus stop, where many office and factory girls would pass, for the people to see our creation. A few of the kids would beg for a copper or two, giving much annoyance with their continuous chanting of 'Please remember the guy'. I did my part in whistling Laurel & Hardy's signature tune in time with the girls steps. If they walked faster, I would whistle faster. This used to embarrass them and they would nearly always stop and give me a penny just to get rid of me. With these efforts I managed to have some money in my pocket and when I was hungry, which was often, I could then afford to buy a penny's worth of stale cakes from the baker's just before closing time. Sometimes, when my Mother had been busy finishing off a customer's dress, she would send me with an enamel basin to get some pease-pudding and faggots from a nearby German butcher in New North Road. I usually managed to eat a fair amount of it before returning home.

I have also many unpleasant memories of my childhood, like lice in both my sister Vera's and my hair. Mother, using a fine tooth comb, would search for them in our hair, comb them out onto a newspaper and I took great delight in squashing them. A nurse periodically visited all the local schools and she would carry a basin full of disinfectant and, dipping her comb into this solution, would proceed to part our hair for inspection. Our necks, too, underwent her scrutiny.

A woman doctor arrived every few months for more examinations. I did not like that at all, particularly when she ordered us to drop our pants in order to prod us. The dentist, too, brought a lot of fear to us youngsters, especially when we had to follow up his visit to our school with a trip to the clinic in Rotherfield Street. One could hear children's screams coming through the closed surgery door and when the door reopened for the next little patient to take his seat in the infamous chair, mothers would try consoling their children by promises of sweets after their ordeal.

I also remember sadness in my life, when my brother Alf was suddenly taken to hospital. He had diphtheria and was given little time to live, being 'on the gate', as they said in the thirties, but he did recover. My only hospital stay during my school years was an overnight one to remove my tonsils. Our Indian doctor, who always impressed me by wearing cream spats and sporting a gold-headed walking stick, suggested I should have them out after yet another painful infection.

My Mother lived by principles, such as attendance in school and Sunday school, 'waste not want not', God is always watching you' and cleanliness is next to godliness'.

Once a week Mother took a scrubbing brush, a bar of carbolic soap and a bucket of water to scrub the entire floor of our flat. Religiously she carried out this task until she became too sick to get down on her knees. Then she would ask me to take a day off school and perform this task for her.

Our galvanised tin bath, which hung on the landing wall, was taken down every Friday night and put in front of the living room fire. Kettles and saucepans were filled at the downstairs sink, carried upstairs, put on the gas stove to heat and then poured into the bath. My sister had first go, followed by my brother and me. I can't now imagine how my mother emptied the dirty bathwater down the stairs into the small sink?

One Friday night a woman came to our flat for a dress fitting while I was having my customary weekly bath and, after looking at me, she earnestly advised my mother to take me to the doctor because of what she called my 'pigeon chest'. Next day our family doctor suggested I should drink a pint of cold water every morning followed by 20 minutes of exercises, lifting my arms up and down and at the same time breathing deeply to develop my lungs and chest. This went on for about six months and I did notice my chest becoming bigger and my whistling getting stronger. I realized, that little me, a small boy for my age, could whistle louder than the other boys.

That gave me great satisfaction, although my continuous whistling often drove my mother to breaking point and she would chase me out of the house, even more so when the family in the flat below us would start slamming their doors, indicating that they too wanted a rest from my whistling. Unperturbed, I would carry on whistling, outside, in the street.

Often when coming home from school, I would see people looking up to our flat windows, listening to my mother playing the piano and singing and I would tell them with pride,

'That's my Mum!'

One day when my sister was singing 'Here we are again', I joined in whistling. My mother stopped playing the piano and called:

'Come here, Ronnie, let's hear you whistle it properly!'

and made me repeat the song over and over again until she was satisfied. From then on I became part of my sister's party piece, with Mother playing the piano, Vera singing and me whistling. When Mother taught me to whistle 'Tales from the Vienna Woods' she wanted me to include some bird trills. She achieved this by telling me to make a noise like a purring cat and put a whistle through it.

It took me a long time to master this trill so Mother took me for a day's visit to Westcliffe Gardens, Southend-on-Sea, where she made me listen to the many different songbirds, all trying to outdo each other with their distinct whistles and trills bursting from their little throats, all in varying keys. I was starting to hear the difference in their songs and I loved being out with my mother.

My schooldays were good. The Headmaster, Mr. Taylor, together with Mr. Jackson and Harvey were all kind to me. In spite of my small size I was good at sports and even chosen for the tug of war team. I also enjoyed dramatic work, art, music and being in the choir, which won the accolade as the 'best school choir' at the *County Hall* in London, although the adjudicator called me forward after our performance and informed me that I nearly lost points for my school through continually moving whilst singing. I stood there, in front of the whole choir, with tears running down my cheeks, quite humiliated by his words. I am sure the adjudicator would have been horrified if he'd seen Elvis Presley or Michael Jackson's movements on stage. I suppose I was before my time.

Years later I was reprimanded again by two Moss Empire Managers who wrote a report about me to the head office's chief booker, Miss Cissi Williams, which read:

'It is disconcerting to see Ronalde's legs and arms moving, beating time with the music whilst performing his act!'

It was generally me the masters picked out if a visitor came to our school, probably because my mother had taught me to always speak up and smile, which won me the nicknames 'Smiler' as well as 'Birdie'. Usually I was clean, although I did dislike one particular suit, cut down from one of my father's. My dear mother put the buttonholes on the girl's side. She also had the habit of sewing up my trouser pockets to keep my hands out.

My cousin Harold, from a wealthier part of our family, was educated at Harrow where he had to wear top hat and tails. Clothes he had grown out of would be passed on to me and I used them when I took off Albert Whelan's Variety Act.

Albert Whelan was a favourite of King George Vth, who had requested him to appear in the Royal Command Variety Show. The time allotted by the Management Committee for this last minute Royal request was four minutes and Albert Whelan, somewhat disgusted even cut that.

He started his spot as always dressed like a Gentleman, immaculate in his full Evening dress, Top hat and a silver topped cane tucked under his arm. He walked around the stage taking off his white gloves, a finger at a time, in step to the chorus music of the 'Jolly Boys', with all the audience joining in with his whistling, including King George in the Royal Box. At the end of the chorus, with his white gloves off, he would then usually entertain, sing or tell a story. Only this time Albert said: 'Good evening' and acknowledging King George, looked at his watch, put on his Top hat and with his silver topped cane under his arm went again into the chorus of 'Jolly Boys', reversing what he had done a minute earlier by putting his gloves back on, finger by finger and walked off the stage to tumultuous applause. Albert Whelan must be the only star who has ever done less than the allocated time given to a performer for a Royal Command Performance.

I also loved wearing cousin Harold's colourful waistcoats, thus enticing the bigger boys to call me more names like 'Robin' or 'Canary'. Chanting those nicknames, they would come up behind me and ruffle my hair, which did make me mad, as I had taken great pains in perfecting a side parting.

My father, who had won a prize in his school for the best kept hair, perhaps handed down this pride in appearance to me. I even went as far as using soap to stick my hair down, so it was understandable that I would have a go at anyone who dared to touch it. I'd fight like the mighty Welsh Atom boxer Jimmy Wilde I worked with years later in a Northampton Theatre and had a friendly spar with.

All in our family were clothes conscious. Father wore a bowler hat and in summer a straw hat or a trilby, sometimes a cap, and he meticulously tied his own bow-ties. He would not wear a white stiff collar if it had the slightest mark on it. I have seen him on a Saturday night leave our flat with a scarf round his neck and walk over the Canal Bridge to Hoxton to buy a new collar, so that he could go out that night, spotless. Once he took a waistcoat back to his Jewish tailor, after having worn it for three years, because he did not like the fit.

My mother would buy a remnant of material off one of the stalls down Stoke Newington's Ridley Road Market for a few pennies and make herself a dress and cheeky little hat, ready to wear the next day, although she would not be going anywhere, because my father never took her to a show or a meal. He did, however, have her join him on a Saturday night for a near closing time drink at the pub. Those were the nights when I often thought the end of the world had come. Drink used to make my father quite cantankerous and it did not take much for him to have an argument, brought on by little things, such as my mother wearing the slightest hint of lipstick. He was deeply jealous of my mother and could not bear to see people touch, let alone kiss her, even relations at Christmas, under the mistletoe.

On those Saturday nights my sister Vera and I used to await in fear the pub's closing time. First we heard Mother coming up the stairs and then Father who was already grovelling at something trivial which had happened during the evening. He would go on and on, becoming more and more sarcastic until the supper, which Mother had prepared for him, would end up on the ceiling and we children were screaming until Mr. Owen from the downstairs flat came up to console us. Next morning all would be forgiven with a cup of tea in bed for Mother.

Once I remember Uncle Jim knocking Father's pride and joy, his bowler, off his head and jumping on it. That was after Father had sat for ages on our landing holding his hat over the steam of a kettle and then tenderly brushing it, smoothing the grain in one direction, round and round, until it looked better than new. My mother was the 'belle of the ball'. Men were forever whistling after her; in fact, if she was walking somewhere to see a client about a dress, she always wanted me to walk with her, to keep away strange men who would follow her.

It was during one of those shopping days at Riddley Road Market that I saw and heard Oswald Mosley speak. He stood above a Corner shop surrounded by his 'Blackshirts', ranting away. A Jewish stallholder who continued to bigot against Oswald Mosley's preaching had his face bashed in by some of the 'Blackshirts', spurting blood everywhere, it was quite horrible to watch. They also turned over his stall, scattering all his wares on the street and trampled over them.

Our school choirmaster, Mr. Benge, was great. It was he who asked us boys to 'whistle like birds' during a rehearsal of the 'Birdcatcher Song' from Mozart's Magic Flute for a concert at Islington's Town Hall. The boys made all sorts of funny noises and when they had all finished I chirped my version of a whistled trill.

'Stop!' shouted Mr. Benge. 'Who did that?'

'It was me, Sir,' I answered.

'Come here and do it again!'

I had to whistle again and again. It was my start – I had begun to perform before the school and my mates. But it was my singing voice that gained me the position as a choirboy in the Church of St Helens at Bishopsgate. On April 1st 1935 I was one of the choirboys singing at the anniversary of James Wylford, Merchant Taylor Master. I enjoyed being a chorister, but as a young boy the sermons on Sunday were extremely tiring, as we had to sit still at all times, no talking, we did not even dare to smile. Mr. King, our organist, used to watch us like a hawk through his mirror so we learned the sign language so we could speak with our hands though we did not dare laugh at the jokes. For me, St Helens, popularly called the 'Westminster Abbey of the City', had a very religious atmosphere and was at times quite eerie, especially if I had arrived early in the evening for choir practice and sat alone in the church among the numerous columns, throwing their dancing shadows over the pews.

For our family and most others in Islington, life was a constant and continuous fight for survival. Perhaps this was one of the reasons my father put boxing gloves on me and my brother Alf, so we could learn to stand up for ourselves. I boxed at the Albion Road Club and later the Hoxton Manor, where the trainer manager, Jack Smith, had great hopes for me. This pleased my father no end as he loved the sport and sometimes took me to Islington's 'Collins Music Hall'; reputed to be the oldest in the world, to watch a boxing match. Charlie Chaplin played it in his early days as I did in mine.

The 'Collins' name came from a relative of Agent Joe Collins, father of Joan Collins.

I felt good when I was introduced to Boxer Jack Bloomsfield and Kid Berg. Immediately I imagined being part of the great world of boxing.

In 1936 BBC Television showed for the first time a live world championship boxing tournament match, Eric Boon versus Arthur Donahaugh. Ferry's radio shop in Downham Road, where we lived, brought chairs into his shop and permitted the 'street' to watch this great contest on their TV set. I sat there, among all the grown-ups, cheering at every punch thrown.

When Mr. Benge heard that I was involved in boxing he reminded me that I might not be able to whistle any more if one or more of my teeth were knocked out. This observation worried me so I decided to give up boxing, much to my father's dismay. Jack Smith understood my choice but regretted my decision, although his tuition was of great help to me as I did learn how to defend myself. During my evening walks home from choir practice I often saw groups of rough-looking boys roaming noisily through the streets, harassing folk they thought were not as tough as them and I was stopped a few times. But using their own language to answer them back accompanied by a few well placed left-handers soon made them disappear.

For years my mother tried to move us out of our small flat and eventually we were offered a house of our own, at no extra rent, in Palmers Green. Unfortunately Father was against the move, he did not want to leave 'his' Trafalgar pub mates, so we stayed put. By then I was sleeping in the tiny attic, bitten nightly by the bugs coming out of the walls. I was told that the lumps and bumps on my body were heat spots, but when the school doctor saw my spots during one of her routine school visits she organised for the Islington Council's Fumigation health officers to disinfect our flat. They swept up the bugs in their thousands. I had often helped my mother to paint turps over our iron bedsteads and stand the four bedlegs in tins filled with paraffin to keep the bugs away and squash them under the wallpaper in the dead of the night.

All this seemed quite normal at that time, as were the mice. They used to come out of their holes on the landing and watch my mother iron and she would talk to them. One day I could not get my foot into my boot and soon realized that there was something alive in it. Hastily I removed my foot and held the boot out the window. Sure enough, a mouse appeared, sniffed around its rim and tried to get back in but sadly took the big drop, falling four storeys down. Often I would catch a mouse with my bare hands, especially when Mrs. Owen, who lived in the ground floor flat, shouted for help. Mr. and Mrs. Owen, both from Wales, were always kind to me. From Mr. Owen I learned a lot about carpentry. I was forever watching him in his workroom. He made a gramophone cabinet for us, the showpiece of our living room. It was wonderful to be able to play our few records, others I'd borrow. Mother loved listening to Grace Moore,

Jeanette Macdonald and Gracie Fields. I was more captured by comical songs and of course Caruso. We also had one of a horse race, repeating the words 'Spine Cop wins' and another by Jack Hylton and his band called 'Party Rhymes'.

The coronation of King George VI and Queen Elizabeth in 1936 was celebrated everywhere with organised street parties. Ferry's, decorated with streamers and hundreds of Union Jacks, used the top of his music shop as a stage, and rigged up a microphone and sound system for the musical side of entertainment. From this 'stage' one could overlook our whole street and us kids sitting at the fully laden tables with drink and food, having fun and singing plenty of 'Land of Hope and Glory' and 'Rule Britannia', helped along by the grown-ups. For the first time in my life I was put in front of a microphone by Mr. Ferry and whistled 'Land of Hope and Glory'. The loud echo vibrating back from the walls of our street's houses made me nearly jump out of my shoes, it thrilled me so much. Years later I received a letter from Mr. Ferry, congratulating me on my chosen career of show business, a letter I still treasure.

As usual, during holiday times, my Mother's singing and playing the piano was in great demand at our local Trafalgar pub. Children were not allowed inside so I was put in the garden. From there I could hear her play and I whistled the tunes quietly with her. A man who had just visited the bottom of the garden and was on his way back into the bar heard me, picked me up and carried me inside where my mother was playing and sat me on top of the piano saying:

'Let's hear him whistle, Ann!'

My mother smiled and started to play 'Tales from the Vienna Woods' and I began to whistle. When I had finished there was first silence, then followed a big roar and shouts of:

'More, more!'

Mother and I continued.

By now the pub's manager started to get worried of losing his licence by having a child in the bar if the police should happen to look in, which they often did. Reluctantly I was sent back to the garden. Suddenly a big surprise. Three men came out to me, each holding a beer mug full to the brim with coins.

'It's for you, Ron!'

I'd again earned money with my whistle and again gave it to my mother and again she shed tears.

Little did I know that due to her working at home making dresses, Mother had, from continually stopping the wheel of her sewing machine with her thigh, developed a nasty bruise. This had grown into an open wound and did not heal because she could not afford to stop making dresses. Suddenly this bruise had turned into cancer. She knew she had little time left. Mother was taken to the Metropolitan Hospital in Hackney where they operated on her, and thankfully she came back home again where, on the first day, though weak from her ordeal, she sat at her beloved piano and sang her heart out. It was a joy to us children, hearing the warmth of her voice in our flat again and to the neighbours who'd all missed her daily singing. Sadly, this was to be her 'swansong'. After a while she became very weak and was taken back to the hospital.

About that time I had the honour of becoming a chorister at the Priory Church of St Batholomew the Great in Smithfield. This church holds many memories for me. I remember the day when Canon Savage heard me crying in the vestry. Upon hearing that my mother was so ill each following Sunday he said an open prayer from the pulpit for her. This made me so sad but also proud, that a churchman of his high order cared.

During my Chorister time at St. Bartholomews The Great, our choir had to sing at many weddings. One was a very high society occasion. It included the English Prime Minister, Mr. Baldwin, several Members of the Cabinet, the Brides grandfather, the Marquise of Salisbury, her father Colonial Secretary Sir David Ormsby-Gore, later to become Lord Harlech. The Bride was Mary Ormsby-Gore and the Groom Robin F. Campbell who was the British Minister to Belgrade. Why I vividly remember this wedding was not for its high profile. Oh no!, the reason was: NO Bridesmaids! We Choirboys felt quite cheated as we always had so much fun making eyes at the Bridesmaids during Service.

Father told my mother in hospital that I had been accepted at St Bartholomews. He told me that she was overjoyed and shedding tears of happiness and asked him to have me photographed in my chorister robes so that she could see what I looked like. When the picture was ready I was allowed to take it to her myself, but only after having been warned by Father that Mother was looking very sick and that this would be the last time I would see her. Giving her that picture and seeing the proud look in her tearful eyes as she gazed at it is a moment of my life I will never forget.

Then, giving me a last feeble hug and kiss, quietly she begged me to 'Look after the family, Ronnie! God bless!'

With tears running down my face, I left the hospital. I never saw her again. She fell asleep on 16 October 1936, aged 40.

It was her wish that Alf, Vera and I should not attend the funeral. Father told me afterwards, that there were so many flowers and wreaths from family, friends and neighbours, that at the last minute a local shopkeeper offered his open van to carry the many floral tributes to the graveside, she had been truly loved by everyone.

Her loss was hard to bear. There was no Mum to play the piano, no Mum singing, no Mum to cook for us. Vera had her meals with the Mayer family across the road, Alf and I went to aunts Elsie and Blanche to eat. At 12 years of age I would often go shopping for my father and buy some meat or sausages and cook them in the frying pan. He ate my efforts with a slice of bread. It all had to be done quickly and be ready for him on time as he had only one hour lunch break and in that time also had to get to and from his workplace in the City. I had a two-hour school break, so had plenty of time to shop, fry and wash up. Even then, his principles would not allow him to eat out. I certainly missed my mother. For weeks, everything seemed to be out of balance until it was my birthday and Father gave me a record of 'The Teddy Bear's Picnic' by Henry Hall's Orchestra. This recording brought a smile to my face and started me off whistling again.

After school hours Auntie Blanche, my Mum's elder sister and a professional club singer, took me under her wing and I used to accompany her to different venues such as the 'Mildmay Park Club'. She often would arrange a short spot on the show for me too. It was on one of those nights that a talent scout, Paul Beverly, approached me and next day asked my father for his approval 'to make a star out of me!' Paul Beverly took me, still only a 13-year-old schoolboy, to audition for Leonard Urry's Discovery Show. This was unsuccessful, but he did not let this incident weaken his enthusiasm and often took me around with him, introducing me to Show people and having me perform at different venues. Then Paul started talking about a contract he had drawn up and wished me to sign, the date: 8 October 1937. In it he offered me £2 per week for the first three months then £3 and 10 shillings for the remaining months of the first year of engagement. For one-night performances I would receive a further 15 shillings or two guineas, according to the venue. I asked to take the document home to show my father. This contract was never signed.

My father, Charles Waldron

Mother, grandmother and me at Southend Beach

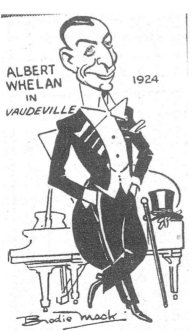

Little Ronnie imitating Albert Whelan (at left)

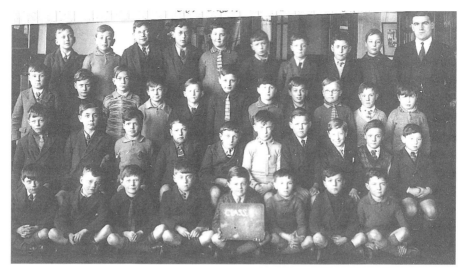

Our class at Ecclesbourne Road School. Phillips, first on the left, gave me my black eye.
I am in the middle.(Mr Harvey, teacher).

Bridesmaid, sister Vera; Pageboy, cousin
Albert;& (in top hat) cousin Harold

Auntie Blanche, who took me to whistle
at the Midway Club

Ecclesbourne School

St Helen's Church

Pawnshop in Islington where my suits were pawned by my stepmother

Choirboy in the church of St Bartholomew the Great, Smithfield

Act Two

A SILVER SONGSTER

I left school at 14 to work with Gerald Brown, Chartered Accountants, in Golden Square off Piccadilly Circus for 15 shillings per week. This appointment was an honour for my school and so important, that my teacher, Mr. Cook, had been instructed to accompany me to the interview.

I had many duties; one was opening the door for our visitors (Lord and Lady Currie, Sir Cecil and Lady Hanbury, Sir Malcolm Rollo, Professor Haldane), another was paying in or drawing out cash from the bank opposite the Ritz Hotel. To do this I would walk through the very select and hallowed Burlington Arcade, where two Beadles were constantly on duty, walking up and down making sure that no one caused a disturbance. My little bit of fun was to let the two parading Beadles pass me. Once they were out of sight I would burst into different bird whistles and hurry on through the arcade. The very elegant shoppers would stop and look up for the bird, not noticing little me. This did amuse me, especially when typical English toffee-nosed gents would expound their ornithological knowledge, stating the specific bird they had just heard. One day I was stopped by a third Beadle who had come up behind me while I was whistling. He gave me a clip round the ear and a stern warning, never to whistle in the Arcade again. Relieved, I took his advice.

In 1991 a farmer was brought to Court and fined for whistling in the Arcade. He pleaded that he did it unconsciously as he was used to whistle when walking, to warn his farmhands of his approach.

So I did get off lightly.

One of the partners of Gerald Brown suggested, I should enrol in an accountancy course. This I agreed to, until Paul Beverly phoned. He had managed to arrange an audition at Bush House for the *Star of Tomorrow* programme on Radio Luxembourg and one with Jack Jackson and his Band on Radio Normandy called *Pond's Serenade to Cream*. After the audition I was not expecting to be accepted, remembering that I had failed before, although I whistled a song accompanied by a piano on the BBC's *Children's Hour*. A week later Paul waited for me outside my workplace. He had wonderful news. I was to be on the Jack Jackson Show. My wildest dreams were about to happen – I was to have my first radio broadcast and a leading critic of *208 Radio News* wrote:

This week's 'Star of Tomorrow' is probably called something quite different by some people. He is an office boy and whistles. Nothing unusual in that, but he whistles really well, so well, that one day he could make his name and his living out of it. The producer of the programme thinks he will, so you can judge for yourselves.'

As a result of this positive reaction, Paul obtained a contract for me to appear for one week in Variety at the *People's Palace Theatre*, Mile End Road, for the princely sum of £8, which of course to me was a lot of money, but I was too scared to accept. I was really frightened to appear alone on stage. This was an unexpected setback for Paul. He then suggested I should do a short stint in a stage act, a boys choir called 'Steffani's 21 Silver Songsters'. This, he thought, would give me experience and self-confidence so that he could then present me as a single act in the Variety Theatres. An audition was arranged at the famous Dominion Theatre, a venue used later for Royal Command Performance shows. I was extremely nervous when the Songsters' boss, Steffani, asked to show him what I could do. 'Please,' I whispered, 'could I have someone play my music?'

Ken Morris, later to become Charlie Chester's 'Professor Ken Morris' on the BBC, was one of the Songsters and accompanied me on his accordion.

After hearing me whistle and sing, Steffani looked pleased and I was taken to the front of the Theatre to watch the '21 Silver Songsters'. First came another group called The Savoy Junior Band with a young George Melachrino as their leader. The Songsters were all dressed alike in short white trousers and blazers with red cravats, white ankle socks and black shoes. Steffani conducted from the orchestra pit. Their opening song was the 'Blue Danube' followed with a solo 'Oh Danny Boy' and 'Il Bacio' and then the 'William Tell Overture' with all Songsters singing together, all their movements in unison. In the finale some boys would each enact something on their own to 'The Lambeth Walk' - tap dancing, banjo playing, long boot dancing, accordion playing, again with singing and coordinating movements. I could see there and then that I would be happy working with these boys.

Gerald Brown was sorry to learn I was leaving, but all wished me luck in my new career. My introduction to the Songsters went quite smoothly, but Steffani did change my name from Ronald Charles Waldron to Ron Warren. This, he said, would be easier for the compare. I used this name for the early years of my career. Soon I started to rehearse new songs for my first appearance with the Songsters, on 5 September 1938 at the *Regal* in Beccles, Suffolk. I was petrified, forever running to the toilet until at last I was on stage. The next day the local newspaper wrote a glowing report and made special reference to my whistling.

September 12th we appeared for a week at the *Garrick Theatre* in Southport, and the following week we were off to Glasgow. This was to be my first performance on the Moss Empire circuit. I caught the early morning train from Kings Cross, my father waving me off with his usual affection, showing a tear which he tried to hide by puffing on his pipe and turning his head, pretending to cough. The train started to pull away, I was on my own and in tears.

By the time I arrived in Glasgow it was dark. Coming out of the station, carrying my suitcase, which was nearly as big as me and rather heavy, I searched in my pockets (a habit I still have today and drives everybody mad) for the digs address I had been given by Steffani. I read Buccleuch Street. When I asked a lady for directions I had great difficulty in understanding her strong Scottish brogue. She kindly put me on a tram for Solihull Street. The conductor then played his part and halted the tram in between stops to save me walking too far with my out-sized suitcase although it still took another half an hour for me to arrive at the digs and climb its endless stairs to the top where, at last, I was welcomed with another Scots voice saying,

'Come in, laddie, the boys are all here!'

Next I was shown where to sleep - with two other boys in a bed in a hole in the wall off the kitchen. Actually it was quite snug, although we had to climb over each other to get in and out. There was a curtain for privacy.

Next day, Monday, we reported for 'Band Call' and it was exciting to watch top stars like Nat Gonella and his Georgians, Dolly Harmer and Wee Georgie Wood, the Diamond Brothers and the Winter Sisters from America during their rehearsals. In awe I stood on the side of the stage and watched, especially Wee Georgie Wood who was only four foot nine inches tall. Often I had been called Wee Georgie Wood by my street mates and many workmen because I was small too and I think it was also my cheeky face which bore a similarity with Georgie's when he did his stage act portraying a very mischievous boy dressed in a school uniform with short trousers, grey socks, one up and one down and a cap with its peak on one side talking in a kitchen scene to his 'stage-mother' Dolly Harmer asking very inquisitive questions indeed whilst she appeared to be ironing. This scene brought flooding back memories of my mother standing on our landing, ironing, whilst I used to kick a ball with other children from our street, like Billy Sparks and his cousin Benny Dean. They were both older than me and always talking about boxing. One afternoon the father of one of the street boys came up to us and hit Billy, because apparently Billy had hit his son. Immediately Billy put his fists up and started to box like a prizefighter, giving blow for blow. I have never forgotten this incident.

The war separated us when our families were bombed out of Islington by a German land mine which fell right where we used to play. The bomb crater, big enough to take six London buses, was featured in the *London Illustrated* as the largest of the war. You can imagine my surprise when years later I read that one of the courageous 'Cockleshell Heroes' who penetrated enemy country was none other than my old street pal, Billy Sparks, the highly decorated Corporal William Sparks and with interest I read the article which was printed in the *International Express* during 1995, the year of remembrance.

'Which was the most famous naval action?' the paper asked.

'Beyond any doubt, the brilliant British Marine Commando raid which took a midget submarine 'HMS Georgie Wood' to within five miles of the enemy coast at Fuglaskar Cove. Cleverly painted to resemble a giant pilchard, it was able to slide in at night under the very noses of the shore batteries and capture a dozen prominent Icelandic herring. They were grilled by the MI5.'

In our Silver Songster's act I soon whistled a chorus of the 'Lambeth Walk' on my own, under Steffani's tuition my confidence slowly began to grow. When Steffani booked the American Whistler Fred Lowery on our same bill I was quite excited when he showed me how he relaxed his lips to control the blowing of air to produce his unique style of whistle. Fred Lowery was assisted by a lady who guided him nightly on and off the stage, as his vision was impaired. In America he was with the Vincent Lopez orchestra and later joined the Horace Heidt's orchestra. During one of my first seasons at *Radio City Music Hall* in New York the Horace Heidt's orchestra appeared at the *Strand Theatre* on Broadway and after catching my show Horace sent his Manager to see me with the offer to join his band. Later I was told why? Fred Lowery had just left him.

After Glasgow we travelled to Bolton, Morecambe and on to London where we played three shows a day at the *Premier Theatre* Eastham, alternating with two at the *Broadway* Stratford. This was my first introduction to five shows a day, the first to start at 2pm and the last at 10pm. To be on time at every theatre, Steffani had a coach ferry us through the London traffic. Naturally we had lots of fun whistling and shouting at passing girls and found it fascinating to see the City and West End lights coming on, turning the night into a blaze of colour.

As mentioned before, my association with Steffani as Paul Beverly's 'protege' was to be temporary, but I sensed, in the many talks I had with Steffani, that he would have liked me to stay. He assured me that he did not wish to upset Paul in any way although he could not pay me as much as Paul had offered, which was eight guineas per week if working. But Steffani could guarantee 50 weeks work a year with everything paid for – food, lodgings, travel, costumes and 15 shillings cash per week. He must have watched my face because very quickly he increased this amount to 17 shillings and sixpence and produced a prepared contract from his briefcase. I decided that staying with Steffani would be better for me, because I would gain more experience through nightly performances and learn more musically. I asked my Father to sign Steffani's contract on my behalf, as I was still a minor, on 17th October 1938.

The following week we played the *Empire* in Nottingham, another Moss Theatre, where Billy Cotton and his Band were topping the bill and Steffani had to take the 'Lambeth Walk' out of our programme, because Billy was featuring Ellis Jackson dancing to that music. 'Tops' of the bill always had priority. I was thrilled when Billy gave me credit after our first show with:

'You've got a good whistle kid!'

Later, when I was becoming famous his son Bill Cotton Jun., who was in the music business plugging songs, would offer me many top song titles of the day to broadcast or record for EMI.

The *Theatre Royal* St Helens was followed with the *Dominion Theatre* London, where, naturally the family and many of my school friends came to see me. I was very proud. Again we doubled that week with the *Granada Theatre* Clapham, doing five show a day.

During these hectic weeks, Steffani received a message from his agent, Michael Lyon of Panton Street, that Sandy Powell, one of Britain's top comedy stars wanted a boy singer to act as his 'nephew' for his BBC radio series *'Can you hear me, Mother!'*, who could talk too. Unfortunately our best singer spoke with a distinct Welsh lilt, which would not have sounded right with Sandy's North Country accent. To overcome this, the BBC producer decided that, as it was for a radio show, they could use two boys, one singing and one talking. So I was chosen as the talker. The two of us were driven by Sandy Powell's chauffeur in a huge American limousine to the *Elstree Studios* where Sandy was filming and shown into the 'Star' dressing room where Sandy's mother sat. There was also a budgie in a cage, so I casually whistled at it and she laughed when the bird chirped back at me. Sandy soon arrived and as I told him of the producers singing and talking arrangement, his mother interrupted:

'Sandy, you should hear this boy whistle to your bird!'

He looked at me –'EE, lad, show us!'

So I gave him a few bird whistles and, laughing, he asked if I could whistle a tune? I did. He put his hand up to stop me and announced that he wouldn't need the other boy singing, just me to play his 'nephew', whistling and talking. This turn of events was very exciting for me but not for my friend, who looked so disappointed.

I couldn't wait to tell my father; but really I wanted to tell my mother.

Following these successful BBC radio programmes Sandy expressed the wish for me to tour with him, portraying his 'nephew' and Nat Gonella, who played the music for Sandy's show, also wanted to include me in his band, the Georgians, but I preferred to return to my nest and stay with the Songsters.

After London the Songsters returned again to Scotland, this time to the *Empire* Edinburgh and were featured in a Revue, which was presented by Music Hall Star Gerti Gitana and her husband Don Ross, with a cast of 65 artistes and my 'Monastery Garden' number was carried as 'excellently' in the newspapers.

Gerti Gitana had started out on stage when she was only four years of age with the Tomlinson's Royal Gipsy Children troupe and by the age of eight had already appeared as a single act at the *Tivoli* in Barrow-in-Furness. She made 'Nelly Dean' one of her most famous songs.

During December I made more radio programmes with Sandy Powell and the Songsters finished a fully booked 1938 by entertaining in a Cabaret at the *Mayfair Hotel* in London with Harry Roy's band. A truly exciting year and an unbelievable experience for me, seeing so much during my first few months in the Theatre.

Winters can be cold in Britain and it was certainly cold when we Songsters arrived in Yorkshire. The town was Barnsley. The theatre was not palatial, but it was not the theatre that stayed in my mind, but the Chorus girls. To my surprise the eight Millie Jackson Girls, who were to appear with us in the Show were also staying at the same digs, it surely must have been 'Full House'.

The landlady had made us all welcome with a hefty supper and soon we were off to our beds. My freezing room had two double beds, three boys for each bed! Some of the girls were in the next room. I got quickly undressed and jumped into one of the beds between two of the boys. We all cuddled up for warmth and were soon asleep when suddenly I was woken up by one of my bedmates breathing heavily into my face. This draught from his mouth caused me to turn to face the other way and, putting my arm around the other boy, tried to go back to sleep. But I was confused, was I dreaming? Something felt different! This boy has large, soft breasts!

Hey! I wasn't dreaming! I wasn't cuddling a boy, but a *girl*!

I could smell her, it was fresh and clean and oh, so nice.

I lay still and felt the warmth of her body coming closer and closer until we touched.

She started to cuddle me, she kissed my forehead, my lips and her hands began to wander, slowly down my body. Something was happening to me I had never experienced before. Nature was spurring me on and taking over the running of the show when suddenly, in the quiet of the night a dog barked, a man was shouting. I heard a door open and close and I was in bed in the middle of two boys again. The 'Lady of the Night' had taken flight. I never did find out which chorus girl it was but at that early age I realized that I liked to be in bed with a girl.

During the late thirties Ivor Novello's romantic shows The Dancing Years, Glamorous Night, Careless Rapture and Noel Coward's Bitter Sweet with their Viennese-Bavarian atmosphere were packing every theatre. Steffani thought that the Songsters too, could add a little continental flavour so he dressed the boys in Lederhosen and feathered velour hats to perform the 'Shoe Plattler'.

This called for a trip to Austria with a few of the Songsters to see a team of dancers who were Gold Medallists holders of Marquorstein Dance in Hoch Schneeberg. After the ship's crossing from Harwich to Hook van Holland the tour continued by rail first to Berlin and then on to Prague, Vienna and via Southern Bavaria, Switzerland and Paris back to London. The train journey through Germany was not pleasant, as it seemed to confirm the fears held in some quarters that Hitler was gaining on momentum. Many train compartments were full with soldiers, wearing uniforms or 'Blackshirts', complete with badges or armlets adorned with Hitler's swastika.

During a railway stop one of the Songsters ran to get a cup of tea and was surprised to be told, when asking for two spoons full of sugar, that there was an extra charge for the sugar. When he asked why he was told it's going towards the 'Hitler's Winter Relief Fund'.

Although the stay in Austria was short, Steffani booked seats for Franz Lehar's 'Land of Smiles' with Richard Tauber at the Vienna's *Opera House*. We wished we could afford Richard Tauber for our Shows but were able to book Darroll Richard, Tauber's understudy. Years later I met Richard Tauber and bought the grand piano he used to play on stage at the *Cambridge* Theatre. I have kept the piano keys embroidered felt cover and it graces the keyboard of my grand piano in New Zealand.

Richard Tauber, married to Diane Napier, loved entertaining well into the early hours sitting at a piano, singing. He also had a nurse looking after him and if he ever started to feel cold she would immediately run a hot bath for him. He lived the life of an Austrian Aristocrat to the full.

A Bavarian scene was soon drawn up and constructed by one of Harry Drury's scenic artistes whilst we Songsters learned the various hand and thigh slapping routines which was enjoyed by the audience as much as by us boys, as we often planted a 'missed' slap on our partner.

When I told Steffani that my grandparents used to yodel a song together called the 'Yodelling Boy' he thought I should be able to yodel too. Very quickly I found that I could do it so he started to rehearse the song with me for this new scene. It became a showstopper.

Albert Ketelby's 'In a Monastery Garden' was soon to become my showpiece (I was proud when I received a letter from him personally, congratulating me on the interpretation of his music), especially with a spectacular Cathedral scene behind me, featured as the finale of the Songsters' act. To achieve this 'holy atmosphere' the boys had to look innocent and religious. One giggle would have ruined the whole picture. The scenery, bought from the Folies Bergere in Paris, consisted of an enormous backcloth painted in sombre colours, illuminated by stained-glass colourings. The entire scene was designed to lend great depth and height to accomplish this church effect.

There were two 'book wings', one representing an organ with huge pipes, the other Gothic pillars placed on each side of the stage. In addition, the Gothic pillar wing had an octagonal stained glass window painted on muslin near the top, from which the strong beam of an arc-light, placed on a high platform behind it, filtered through to the Songsters, who were standing behind a church pew on stage giving a most realistic impression of a shaft of sunlight cascading into the 'Cathedral'.

This scene also introduced Bert Collins, an actor as well as our Touring Manager. As his hair was snow white, it was easy for him to play the character of a very old churchwarden who was becoming forgetful and frail.

The stage curtain opens with Bert sitting hunched on the steps by the altar, polishing a silver chalice. The priest enters to tell him that his services are no longer required. The old warden, in despair, tries desperately to plead with the priest, but sadly without success and slowly sinks back down onto the steps, sobbing heartbreakingly when suddenly, he 'has' a heart attack and dies.

Before his entrance Bert is fitted with wires fastened to his back, which should lift the 'dead warden' serenely up to heaven.

Unfortunately, at one performance the wires somehow got caught around poor Bert's ankle. The Stage Manager, standing in the side wings, watched in horror as Bert's leg started to move sideways and then slowly lifted off the floor, higher and higher. He frantically hit the emergency button for the stagehands working in the flies to stop pulling up the wire while Bert tried his best to act dead and save the tragic moment. Suddenly all reverence of the scene was broken with a horrendous cry of

'Christ, my leg! Christ, you're taking my bloody leg!'

The audience broke into fits of laughter as the 'dead warden', by now very much alive, was seen flying, upside down, to heaven and using words not normally heard in church.

Many years later, Eric Morecambe and Ernie Wise, in one of their TV shows dressed as monks in a monastery garden were chanting and attempting to whistle to each other, when suddenly one of them was airborne, flying about to my 'Monastery Garden' with all its birdcalls.

We had another angelic scene, depicting the Harp of God. Again this was a backcloth set, with the outlines of an enlarged harp painted on it and twenty-one holes cut out, each large enough for a Songster to put his head through. In this scene we would sing 'The Last Chord', bringing tears to many mothers eyes in the audience. Of course you had to have 21 heads to complete the picture, but at one performance three boys were missing. Steffani immediately asked the Stage Manager for three of his stagehands to put their heads through the missing holes. The front tabs opened, all 21 holes of the harp were full, but Steffani, conducting in the pit, had a look of horror on his face. One of the 'dear little angels' sported a beard and the other two wore moustaches of varying sizes. You can well imagine the audience's reaction. First there was the isolated snigger, which quickly built up to one mighty roar of laughter. Steffani was furious. His first words after the show were:

'Why didn't they bloody well shave?'

Sundays were the days we travelled from town to town and one theatre engagement to another, usually by train. Sometimes journeys were short but others took hours, with the train stopping at every one-horse town. The theatrical landlady's few sandwiches were soon eaten so, when the train stopped, one of us boys would run like mad to the kiosk to get some sandwiches, but if grown-ups were at the stand first he would get pushed aside. We tried to support him by hanging our 21 heads out of the train windows with our mouths wide open. The kiosk holder would take one look and conveniently not notice our messenger who would return empty handed. After a few such incidents I devised a way to overcome this problem: I learned to imitate the stationmaster's whistle. As the train stopped a few boys would rush to get to the kiosk and if the queue was too long I would give my whistle and some boys would shout,

'Train's going, quick', so that the people immediately boarded the train, allowing us to be served very promptly.

I also used this trick if we were late getting onto the train when the stationmaster had already blown his whistle. I would whistle my version, so the train would immediately shudder and stop again, much to the amazement of the station master, who would look down on his whistle in bewilderment, but to the relief of the last boy who was trying to make the train.

One particular travelling day when it was extremely hot we began tantalising each other with who could think of the most types of drinks. Suddenly a new boy spoke up from his corner seat. Having recently attended his first rehearsal with us, he must have heard the titles of several songs mentioned, among them 'Handel's Largo'.

'I'll tell you what I'd like to drink now!' he cried, and we all turned to him.

'A lovely glass of Handel's Largo.'

He seemed quite perplexed at the roar of laughter that greeted his outburst for it was evident that he had been under the impression, that 'Handel' was the brewer's name of fine ales and that the word 'Largo' referred to some sort of 'lager'.

Steffani's Silver Songsters

Cathedral scene of 'dead' church warden

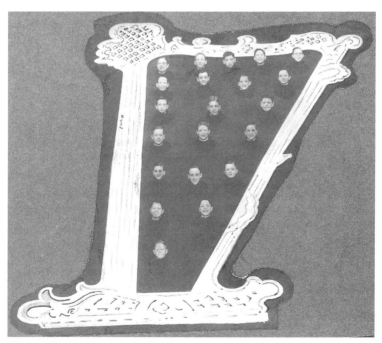

The Lost Chord harp with the heads of 21 Songsters

Train travels –
Top: Conrad Burnett (South Shields);
Denis Ridding (Birmingham);
Paddy Walto (Ireland)
Bottom: Albert Thompson (Scotland);
Auldwyn Humphries (Wales)

First stage photo, aged 14

The Songsters

Nat Gonella

Wee Georgie Wood & Dolly Harmer

Songsters – Ken Morris on piano, Cox twins on guitars

Act Three

THE SCANDINAVIAN TOUR

A Danish impresario wished to present our Songsters' act in Scandinavia.

'It will be a herculean task', said Steffani to his agent. Licenses had to be secured, passports and visas obtained and magistrates, registrars and even Bow Street Police Station had all to play their appointed roles as dates and venues had to be clearly defined.

Arthur Short, Steffani's partner, travelled as interpreter, John Harper was Stage Manager and Professor W.H. Williams from Barry, South Wales, Musical Adviser. It was said that we 21 boys were the finest combination of Songsters Steffani ever presented. Our group included George Wilkinson, a wizard on the banjolele, Les Roy, the only boy long-boot dancer in Britain, Norman Walsh an accordionist and me as siffleur. Vocalists included David Walton, the Irish boy soprano, Aldwyn Humphries, who had made several recordings such as Bishop's 'Lo, Hear the Gentle Lark' and Scotland's Albert Thompson. Many of the boys held Welsh singing awards.

On 7 January 1939, the day before we left for Scandinavia I made my first entry into the recording world with the Songsters at London's *St George's Hall* on the REGAL-ZONO PHONE label. This was quite an experience and I still enjoy playing the old 78 records to hear my first recorded whistle. The purity of this record was confirmed by a music critic with the words: '*of the Highest Standard*'.

When we departed from Liverpool Street Station for our tour of Scandinavia the London press reporters were there for a story and the newsreels took pictures; this was an important event in the world of music. For the first time in history an English boys' choir was setting out to perform before continental audiences with whom, until now, the Vienna Boys' Choir had held undisputed sway with their offering of boy vocalism of mainly religious works. We took comfort, however, from the fact that we were something different covering a far wider field and either thrill or shock our Scandinavian audiences with our act.

We sailed from Harwich on a cold winter's night. On board was a group of similar aged girls going back to school in Denmark. They carried accordions and guitars so it did not take long for our musical instruments to be brought out and we all sat together on deck, making merry, well past midnight. It was all quite romantic, with the bright stars shining and us boys enjoying the first sight of our fair 'Viking' maidens. Naturally, some of the older boys had to find out how they kiss the 'northern' way?

About 2 in the morning we ran into a storm. The ship did everything. Holding on for dear life to the siderail of my bunk, I was sure I was going to die and started to pray for God's forgiveness for everything I had done and not done. When morning came we heard that everyone had been sick and Steffani looked deathly. Had I heard? The boys shrieked, he'd asked for the last rights to be read.

As soon as we docked the Danish impresario Emilio G. Jacobson came on board and escorted us to a quayside cafe where a long table, decorated with Danish and English flags, had been laid out with a smorgasbord. Speeches of welcome were made during the meal, we all clapped and cheered, even though the speeches were in Danish and none of us understood a word of it.

Travelling on the 'Englanderan' express train across Denmark to Copenhagen brought home to us again some of the reality of Hitler's Nazi regime, for on the train were many Jewish families who had managed to escape from the iron hand of Nazism. Many had left their homes with nothing, some were pleased to accept a sandwich or chocolate from us. Their sadness was hard for us young boys to understand.

In Copenhagen the *Hotel Cosmopolite* was the Headquarters for our tour where, for the first time in my life, I had a bedroom with bath all to myself with a maid always entering just as I took a shower to chat.

Our first appearance was in the '*Odd Fellows Palet*', the Concert Hall of the capital, a beautiful building with crystal chandeliers hanging from the lofty ceilings, and elaborate carvings everywhere. We felt that we were in the highest possible sphere of the concert world. For me there was a great feeling of pride – here I was, a 15-year-old London boy, treading in the steps of the great and famous.

When the day of our opening performance arrived, everybody stood anxiously on side of the stage, nervously checking cravats, pulling up socks and then the magic moment was upon us with an auditorium full to capacity. We started with the 'Blue Danube' followed by 'Invitation to the Waltz' and the 'William Tell Overture'. At the end of our act we received thunderous applause and for the first time I heard the 'stamping of the feet'. Encore after encore followed until the House Manager came onto the stage accompanied by four young Danish girls dressed in their national costumes who carried bunches of flowers, handing one to each of us 21 Songsters. Steffani was presented with a huge bouquet. We all stood there, holding our posies, feeling quite embarrassed. We knew of ladies receiving flowers, but men in Britain weren't given flowers!

A review the next day mentioned '*a Boy Whistler, who filled the Concert Hall with the song of the Nightingale, so real, that one could easily imagine being out in the woods among live birds*'.

That first concert on 13 January very quickly brought forth a request by the Danish

Radio to whistle over the air before our tour commenced to Alborg, Odense, Norsens, Aarhus, Nykobing, Randers then onto Oslo, Trondheim, Stockholm, Orebro, Linkoping and finished again with a concert on 18 February in Copenhagen. Looking through my diary now brings back many memories. For instance making a record with the Danish Boys' Choir; visiting the Toborg Brewery where we were all made life members; seeing the Hans Christian Andersen House and a very moving visit to a Blind School where one of the boys held his hands over my fingers while I was whistling and then tried to explain to the others how I did it. This visit triggered the beginning of a life long association with many Vision Impaired Societies in Britain, the USA, Africa, Australia and New Zealand.

We visited the famous 'Kro Inn' where I was presented with a linen napkin, embroidered with all their family names. During the war years they ran an underground movement and as a result some were brutally executed by the Germans. And then I met the 'Olsen' family whose son, Oluf, took me tobogganing. This I did enjoy until I nearly fell off the sledge whilst we were turning a corner coming down at great speed a steep mountain path. Oluf managed to pull me back on his lap where I held on for dear life until, at last, we came to a standstill.

To cheer me up next day he suggested a two-day trip to go polar bear hunting.

'And where would we sleep'? I asked.

'No problem, after we shoot the bear we skin him and cuddle up inside his coat for the night.'

It should not come as a surprise to anybody that I declined his grand offer.

Oluf Reed-Olsen became one of Norway's greatest war heroes, rowing from Norway to England where he then was trained to parachute back into Norway and cause havoc within the German installations. He later wrote a book, 'Two Eggs on my Plate'.

Steffani, suffering with cold feet due to the bitter weather and thick snow, bought himself a pair of galoshes that fitted over his black shoes. You can imagine our giggles when Steffani walked onto the stage in Trondheim's Concert House, sat down at the piano in full evening dress and started to play the piano with his galoshes still on. Again we laughed when Steffani was complaining one morning down the hotel's telephone that his boiled eggs were not cooked enough. A 'don't understand' reply caused Steffani to shout:

'Doesn't anyone speak English in this country?' to which Professor Williams casually remarked, 'How dare they speak their own language in their own country!'

Yes, we boys did have some language problems, although this was usually quickly overcome when we took the Scandinavian girls out; we let our hands do the talking.

Soon the time had arrived for our return journey to England. Although the tour had been a great success, we had collected many fantastic newspaper notices, the Danish impresario proved to be unreliable; he failed to come forward with our return tickets. It was decided to put all us boys aboard the train, without the tickets, and Steffani would stay behind to finalise these last details. We were bundled into the train almost as it was moving out and Steffani hurled last-minute instructions at us to get to the boat at all costs. The fun commenced when a ticket collector came to inspect our tickets. Pretending not to understand him we all began to sing 'Abide with me'.

A second ticket inspector arrived we 'couldn't' understand either but we continued the fun and began to sing the Danish national anthem. After listening to us, he had forgotten why he had come and smiling, carried on with his duties. Some time later a very official looking inspector with all his gold braid came and in beautifully spoken English requested to see our tickets. As quick as a flash a few of the boys from Wales stood up and answered him in Welsh, then the rest of us jumped up and we all sang the Welsh national anthem until, with a shrug of his shoulders and an expression which clearly indicated that he thought everybody had gone crazy, he too gave up.

Fortunately, by the time we reached the port, Steffani had tracked down the impresario and obtained the tickets. This information was telegraphed to the port authorities and we were allowed to board the ship to take us back to England.

It was good to be back on home soil again and to see our families. We had been out of Britain for nearly two months and had experienced so much.

Tuborg Brewery. My first pint

Blind school in Norway

Whistle and be
be glad all
through life

Above& below:Kro Inn mementos

Friend Oluf Reed-Olsen,
Norway's greatest war hero

Being entertained by
the Danish Boy's Choir

London's Liverpool Street Station – departing for Scandinavia.

Act Four

TRAVELS AND ANTICS

Back in England we were given no time off but had to immediately start again travelling the length and breadth of the British Isles, working every week. We also crossed the sea to Ireland, where we appeared in Dublin and Belfast. Our first performance in Dublin was at the luxury *Theatre Royal*, a cine-variety theatre, presenting films, interspersed with combined symphonic orchestral interludes by their resident orchestra, and Variety offerings, usually booked from England. I had always known that the Irish were musical, but I had no idea of the extent their enthusiasm would go to when roused.

We received an astonishing ovation in spite of a rough overnight boat trip on the Irish Sea, where most of us had been seasick, which caused us to arrive in Dublin feeling rather tired for our matinee appearance scheduled for 2.30pm the same day. Yet this performance received unprecedented applause. We took call after call and, as the last curtain fell, the audience would have none of it. They whistled and shouted for more and more, even after the orchestra attempted to play an interlude – they had to give up. The lights went out and the film commenced—but no, they hooted the picture off the screen, compelling the Theatre Manager to put on the houselights again. He attempted to pacify them from the stage, but this only added to their determination to have more of the Songsters.

We were quite unaware of what was going on, when suddenly the Stage Manager came running into the dressingroom and shouted to Steffani:

'Oh, b'Jesus bring the boys back out there or there'll be a bloody riot!'

'But the boys are half undressed!'

'It doesn't matter,' was his frantic answer, 'get them on before they wreck my building!'

We raced onto the stage, Steffani leapt to the piano and the curtain rose again to cheers that lasted several minutes. There we stood, in an array of different attire, singing some more numbers. Words cannot describe the enthusiasm of the audience but at last we managed to get the curtain down.

The Manager, thanking us for our help, informed Steffani that he had phoned the Chief of Police, asking him to send some policemen to be on duty at the stage door for when we left the theatre. We did not understand why all this was necessary until he told us how the overwhelming joy of Dublin people could easily become a source of definite danger. His words proved only too true. Huge crowds had gathered at the stage door, all wanting to show how much they thought of us. In fact we almost had to run to our coach between two rows of sturdy Irish policemen, while equally sturdy Irish men and women tried to pat our heads to give us their blessings. It truly was a week of triumph.

It is said that number 13 is unlucky, and it proved to be so for us Songsters after a very successful variety show at the *Queens Theatre* Rhyll in North Wales. We travelled on a 13th train towards London and made a stop at Crewe Station where our reserved carriage was unhooked to wait for a later pick-up by the London Scots Express. Unfortunately the tail-end of our carriage was left lying across the path of the oncoming Express. Jee were we hit! it knocked us for six. My large suitcase came down onto my head; I remember putting the case back up again and then opening the carriage door and jumping. I saw other boys diving through the broken windows, some were badly cut. The train's engine, still running and emitting steam, was only inches away from me. Doctors, ambulancemen, helpers and newsmen appeared from nowhere. Fortunately I was not injured but even today I feel tension and fear if the ticket inspector opens or closes the carriage doors with a bang or the train fumbles when it starts and stops.

At last, the Songsters had made it onto the front page of the *Daily Express* .

Touring weekly was made more interesting because at the Theatre's Monday morning Band Call, we met many new artists also rehearsing their act. My introduction to Stephane Grappelli came about when I rehearsed whistling the 'Can Can'. That's when he told me the story that the dance, translated meaning *scandal,* had been originally performed by men as they liked to kick their legs with tight fitting trousers into the air and perform splits although it did not take the ladies too long to done their long skirts and replace them with sexy black stockings held up by suspenders, often red, and with their frilly skirts and panties soon entertained the audiences with their high kicks, splits and shrieks.

Stefane also tried to make a little fun with me when he answered my birdcalls with his violin. Often Steffani was mistaken for Stephane Grappelli and asked how his fiddle playing was coming along.

During those Band Calls occasionally one came across a bad pit band or an awkward musical director who would sarcastically criticize the band-parts. This particular MD was quite a bully, acting like a tyrant putting all the acts on edge, especially when, without looking up from his Orchestra Pit to see who was to be next, shouted:

'Right! Next! Chuck 'em down!'

The next 'chuck 'em down' was to be Frank Randle's turn and using a very soft Lancashire accent Frank asked:

'I beg your pardon?'

'Chuck 'em down' repeated the MD, still not looking up.

That's when Frank caused the laugh of the day when he stepped forward to the edge of the stage, lifted his arms with his music sheets above his head and 'chucked' them down into the Orchestra Pit.

'Now' Frank said quietly, 'pick 'em up!'

And then there were unhelpful organists, such as the one that thought he didn't need to rehearse our music. He took his time looking through it while we patiently waited and waited.

Steffani ventured to remark: 'When you are ready?'

'Ready for what?' asked the organist.

'For our rehearsal,' replied Steffani.

'I don't need to rehearse, it's all quite simple'.

Steffani pointed out that such a course was most inadvisable. Our act was a very tricky one to accompany, and he firmly insisted that we should have a 'run-through'. The organist still maintained that it was a waste of time but eventually agreed. He played, although oblivious of Steffani, who was trying to give spoken directions into his ear. At the finish, the organist slammed our music folder together with a confident, 'Well, that's that.'

Steffani complained to him that his playing was far from satisfactory, but the organist replied:

'It'll be all right for t'night. You do know that I am a pupil of Cortot?'

'It had better be,' answered Steffani. He was not concerned under whom the MD had studied, only with the correct interpretation of our music.

During first house, as we were singing and moving to the 'William Tell Overture', we could sense a tension in our performance. The organist was totally ignoring Steffani who stood at his side conducting us. We instinctively knew that there was going to be trouble. We could lip-read Steffani's words:

'Come on! Come on! Faster!'

The organist took no notice.

'Faster! Faster!'

The whole thing was rapidly degenerating into a hopeless fiasco. We were at cross-purposes with the organ. Our faces registered anxiety. We could see Steffani desperately trying to deal with this unhelpful man. Abruptly the organist turned his head and told Steffani to:

'Shut up! Will you shut up!'

That was more than flesh and blood could stand. Steffani, lifting his powerful voice to its limits, shouted:

'Shut up? Shut up? I will knock you off that f.....g organ!'

Unfortunately these very appropriate words went right through the organist's microphone into the audience. Well, first there was a hush followed by a mighty roar. It was like a goal scored at Wembley Stadium. There was pandemonium, we had come to a standstill on stage and didn't know whether to laugh or cry, the organist looked furious, the curtains came down. He and Steffani were called to the front of the House Manager's office for an explanation and the cinema's area director was informed.

The result?

Instant cancellation of all our future bookings of the Gaumont circuit. That one word, so fitting for the occasion, had cost Steffani many thousands of pounds. He and his agent worked frantically to fill all the empty dates whilst we Songsters managed to visit, in our unexpected 'free' time, other shows and usually obtained free seats after showing our 'cards' which we had printed ourselves with our own, agent and act name written on it and some of us also had the letters 'VAF' (Variety Artists Federation) added, proving that we were Theatre Union members. When touring it was not unusual for us boys to see a matinee or film in the afternoons, of course with showing our cards we never paid and therefore I do class myself very fortunate that I was able to see and learn so much about the 'live theatre' at the age of 14, a treat not many youngsters have today.

That's when I saw Harry Lauder (keep right on the end of the road) at the *Blue Hall* in Islington, Talbot O'Farrell at the *Met* Edgware Road, Sam Brown and Elsie Carlisle at the *Hackney Empire* and so many more of our famous artistes.

Soon we were working again and during our engagement at the *Royal Court* Warrington one of our boys had a birthday, so the landlady was asked if we could have a party. We told her that Taffy was from Wales and, as his father had no work, he had to send his entire earnings home.

'Certainly, my luv, I'll give him a party!'

So on the Friday we had a slap up North Country high tea. The landlady had told her neighbours and they brought him gifts and a cake. We really did enjoy ourselves.

In a group of boys such as ours you had many different characters so it was not surprising that the following week at the *Empire Theatre*, York one of them suddenly asked:

'Anyone having a Birthday this week?' There was a pause and quietly a voice whispered:

'Let's invent one!'

So each Friday we acted that it was somebody's birthday with an unsuspecting landlady giving us a party.

Another character was Songster Frankie Couburn, a real 'actor'. He could adopt any mood required to suit his purpose and was sacked many times for doing so. During the war he was taken prisoner in Germany where his chief occupation was to organise their shows. Eventually, using these very costumes, he successfully escaped from prison disguised as a woman and this story made headlines in the press.

Di was our 'studious' Songster. He couldn't wait for our engagement in St. Helens, Lancashire.

'Why? Do you have relatives there? we asked him.

'No but I always wanted to visit Napoleon's grave' he replied earnestly. When Steffani heard of this 'Howler' he reported it to the local newspaper who duly printed the story with the outcome that a day later a letter arrived with some photographs showing Napoleon's grave and was simply signed:

'An old St. Helenean.'

'Oh horror!' – one of my back teeth had started to ache. Even at that early age I had already realised, that my teeth were my 'props'; without them there would be no whistle. I needed a good dentist that would not cost too much.

I remembered my father telling me that when, during the 1926 General Strike, he had a toothache, his two brothers Bill and Jim told him that he should go to the Training Centre of Dentistry at London's Guys Hospital, where they would take his tooth out for free, although if he wanted gas the cost would have been one shilling which his brothers wouldn't allow him to spend as they needed that shilling, the only one they had, to pay for their beer.

That's the place I was going too. Soon I sat in the chair and seven students with one teacher started. After he had a look at the tooth the students were instructed to prepare to extract. I protested.

'Nobody is going to take my tooth out, I just want it filled!'

I too declined the offer of gas and after much to and fro the students started to drill, and drill. After a while the teacher looked again at the tooth, shook his head, looked at me uncertainly, then nodded to the students to carry on drilling, and drilling. Finally he gave the order to start filling the cavity. I was still the owner of my tooth. The students helped me off the chair and had to steady me, one of them asked if I was still able to whistle, I tried, but the result was very feeble and weak. My whole head felt as if it had been under a rolling train for hours. I managed to get to the theatre in time for the matinee. Our Touring Manager, Uncle Bert, passed me on the stairs and stopped – 'I didn't realise that this theatre has ghosts as well!' He told me to get the hell out of there, back to the digs.

The sequel to this story was, that when I could afford the best dental services, my dentist, Mr. Cunningham of Devonshire Place, speaking about me to fellow dentists at his club about the importance of my teeth for my work, was interrupted by one of his colleagues who thought he could remember a 'little chap' coming into Guys and being adamant that the tooth be filled and not to be taken out - 'and that little chap whistled!' Needless to say, my dentist immediately made an appointment for me to see him and this famed back tooth was refilled, but this time capped with gold. Because my teeth are so important to me, I prefer the dentist to work on them without injections, so that I can feel that I am in charge of what he does to them.

There is one thing I am sure all of Steffani's Songsters will agree upon and that is that he treated us boys as 'The Star Act' which we usually were. He would not allow having us called 'Kids'. When Ronald Frankau began making some sly remarks on stage about the 'Kids who come from the wilds of Wales' as we were about to go on, Steffani, who was already in the pit ready to conduct us, heard it and shouted up to Frankau to 'get off the stage, let the Stars commence.' Frankau later apologized.

It was often difficult to find accommodation for us Songsters, so our Manager would go ahead and inspect the booked digs. This time it was Oldham.

'Come this way,' the landlady beckoned, whereupon our Manager followed her through a spotless kitchen towards the back of the house and out to the backyard. There she proudly opened the door of a low built brick house. No sooner was our Manager inside than the meaning of all this peculiar behaviour dawned upon him! The inside had been freshly lime washed, there was sand on the floor and three sturdy perches stretched along the whole width of the building. There were drinking trays with water and square mesh netting covered a window at the far end.

'My husband did it all out for you, it took him over a week. Took real pains with it. I'm sure the Songsters will like it!'

Then, no doubt seeing the look of horror on our Manager's face, she asked anxiously: 'Why, isn't it suitable?'

'Heavens no!' he exclaimed,' This isn't what I requested. Don't you know the Songsters aren't birds, they are all boys!'

'What?' she stuttered. 'Boys?'

'Yes,' he retorted, 'and they will be here soon!'

'Oh my God' she cried, 'Harry, come here a minute, listen to this!'

The poor fellow stood there quite bewildered, scratching his head. We walked into this situation and immediately saw the funny side of it and none more so than Master Eddie Bartholomew, whose cousin, Freddie Bartholomew, was the very famous boy film star.

'You whistle like a bird, Ronnie, you can have the whole aviary to yourself.'

Eventually digs were found and again we slept, five crossways in a bed; one moved, we all moved, however, there were the odd occasions when I had my own room, the bathroom, on condition that I had to be up and out before the first morning riser.

Our date book was full for every week of 1939, including many Sundays, and we even had another trip overseas! A week's engagement during August at the *Derby Castle* in the Isle of Man, made famous by artistes like George Formby and Florie Ford. Many of the boys were interested in the TT motorcycle races and looked forward seeing the island. We went by ship from Liverpool and were soon introduced to Manx folklore as the bus driver told us about saying 'Good morning, fairies' to prevent an accident when crossing a local bridge. Naturally we all thought this hilarious, but when we did pass over the 'Fairy Bridge', we all lifted our caps and chanted 'Morning, fairies!', just in case.

29 August 1939 my 'Monastery Garden' again made headlines in the Manx papers.

Our return journey to Liverpool by boat in September, before travelling on to Blackpool, was interrupted about three in the morning. The whole ship shuddered and then all engines stopped. There was much activity, the crew were moving us boys in all haste up to the top deck from where, through the darkness, we could see a massive submarine floating about a couple of hundred meters off our starboard side. We heard the submarine's commander talking through a megaphone to the captain of our ship. He warned us to proceed from now on with care as there may be other submarines in the area, enemy submarines. We should keep all lights down to a minimum and cut the noise above and below deck. It was exciting for us boys as we watched the submarine slowly disappear beneath the waters of the Irish Sea.

Eventually, after arriving at Blackpool Central Station we were told to cross the road to *Feldman's Theatre* and await instructions. Sitting on our suitcases, we could sense an unusual tension in many passers-by. There were crowds spilling out of the station and groups of children, all carrying gas masks. Each child had a label pinned onto their clothes with their name and address; they all looked sad and lost. Officials with armbands ushered crying children into buses, adults were shouting instructions: 'Come on, hurry up, quickly, quickly!' And then everything came to a halt as people listened to the radio. The British Prime Minister, Neville Chamberlain, was making his historical announcement:

'We are now at war with Germany!'

Strangely, folk seemed to be relieved at the news; I'm sure they all expected it to be over in just a few months.

And then Bert Collins was advised:

'All places of entertainment in Britain were to be closed!'

This, naturally, was a shock – our act was disbanded and we were all sent home.

Steffani, an East Anglian, returned to Beccles in Suffolk to await events. Some of us Songsters never met again, including Conrad Burnett, a nice lad who was lost at sea. It was reported that he sang as he was being carried away by the waves; I was proud to have known him.

Many of my relations were immediately called for wartime services. Cousin Harold lost his life as a RAF Air Gunner, Cousin Albert Kimpton and Cousin Derek after the war went to Canada, Cousin George became a Major in the British Army and stayed in Germany and Cousin James Waldron I never saw again.

I had left the Isle of Man in peace and arrived in Blackpool at war. The Isle of Man was to be closed for the complete duration of the hostilities and used as a prisoner of war camp for captured foreign enemies and all European aliens living in Britain. Many of our stage performers were interned on the island because of their nationalities, causing the break-up of the brilliant piano duo, Rawicz and Landauer, as one of them was not British.

My journey home to London was depressing and slow. The train kept stopping and one could already hear the words:

'There's a war on, don't you know?'

With the order to close theatres I had to think about what I was going to do. It was all quite disappointing that, just as I was beginning to feel confident, everything had suddenly collapsed. After a week at home a telegram arrived from Steffani, bringing a ray of hope. He asked me to join him in Beccles.

Songster Frank Couburn – German prison escapee

with Songster Leo Yarr

Mona Queen

Resting in front of Derby Castle Theatre, Isle of Man

George Formby

Act Five

THE WARTIME

Steffani had hired a houseboat. Due to the fact that my father had recently remarried I felt somewhat at a loss in London, so this invitation could not have come at a better moment and I felt soon at home on the beautiful River Waveney, where waking up in a bunk, to the slight movement of the water as the sun started to rise and birds singing, was like being in another world.

Life was bliss, but reality had to be faced. Nick, Steffani's elder brother, the life and soul of our party, saw that we were short of money and suggested that we should go on the dole. In his friendly and comical way, he managed to have us receive our weekly allowance without having to go and sign on daily. This was in spite of Nick volunteering to bring his shotgun to clear the pigeons off the Unemployment office's roof. Unfortunately it all went a bit wrong when he accidentally shot nearly all the roof tiles off, missing the pigeons.

He had signed on as an unemployed bookie's runner, but was soon reminded by one of the officials of his previous job: a shoemaker.

'There's a war on and there's a shortage of shoemakers!'

Nick laughingly retold the story, but to our surprise Steffani suggested that we open a shoe repair business. He leased a double-fronted shop and a beautiful Georgian manor with a couple of acres of garden behind them. Vi, Nick's wife, was mother, cook and bottle washer. I was tea-boy and did a bit of hammering on the bench when any potential customers were near, so it sounded as though we were very busy. Then Nick had another idea.

'I'm going to see an Army quartermaster at the nearby Norwich Barracks and Ipswich

Army camps about boot repairs for the soldiers!'

The meetings were successful and knowing Nick it would have been all arranged with a hell of a laugh over a bottle or two of something. From then on it was all go from early morning to late at night so much so that in desperation Nick had to go back to the Army and ask for assistance which meant, that a few soldiers came every day and repaired their own boots. Only Nick could have arranged this.

The business grew, we added the outlying districts such as Bungay, Diss, Worlingham, Barsham and Lodden to our shoe-repair circuit and engaged the local buses to pick up and deliver our sacks of shoes at the different locations.

Germany had started to drop leaflets about the war, so we had a leaflet printed, stating:

'This is not a German leaflet, but one to tell you that WHILE-YOU-WAIT SHOE REPAIRERS ARE OPEN.'

I can't say what financial arrangements existed between the Army and Nick, but soldiers and officers alike loved to be in the shop, and drink, brought in by the local Kings Head Hotel, was always available in the lounge at the manor.

I was enjoying myself becoming a real country boy and was sorry when Michael Lyon phoned to say that he had started to book us into theatres that had reopened. The government had realised that people must have entertainment, that it was good for the country's morale. Steffani had been excused the call-up, as were many of the theatre impresarios.

We started touring again almost immediately with some of the old but also many new Songsters. Steffani, realising that there was going to be a shortage of artistes, as many had gone to serve their country, thought that I could do a 12-minute single act. For this I needed a long trouser suit and not a Silver Songsters stage outfit. I expressed the wish for a white tuxedo evening suit so Steffani took me to the theatrical tailors, Morris Angel in Charing Cross Road and I chose an off-white herringbone serge cloth. At the tailor's suggestion, we chose a pageboy style jacket as I was so young, with tight-fitting trousers.

A month later I was the proud owner of my first hand-tailored stage suit but I soon found that it gave me some problems I had not bargained with.

Due to the off-white cloth of the trousers, my white shirt-tails hanging down inside each leg would show up under the stage lighting. To prevent this I had to tuck the front of my shirt underneath my private parts and pull the back of the shirt, carefully pleated, between my legs towards the front before pulling up my tight trousers, taking care not to ruffle my efforts. Of course I had to make sure to visit a certain 'little room' first otherwise it would have been a catastrophe to start all over again.

There was another problem. I was a growing lad and having added all those layers of material accentuated a few contours which the chorus girls took a delight in accidentally brushing past when they came off stage, making it at times quite hard and distracting for me not to miss my cue.

Soon I learned to use a pair of scissors and on every new shirt I cut the bottom off just below the waist.

When we arrived at the *Savoy* Kettering on Sunday November 19 I was intrigued to see that Eddie Sharp, the whistling mimic, was appearing that night with Billy Reid, Dorothy Squires, Peter White, Audrey Knight and Sonny Day, Harry Moore and a Dutch Yodeller, George Van Dusen.

Some years earlier, as a schoolboy and just having won a talent competition at Islington's *Carlton Cinema* in Essex Road, the professional whistler Eddie Sharp was to appear. I had asked my Mother to take me and was overawed listening to the man and thrilled to be brought to his dressingroom and allowed to whistle before him, hoping that he would give me a little encouragement. Alas, I came away very despondent, he had told me that I was no good and would not even let me finish my piece. So it was not surprising that I had to see the Sunday concert with the fantastic whistler. Steffani, after hearing his act gave me a quizzical look and I had to agree, Eddie Sharp was not as good as I had told him.

'No' said Steffani, 'he's stayed the same but you, son, you have passed him'.

This time I had no desire to go backstage.

My first pantomime, *Mother Goose* with Miriam Lester, Neil McKay and Arthur Lowrie, opened in December 1939 at the *Globe Theatre* in Stockton-on-Tees. It was also the first time that the Songsters played a six week long season, although we still gave Sunday Concerts, introducing me with my own little act.

It was difficult for the Songsters to stay in one place for long without becoming full of mischief, specially having to spend much of the day in the theatre, as a pantomime was completely different in its running times to the Variety Bills.

One of the boys had taken a great dislike to one of the performers, so when this particular artiste was on stage, performing his love scene to his leading lady, our boy tossed a stink bomb onto the stage. It landed exactly where he wanted it to, between the couple, as they were entwined and engrossed with emotion, delivering their duet. Suddenly you saw her drawing away from her 'lover', her face showing a look of disgust and his turning as red as a beetroot and just as he had declared himself! Fortunately this all happened towards the end of their act, the tabs came down and he sprinted into the wings to find the culprit, but alas we were gone.

Bert Collins had another problem on his hands. One of the bigger Songsters was always after chorus girls and many a time found with one of them behind the tabs in the darkness of the backstage. Bert was worried that one would become pregnant so it was a relief to him, when the pantomime season came to a close and the dancing babes were still babes.

The war was looking as though it would not, as people first thought, be over quickly, especially with the tragic event of Dunkirk. I saw many wounded soldiers with their red ties, showing them to be under hospital care, in the streets of Morecambe, where we were to appear at the *Winter Garden Theatre* with Reginald Foort and his Two Ton Organ. Steffani thought that we should include something patriotic, such as 'Land of Hope and Glory' and chose me to sing it on my own.

'I don't know the words of the verses!' I stuttered, already scared. Whistling solo was okay, but no, he wanted the 'words sung'.

Steffani, seeing me nearly collapse, simply informed me that he would 'fix a card with the words onto the microphone!' The evening show came, Reginald Foort's organ struck up, I walked forward to the microphone in front of a packed theatre and started to sing. Suddenly my nervousness was gone, I sensed the electricity of the audience, and when they all joined in singing the last chorus with me, I felt a shiver running down my spine.

After the performance Reginald Foort came to praise me and suggested that we should record the song together. Steffani, too, was very happy with my singing. The voice I'd had as a choirboy had broken into a man's voice. All my past singing numbers had to be changed and Steffani began to rehearse me as a juvenile lead of the show with songs like 'Ramona', 'Because', 'Marta', 'You are My Heart's Delight' and started to introduce me to songs about birds which he rearranged and the 'The Nightingale Song', 'Song of the Thrush', 'Blackbird' and 'The Lark' were then combined into a medley which took seven minutes to perform, both singing and whistling.

During the late thirties and forties many landladies would be waiting at railway stations to meet in the trains with various artistes on board who were to play their town for the following week. Some offered their homes for extra money, others were genuinely interested in our profession, but all of them were kindly folk. Often they would sleep in their own kitchens, not only if their house was full but also to stoke the back-boiler during the night to provide warmth and hot water.

Toilet facilities were usually situated through the kitchen out the back, nearly all of them right at the bottom of the garden. I have gone through many a kitchen to reach this commodity when, in passing, the landlady would give me some sheets of newspaper with the comment, that there might not be any left out there. This I found most embarrassing and I used to train myself for an 'early morning call' to the Theatre, to see 'if the post was in'.

Playing the Alhambra, Bradford was even more embarrassing when I found that the dig's toilet was situated directly off the kitchen. On top of this the landlady kept her birdcage in the kitchen, close to the WC door.

Unfortunately it was a Minah bird, well known for its capability of imitating with uncanny accuracy any noise or sound it hears long enough.

This bird always sat on its perch with its eyes shut, but as one tried to make an unobtrusive move towards the toilet door, his right eye would open, then, suddenly, all hell appeared to break loose. There were deafening sounds of water running, paper tearing, chain pulling and the most private of noises, wind breaking, to such perfection that one felt obliged to shut the door immediately and make a hasty retreat. The closure of the toilet door brought forth instant silence from the bird, making people believe you must have overdone it with your measure of syrup of figs.

Again, another week lay ahead of going to the Theatre to see if 'the post was in'.

Mother Goose pantomime had finished and we returned to our weekly performances in Variety.

During that time we were also rehearsing for a REX DECCA recording called 'Gulliver's Travels' and the 'Wizard of Oz'. On this I sang with all the Songsters and whistled a few bars of the melody and did some birdcalls too. I also had to speak the words of the town crier. During the following three months, again travelling and performing every week, Steffani was rehearsing us for yet another recording session with DECCA. The themes of these records were: 'A Day With The Army' and 'A Day With The Navy'. For the Army record I was given a cardboard container the size of a shoe box, filled with small stones. This I had to hold and shake in strict rhythm with the music, making it sound as if soldiers were marching past.

On 14 October I began to rehearse for my first Revue, *Nature on Parade*. Bill Parkin presented this show in association with Steffani and during the run I was both performing and assisting the stage manager. We opened October 21st at the *Hippodrome* Bury.

In the show was a 'nude act', La Moya, who asked me if I could draw the tabs on and off for her poses. This worked well until I cut my finger. She immediately offered me one of her 'stage costumes' to cover my wound. It was one of her Elastoplast strips, about three inches long by one inch wide, which she used nightly to cover up a certain part of her lower anatomy. Naturally this brought about a lot of laughter and joking from the boys, but the thought of 'her dress' on my finger affected me very deeply and I became quite infatuated by her. La Moya often invited me for afternoon tea and we became quite happy together. After a few weeks had gone by she told me that the other artistes and my boss Steffani were not happy with our association and this, I think, brought the show to a quick end, as he tried to separate us. My father had entrusted my welfare to Steffani to look after me, and that he did.

Quite a few theatres included 'Nude Acts' on their bills and it was only natural for the Songsters to stand in the wings each night and watch them take their costumes off. I had developed a keen sense of timing and so had been given the job of working the tabs for them.

One night Phyllis Dixie, who with her husband Tracy was a Comedy double act on our bills, stood next to me in the wings. I remarked jokingly that she would look far better taking her cloths off than the nude on stage, to which she smilingly replied: 'Thank you Ronnie, thank you young man'.

Actually our Songsters were quite worried because Steffani seemed to be always seen around her, he must have been smitten by her beauty too.

Some time later she did exactly what I innocently had suggested, she became a nude act and rapidly became the Toast of the West End with her beautiful body and face which had the features of a Greek goddess.

I assisted in many stage assignments. One of them was with the 'street singer' Arthur Tracy, whose signature tune was 'Marta'. At one time I really thought he did come from the streets as he had the habit of clearing his throat and spit before he made his entrance on stage. Whilst appearing on the same bill I was chosen to go on stage, carrying a bouquet of roses, while Arthur asked the audience for the oldest lady to stand up. After wishing her well I would have to take the bouquet to her and give her a kiss and Arthur followed this with singing 'It's my Mother's Birthday Today' as a special tribute to her.

In later years Arthur did very well in Real Estate in New York where he came to see me at *Radio City Music Hall*. He was still in good voice when he reached 97.

Steffani had worked on a new revue called the *Big Barrage* and we opened March 1941 at the *County Theatre* Bedford. The comedian was Jimmy Bryant, Barry Barnes with Matt Leamore as straight man, step-dancers Bryant and Spencer, Doris Sherry, the eight Pom Pom Girls, pianist Renara and actor-Stage Manager Bert Attwood, who later featured in the TV soap Crossroads, with Musical Director Archie Stanton, Steffani's Silver Songsters and Ronnie Warren (me) featured as the 'World's Greatest Whistler', completing the bill. We toured the revue for almost the whole of 1941, although on Sundays the Songsters still appeared at different Theatres with their act and I received my own billing.

At this time the air raids were getting thick and heavy and at the Swansea *Empire* I saw a notice above the orchestra that said:

'Air Raid Alert and All Clear Signals will be advised to patrons by means of red lights, which are placed at each side of the stage. The Performance will continue as normal.'

This, I thought, was quite humorous, as was the theatre programme, carrying an advert, as to how to get your Air Raid Shelter painted with a weather proof paint.

During the run of the show theatre receipts would often take a tumble due to the fear of nightly air raids. Steffani realised he had to reduce the production costs and he also decided to sell Songsters photos at threepence each. We were popular because the mothers in the audience loved us; we reminded them of their own once young sons now away in the war. So it was no surprise when the Songsters sang 'A Boy's Best Friend is His Mother', many handkerchiefs would come out to dry away the tears.

Before the interval Steffani would go onto the stage and tell the audience that the boys would come amongst them with their pictures for sale. Steffani had not bargained for the response. The first interval arrived and the pictures were sold in no time. Second house he gave the Songsters double the amount. The boys again sold out. Next day we had to urgently contact Wilson's Printers of Leicester to hurry up with our order to print a further consignment.

At H*er Majesty's Theatre* Barrow-in-Furness, the BBC Radio was to tape excerpts of our show. On Monday morning the theatre's stage staff warned us that the aircraft carrier *Illustrious* was in dock with:

'They'll be over!' – meaning the German Luftwaffe.

All during the week the air raid sirens were going, and sure enough, on the final night of the show the bombs shattered the town. I was woken up by virtually being shaken out of bed. I tried to get down the stairs as fast as I could to reach the 'beer cellar' which doubled as the hotel's air raid shelter, while flashes of light lit the hall area, when I saw a trembling hotel maid crouching in a corner. Grabbing my arm, she followed me behind the bar where we saw the trap door to the cellar close before our very eyes. I pulled her with me under the staircase and hanging on to each other, we prayed. I had been in raids before but this one seemed to be the worst. With every new explosion I felt her body tightening with fear; I could not possibly tell her that I was afraid too. At last the all clear siren went and I darted to the bar counter to pour us each a stiff whisky. Then I ventured onto the street and felt relieved when I found the Songsters were okay.

Leaving for the *Hippodrome* Chesterfield we were told that the Barrow-in-Furness Railway Station had been badly hit, so a bus took us to the next undamaged Railway station. Eventually we arrived in Chesterfield, alas minus all our scenery, props and costumes. They were to follow. Our digs were opposite the famous crooked Chesterfield church spire, the one, Lord Haw Haw proclaimed that the Germans were going to flatten. Steffani could not understand why I was so worried –

'They usually miss their target!'

'Yes,' I said, 'that's what's worrying me. We're too near that bloody spire!'

Early next day we went to the theatre. All was well until our Road Manager informed us that our scenery truck had not arrived. The Railway Authorities could not trace it but said they would phone the moment they had any news.

Midday arrived and no word – this was serious. At last they located the truck, which had been shunted by mistake onto another line. They promised to try their best and deliver the truck. We had four hours to curtain up and started to make provisions in case the truck did not arrive in time. With the help of the stagehands we looked for the best scenery and costumes the theatre had in store, exchanged our own brightly coloured socks and shirts and when 5.30pm deadline came, the theatre doors opened to admit the audience. Thanks to our MD always carrying a duplicate set of our music, the curtain opened and the 'show went on' to the cheers of a full house. The railway truck eventually arrived three days later.

During a Sunday Concert at the *Grand Byker* near Newcastle the orchestra was playing in the pit under a cover of tight wire mesh netting. On questioning why? we were told that the locals had the habit of throwing rotten fruit at any artiste they did not like, so the musicians had demanded protection against the missiles which often fell short of their target, hitting them instead. I was worried walking onto the stage that night, but at the finale my suit was still white.

Their in-house ghosts have made many theatres famous and to be confronted by one is quite forbidding. My encounter with a ghost happened at the *Gloria Theatre* Chaddesdon. Walking down the large staircase in the foyer with Eddie Bartholomew suddenly a strange spectre wrapped in a silky see-through material and looking very ashen appeared, gliding slowly towards us. We stopped dead in our tracks, this apparition seemed to flow right through us.

'Has the ghost walked?' is one of the sayings in the theatre whilst one is waiting to get paid. Well, I never got paid by this one.

The Company moved on to Luton where fate played its part, I caught impetigo and was covered in festering sores. It was well past midnight and waiting at Crewe Station for our connecting train I felt dreadful so Steffani took me to a quiet waiting room in the middle of the platform to rest. I fell asleep and when Steffani called me to board the train I was quite reluctant to leave. Was I pleased I did though! Half an hour later that waiting room was no more. A direct hit from a German bomb had cleared it away and when we passed again through Crewe Station the following Sunday I saw the platform without its waiting room; I said my little prayer of thanks as we went on our way to our next date.

It should be mentioned that Crewe Station was the heart of the British Railway Network, aptly described by 'the fiddling fool' Comedian and Star of BBC's *Rays of Laugh* Ted Ray as: 75% Artistes and 25% Fish.

During December 1941 Harry Drury booked me for his pantomime *Ali Baba* at the *Connaught* Worthing. I was 17 years old, and for the first time alone in a pantomime. The show was even more pleasurable when I became attached to its leading lady, Marie Sellars. I had developed quite a crush on her and was often invited to her family home. Having put me to bed after one of the Christmas parties, feeling quite poorly, she took me next day to the side and told me that I should be very careful where women are concerned, as I was a 'good looking little blighter!'

The pantomime was a great hit and I received good press notices and comments on my performance.

When the show closed I said a very sad goodbye to Marie, but I appreciated what I had learned from Harry about pantomime production. He had shown me his fantastic stores, how they set up a palace or woodland scene, trick sets, and all his different stage costumes. The seed must have been planted in me there and then, for within a couple of years Steffani and I, in partnership, presented our own *Cinderella* pantomime.

In the meantime Steffani had put together a new show, called *Revue of Nations* and I joined him again, but as the juvenile lead and also acting as his assistant. A juvenile lead could be 30 years of age or older, so as I was very young my leading lady had to be chosen to suit my still small stature. One night I fitted lifts into my shoes, making me one inch taller, this was fine until my leading lady, singing as usual that special song with a cheeky smile on her face moved up to me to look straight into my eyes. But this time she was not looking into my eyes, she was looking straight up my nostrils. She finished the song as if nothing had happened but couldn't wait to reach the safety of the side wings, bursting into laughter.

In another show I sang 'Ramona' to my leading lady with the words:

'I *bless* the dawn when I awake to find you gone' for 15 weeks when, during the last week of our Show I heard the song on radio with the words:

'I *dread* the dawn when I awake to find you gone'.

Well, that evening I sang to her the correct words, she nearly collapsed. Afterwards she told me that she knew all the time I was singing the wrong word, but as I was putting so much sincerity into it she did not dare tell me otherwise.

Revue of Nations proved to be a winner. The first scene incorporated one of Billy Butlin's huge beach balls, painted like a globe. This ball, connected to a motor, rotated slowly to the music of 'Let the great big World keep turning'. Each Monday morning the ball had to be blown up by the local garage. That was fine until we came to the *Grand Theatre* Bolton.

The Songsters pushed the blown-up ball through the streets back towards the theatre at the same time generating great interest for our show. When they arrived at the *Grand's* dock doors, would you believe it, they were not wide enough to let the ball through so some air had to be let out. When the deflated ball was at last positioned on stage, we all had to blow to bring the 'world' back up to her full size.

Steffani often incorporated 'specialty acts' on the bills as they would be very entertaining and not upset any comedian's style or patter. A ventriloquist act was often chosen for this purpose. Arthur Prince used to appear dressed in a naval uniform, Bobbie Kimber used a family of dolls, Raymond in full evening dress and Johnson Clarke as a sportsman but Arthur Worsley I gave top marks. He let his doll do all the talking whilst he stood there, facing the audience full front and never moving as much as a muscle in his face. When it came to the most difficult words for a ventriloquist – wet my lips or bottle of beer – Arthur would repeat these words until the audience started to applaud.

Savenne with his doll – Daisy Maye – would become so engrossed with the doll's character that he continued the illusion in my dressing room. If I spoke to Arthur the doll would answer me back and ask me questions which Arthur would finish asking. Sometimes I would become so confused and stop changing my stage suit as I thought there was a girl in my room.

Wences, a Spaniard, was another great act. He used boxes which he opened and shut whilst talking, hence making his voice sound either free or shut in. He also used to paint with lipstick his thumb and forefinger, clenched his hand into a fist, held two black buttons between two fingers as eyes and draped a cloth over his hand, creating the illusion of a ladies face. Then he would light a cigarette, put it between the painted lips (fingers) and sure enough the 'lady' puffed and exhaled smoke rings.

Wences always demanded utter silence behind the scenes which of course was difficult with so many Songsters waiting to make their entrance after his act. One evening they must have been really noisy and that upset Wences so after his act he rushed off behind the curtains where the Songsters were ready to start their act and began to yell in his broken English when suddenly the curtain rose and there he stood furiously waving his arms about and shouting:

'Theyer maker mucher noiser when I am oner, and nower I maker mucher noiser when theyer oner.'

After this outburst he stamped his feet, stuck out his tongue and strode off like a Matador just having killed his bull.

Steffani did make the Songsters apologize after the show.

Touring this show during 1942 in the many towns I was not only receiving great press write-ups but patrons began to ask me, why they didn't hear me over the radio. So one fine day I typed a letter to London's Broadcasting House, to the BBC Head Variety Producer, asking for some BBC Radio work, reminding him that my first broadcast was on the BBC Children's Hour five years earlier.

I did receive a thank-you letter, but they did not use me apart from one or two *Northern Music Hall* excerpts they taped from various theatres for their weekly radio programme.

We were working in the years when all shows had to undergo the scrutiny of the Lord Chamberlain's Office for their Theatre Licence.

We had a bedroom scene with a soubrette, awaiting her lover, standing in her silk dressing gown next to the bed. The Lord Chamberlain's Inspector demanded that she be fully dressed underneath. Also the 'lover' should not accidentally kick the pot under the bed, as it reverberated through the microphone. There were many other stipulations one had to adhere to, otherwise the licence would be revoked.

We had been sent warnings regarding our show licence, the reason being that, when a show is written, especially the comic's lines, the actions that go with the spoken word could cause the inspector to get his blue pencil out. For instance, the comic's line might be:

'Oh, it's nice and round'.

Those words, spoken on their own, were no problem, but if the comic happened to have his hands on a lady's bottom while speaking, that line would be banned by the inspector so it was understandable that each Monday, when he was usually in the theatre, we feared that the comic would deviate from the licensed script and we would be closed.

Some of the rules were quite ludicrous, especially concerning Sundays. Comics like Jimmy Jewell and Ben Warris could not cross talk. Tommy Cooper could have a table on stage but no tablecloth. Jack Buchanan told me he couldn't dance but was allowed to sing. The stage could not be dressed - no carpet, no stage sets, just drapes. Little make-up was to be used. All those rules and regulations have been lifted now, although whether for the better I am not so sure.

My single act in Steffani's production was going well, but I felt the need to be more on my own so I began to book my own digs to separate myself from the Songsters and problems of overcrowded digs and queues to get into the only toilet, or of landladies like the one in Wigan who served us Songsters the rice pudding out of a chamber pot. Noticing the look of horror on my face, she quite calmly declared:

'It's perfectly clean, I washed it!' and continued sloshing it out onto our plates.

The first digs I booked were in Dundee. The room was spotless with a brightly burning coalfire in its hearth and a beautiful brass bedstead and in the centre stood a table with a snow-white tablecloth already laid for supper. In no time a pot of tea appeared, adding to the most pleasant of welcomes. I did enjoy being on my own. The landlady herself was young but looked rather ill. Next morning, she woke me with a cup of tea and asked if I would like the fire lit. I told her not to go to so much trouble. Looking at me, she asked if I was new to being on my own? I nodded.

'Well lad,' she said, 'I want to give you a wee bit of advice. Whenever a landlady asks you whether she shall do something for your comfort, always tell her to get on with it. You will find as you travel around, that landladies will do little enough for you, without you stopping them from doing what they are paid for.'

I took her advice.

Naturally living in digs on your own, not only apart from the company of your fellow Songsters but also from the supervision of Uncle Bert and his wife Auntie Nan had both good and bad points and I soon learned that being treated as a 'grown-up' meant more than just a private single room. One night I heard a knock on my bedroom door and there stood the landlady in her night attire, carrying a bottle with two glasses.

'Would I want a nightcap?'

'Thank you very much, but I'd rather not.'

Another time I was woken up with the sound of an organ. The landlady was playing the tune of 'Sweet Sixteen' and singing 'I love you as I never loved before'. I managed to keep my virginity on both accounts.

Performing twice nightly for many weeks, receiving a genuine audience reaction and an encouraging press, I had developed a good act of singing, yodelling and whistling, finishing on Albert Ketelby's 'In a Monastery Garden' with bird calls. There was also an acute shortage of acts and stage staff so I was kept quite busy in assisting Steffani, especially when he had to be away in Beccles attending to his shoe repair business. Then it was my responsibility to put a Variety show together, draw up the programme and running order, allocate dressing rooms - in short see that everything ran smoothly.

I also learned to look through the stage curtains or tabs into the auditorium before curtain-up and assess the takings of the house. This knowledge was useful when the front of the house Manager brought the returns' sheet backstage. I was pretty accurate regarding the figure it should show, and if it did not, I asked for the boxes with all the half-tickets sold to be brought to me, so I could see if they followed in sequence. Sometimes one heard jokes about these shady Managers, like 'he isn't fiddling the returns, he's doing better on the Red Cross boxes!'

Our touring company was on 55% or higher of the Theatre takings, so I am sure my fiddly ways saved Steffani hundreds of pounds. He gave me the title of Secretary and added this to the programme credit list. There I was, a very young looking 171/2 year-old, officially booking and putting together Variety bills and touring them.

After a while I asked Steffani if I could have a financial interest in the shows I booked.

'All right, I'll give you 25% of the net profit, but remember, you might lose!'

I didn't mind; knowing that I had a few pounds saved, I felt very confident. As the months went by more and more Variety acts were called up and often we had to make do with quite unsuitable acts for our family type show, headed by the Songsters. I came to the conclusion that if each of the acts could do an extra minute, or indeed one could do an extra spot, we could run the bill with fewer acts and still be able to put a full-length show together. This rationalisation worked very well; I had changed from employee to employer. It was spring 1942.

Agent Michael Lyon had seen my act many times and suggested that I should do some film work. For this I needed some 'stills' that he would circulate among the executives of Wardour Street. A month after the pictures and biography were sent off I received an invitation to go to the Anglo-American film producer John Baxter. He needed an actor to play opposite a young actress, Deborah Kerr, for the film *Love on the Dole*. For the audition I had to learn Rupert Brook's poem 'The Soldier'. I felt sure I had the film part until, out of the blue, I received a letter from His Majesty's Forces – I had been called up to serve my country.

Steffani tried to get a six months' postponement; I got six weeks, not sufficient for the film producer. Deborah Kerr still made the film and became world famous and I got ready to join the Royal Engineers.

Our houseboat

Auntie Nan

In front of our shoeshop

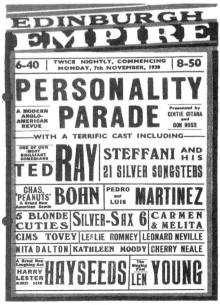

Moya

Phyllis Dixey

My brother Alf and me in Beccles

Act Six

IN THE ARMY

Steffani drove me to the Britannia Barracks in Norwich. I got out of his car and walked despondently through the large iron gates. Next morning I had to report to the barber, and alas my pride, my hair, was shorn off. I looked like a prisoner from Alcatraz and felt like one. My world had collapsed.

Six training weeks later I was classed a soldier, although how I achieved this status I do not know as both my commanding officer and I had many problems, some of which we could overcome, others not.

I did get excused by the CO from having to fire a rifle, because I could not lie down, putting pressure on my chest and private parts when I had to lift the rifle to shoot. He also excused me carrying a full kit, it was too heavy. During a running exercise I stopped after the first mile because I had developed a stitch; I was holding up the whole battalion. After five minutes we resumed our run, but I stopped again. I heard the Sergeant exclaiming to the Corporal:

'What are they sending us as men?'

'You! Walk back!'

'I can't walk back with this stitch,' I told the sergeant.

'Get on the bus!' he bellowed in exasperation.

'I haven't got the fare, Sir!'

The Sergeant, after referring to Jesus Christ, gave me the bus fare out of his own pocket, just to be rid of me, and I was issued with a document stating that I was to be excused from any further running exercises.

I was posted to Liphook Longmore Army Camp in Hants. Set in complete isolation amidst acres of woods and sandhills. A peaceful spot - until the firing of guns started, making me jump like a Jack in the Box.

On the second day in the camp we had to go to the railway station to collect our kits, which had been forwarded from Norwich. The Sergeant Major in charge ordered us to:

'Pick it up!'

Well, that was easier said than done. My baggage looked bigger than the rest of the men's and I knew I was going to have a problem carrying it so I had to quietly inform the Sergeant Major that my kit was 'too heavy for me to carry, Sir'.

'Heavy?' he queried and lifting it with one hand threw it over his shoulder and carried my kit back to the camp. Years later, this very same Sergeant Major Hill, a policeman in civilian life, came to see me at the *Empire Theatre* York reminding me of that incident and he recalled another occasion, when, during a boxing competition, I put his then Sergeant flat on his back with my left-hand punch.

During one of the live ammunition manoeuvres I was given a hand grenade and told to pull the pin just before throwing it to the marked target. This was too much for me. I managed to draw the pin but the grenade fell somehow out of my hand onto the ground, rolled towards the CO who petrified kicked it away. Then the RSM dived to the floor, picked it up and managed to throw it to safety just in time.

Needless to say, I was already down in the trench when I heard the explosion.

The RSM's thundering voice soon broken the silence that followed:

'Sapper, get up! Get up and get off this field, you bloody fool!'

The ashen CO said nothing. Again I was given a note to be excused from any further field training with live ammunition.

On another training exercise I was told to hold a rope that was attached to a derrick the size of a telegraph pole. It was quite simple to hold, but I got distracted by a blackbird singing and forgot I was holding the rope, which started to slip through my hands, burning them, so I just let go when I heard the men shout:

'Christ! Look out! Timber!'

The huge derrick was falling, luckily missing the soldiers scampering left and right. I was given chit number 3:

'Excused of all Field Duties' and, in brackets: 'Danger to the men'.

It is hard to understand that, after eight weeks in the Army, the Sergeant Major called me to his office to inform me that he was putting my name forward to the Officers Training Corps, with the remark that I would walk it. He was, I am sure, being sarcastic as I was not a good soldier; I even had the battalion feeling sorry for me – because I looked so young they all thought I had volunteered.

I had to do something, so I was ordered to set up the new practice target cards. Looking back I saw the men lining up their sights. Immediately the picture of one itchy finger pulling the trigger crossed my mind so I walked back to the Sergeant and told him, quite reasonably I thought, that I would not put up targets while the men were pointing their rifles at me. He stood still and looking at me suddenly, through his clenched teeth, the little word 'shit' was spat at me.

Again, I was relieved of that duty and put in the quartermaster's stores to look after the Army clothing. That job I did enjoy. I changed all my Army uniform and managed to match everything by colour and quality, even the coat. I looked more like an officer.

And then came the alert – a German invasion was expected and every soldier was ordered to carry a rifle, 24 rounds of ammunition and full kit when leaving the camp. I had just received my 48-hour home-leave pass. Never having fired a rifle nor carried my kit, I went to the SM's office asking if I could be excused from these government orders.

'NO' was the answer. I still did not give up and went to the CO. He took one look at me and told me to 'GO'.

I must have been the only soldier in England on leave that weekend without rifle or kit.

Being in charge of the Army stores also gave me a little bedroom at the back, where in the mornings my helper and early riser, Scotty, always brought me a mug of tea. The Quartermaster, Sergeant R.J. Harrison, became a good friend. After the war he and his wife often came and visited me at the *Hippodrome* Ardwick Green near their home in Cheshire. He told me to go and see the doctor as he watched me becoming more and more depressed. At the surgery I befriended the Medical Orderly, who was also interested in music and the theatre. He had a record player in his room and we spent many enjoyable evenings together. Soon the day arrived where I had to tell him that I wouldn't be able to visit him again, as our regiment was off to France. One could see in his face that this news had hit him very hard.

As I was packing my kitbag, the sergeant came to tell me that I had been taken off the rota by orders of the MO so next day I watched as my Army mates marched by, many never to return. I stayed on at Longmoor waiting to be called for the medical. The call never came.

During those evenings I used to entertain the new lads in the camp and this brought me a new position, Attendant to the Army Music Room. Our RSM also arranged charity shows outside the camp, which I took part in, and organised my over-night's accommodation too. He really was very kind to me.

At last I was doing what I was good at, entertaining.

Shortly afterwards I was posted to Peterborough and there given my discharge which stated:

'Unfit for the Army, his services too short to assess.'

I often wondered if the musical evenings spent with the MO stopped me going overseas? Was it him who'd phoned the SM's office?

Perhaps this saved my father receiving a second 'with regret' War Office telegram, when my brother Alfred lost his life serving in the Royal Welsh Fusiliers at the tail end of the war, barely 18 years old.

It was not until 1994, when my New Zealand doctor, Paul Milton, during a routine examination, told me, that, with my crooked spine I should have never been made to enter the Army.

On leave with army hair cut

John Harper

Arthur Prince

Act Seven

A NEW NAME

It was a strange feeling to be told one wasn't fit for Army service. Depressed and worried, I was wondering, could I ever start in the entertainment world again, when the theatrical agent Hyman Zahl came onto the scene.

There it was, one week's work at the *Palace Theatre* Nelson, on a Variety bill. Suddenly I had to sort out my music, prepare my stage suit and write my own lighting plot. This lighting information had to be passed on to the so-called 'Electrics' or 'Mr. Electrics' and to the 'Limes' or 'Lime Boys'. These limes were powerful lights illuminating my face and I made special stipulations not to change these while I was on stage, often in the second half of the show, as they could start to lose their brightness at that time although they could be restored to full strength within seconds. Steffani had realised early on that people did not believe I had no mechanical device in my mouth to whistle, especially my bird-calls, unless they could see my face clearly, so to 'light my face' was vital to my act.

The show went so well that Herbert Hartley, the owner of the *Palace*, extended my booking for another week. Then followed the *Hippodrome* Wigan. During Band Call I sang quietly to save my voice for the night. Coming off stage I suddenly heard someone in a very broad Lancashire accent say:

'You'd better sing louder than that t'night, otherwise thee won't bloody well hear thee!'

He was only the Theatre's boss. These dates brought me back into the theatre as an act in my own right and I felt the need to change my image. To achieve this I began to think of how to alter my name. Previously, when working with Steffani it was one of my duties to set out the theatre bills and that's when I learned about all the problems associated with this task. Each artiste would be quite emphatic how he or she should be billed, what size and position their act's name should have on the double crown bill; either Full Top of the bill; First Top sharing with Second Top; Third usually was bottom and Featured Middle; others made up as needed; Bottom sometimes cut into three acts; and then there were the Wines and Spirits (meaning the lowest).

These positions would reflect the number of the dressing room, and the size of the salary. With double-act names one had to be especially careful as to which one came first, like Ford and Sheen, Billy Caryll and Hilda Munday, Nat Mills and Bobbie, and Forsythe, Seamon and Farrell. And don't ever think you want to be polite in putting the wife first – that would have caused a rumpus!

I had also realised that a long name like 'The Eight Russian Cossack Dancers' looked quite squashed and difficult to read in the allocated space on the bill, whereas names like 'Renara' or 'Coco' stood out. Ron Warren had to be shortened, so I chose 'Ronald', but I wanted to emphasise the second syllable and achieved this with the addition of a silent 'e' to my name:

The result: '*Ronalde*'.

Now I had to change my stage clothes, bearing in mind that during the Army training I had grown somewhat and the white page boy suit did not fit any more.

I chose white trousers and a red jacket but something was missing so I cut the letter R out of cardboard, about 10cm high, covered it with white silk and fixed it onto my jacket's top pocket. I still was not satisfied. I cut out another R, one meter high, covered it with glitter and attached it to the centre leg of the stage back drapes, so that when the curtain opened, the limes would focus on the 'R' reflecting the light whilst I would start whistling in the wings, slowly making my entrance onto the stage. Usually the audience would applaud at that moment; normally only great stars received applause already at the beginning of their act, so it was really a little cheeky expecting them to do the same for me.

I was appearing at the *Shakespeare* Liverpool when Hyman Zahl came to see me with the news that he had arranged a 12-week summer season for me at the *South Pier* Blackpool in Jack Taylor's production, *The Show That Jack Built*. Mr. Taylor was one of the top impresarios of the North of England and his forte was lighting; his scenes took on a completely different dimension once lit by him. The show opened with all its usual aplomb, a packed house with the Mayor, Ald. P. Round JP, in attendance. Appearing in the show were Frank Randle with his entourage, Billy Scott Coomber, Jeannette Haley, the Anglo Polish Ballet and myself. A few days into the show and down came the curtain following a letter from the Chief Constable of Blackpool, H. Barnes, about 'unsavoury stage business'. Next day Frank Randle had left the show.

My wife would laughingly swear that she looks at the moon whenever I am being strangely disagreeable once again. Frank Randle was a comedian/actor really second to none when he was on form – but he did have a moon problem. I assumed that was the reason when he told me, whilst we were having our late night supper at the Grape Hotel cum Pub in Oldham – I was appearing at the time at the *Empire* Oldham and Frank at the *Manchester Hippodrome* Ardwick Green – 'that he had sacked the lot', meaning his entire 'Randle's Scandals Show'.

Rather shocked I asked him 'why?'

'Well' Frank said, 'they weren't singing the correct harmonies' and he blamed the leadsinger as the culprit whom he had only two days earlier invited to have a meal with us as gratitude for all his hard work.

During that week we often went together for a walk in the mornings when he used to suddenly stop in his tracks and look at a passer by.

'Eeeee, what a character to use!'

Its from the streets he drew his eccentricities from, he even went so far as to have all his teeth out so he could enhance his funniness on stage with different sets – one with just a front tooth, another with one tooth either side and finally a beautiful set of pearl-white teeth just like Clark Gable used in his films.

Frank also liked his Guinness and had the habit of dropping his teeth into the full glass which sometimes he offered to his unsuspecting dressingroom visitors. They were horrified when after a few swigs they saw what was smiling at them from the bottom of the glass, I am sure did not fell like smiling back.

Jack Taylor put another show together, called *How Do Folk*. He kept me and reopened successfully with Norman Evans, famed for 'Over the Garden Wall', Harold Ramsey on his organ, Vic and Joe Crastonian, Australia's Patillo and Pesco, Billy Scott Coomber and Janet Haley. To work with Norman Evans was a joy. Often I was invited to eat at his home in Blackpool with his wife and daughter Norma. After dinner he would take me to a special room in his home where he had a superb working model train set laid out.

This show was a success. The only drawback was the lack of dressingrooms as the Anglo Polish Corp de Ballet carried so many dancers. I was fighting for space to put my make-up box, the size of a matchbox, on the dressing table amongst all their clutter. John Stone, a very manly ballet boy, who later became an actor opposite Googie Whithers, tried to move me sideways but I stood my ground. And Michael Charnley's dancing, later known as Karol Novak, took him to America where we met again. And he reminded me that during that show their Director of the Ballet wanted me to join their Company.

As the *South Pier* season was doing well, Jack Taylor started to open on Sundays. The show had to be presented like a concert and I was to do 15 minutes, with 'no extra pay!'

'Well,' I said, 'I'd rather have Sunday off!'

'Sorry,' replied Ernie Coleclough, Jack Taylor's Stage Director, 'you'll have to work!'.

'If there's no pay there's no whistle.' I remained stubborn.

Ernie Coleclough warned me that if I didn't turn up for the Sunday concert I could be out of the show altogether. I gave him my card with the digs phone number on it and told him that he could reach me there until 5 o'clock on Sunday, if they decided to pay me. No phone call came, no whistle was heard.

Next day was murder. Jack Taylor was suing me, I would never whistle again in any theatre. Hyman Zahl, Michael Sullivan, all the agents who had taken up wartime residence in Blackpool, were shouting:

'Ronnie Ronalde has had it!'

I was to be at Jack Taylor's office at 10 on Tuesday morning.

I was there at 9.45 and, when told to go in, I opened the door very gently, ready for all the abuse I expected to receive.

Jack Taylor sat at his desk, writing and without looking up beckoned me to sit down. After a while he stopped writing and looked at me in a severe manner.

'I have been watching your performance.'

He paused and started to fiddle with one of his desk drawers.

This is it, I am going to be fired, I wish he would say it and not cloud himself with silence, it makes me nervous.

Suddenly he spoke again:

'Ronnie, as you are going well in my show I am going to give you a raise in salary!'

I swallowed and managed to mumble a 'Thank you, Mr. Taylor', stood up and was out of the office before he could change his mind.

Back at the theatre Ernie Coleclough asked me if I would be working next Sunday? 'Of course.'

During that period a great friend of Jack Taylor's, the famed 'Pope of Fleet Street', newspaperman of the *Daily Herald* Hannen Swaffer came backstage after watching my performance. He put his hand on my head, patted me and said:

'You'll go far my son!'

Later Jack Taylor told me that Hannen Swaffer who was also a noted spiritualist, had seen angels over my head during my 'In a Monastery Garden'.

The 'Last Night' of the show had arrived and with it not only the usual fun of doing things wrong to your fellow acts, we had also to deal with Mr. Taylor's 'Black Comedy' in which he excelled.

'We have' he started, standing on stage, 'three great people to thank for this show because without them this show's success would have been nothing.'

While the audience applauded, our three stars, Norman Evans, Billy Scott Coomber and Harold Ramsey were looking very proud and growing taller by the minute.

'In fact I would not have gone on with this show without the courage, strength, power and most of all unity of these three great men.'

More applause and looking at the three artistes beaming behind him he spoke with full voice into the microphone:

'They are Churchill, Roosevelt and Stalin!'

The Theatre was in uproar.

With the Blackpool season over I was off again touring theatres in Variety until at the *Metropolitan* in Edgeware Road London, I really hit them for six. On the same bill was Jimmy Wheeler. The father and son sailor act Wheeler and Wilson had just split up and son Jimmy carried on alone as a stand-up comic. One night he had difficulty in following my performance so he told the audience that I had two holes in my head from which the whistles came from. He had skilfully turned their attention from me to him.

While there I received two letters. One was from the Universal Agency, the other from the Variety Presentation's John S. Potten in association with Mike Sullivan, who later discovered Shirley Bassey. Both offered me theatre work for 1944. I also had a visit from Moss Empire's Mr. Lewis, with an offer for a London show called *Strike a New Note* staring Sid Fields at the *Prince of Wales Theatre*. It included many future stars like Morecombe and Wise at £25 per week, the going rate. I did not see the wisdom in accepting less than I was earning. Mr. Lewis came back again but I declined. I was happy with my decision, because having kept in close contact with Steffani and entered a partnership with him presenting shows, I was slowly building up my bank account.

Wartime was a very trying period for the theatre managers as nobody knew when the next bombs were falling so to help them we, the artistes often took it in turns with fire watching. This particular night I was chosen. After everyone had left the theatre I settled myself comfortably on the provided camp bed. Everything was very still and my mind started to wander, when, there psst, I could hear it, a scratching noise. The more I strained my ears the louder the noise became, so I slowly felt for the torch and swiftly turned on the light. Oh dear, there they were, six of them - rats! I threw my shoes at them and that night, with my legs pulled up, I kept vigilance and the torch never went out.

Rats can be quite a problem – they can eat the theatre props, damage violin strings, cause havoc in the dressing rooms with artistes clothes and make-up. At the *Palace* Southampton I saw part of my evening dress shirt torn after it had been pulled out of my wardrobe trunk. Chorus girls often lost their knickers and bras; even their dancing shoes were attacked and chewed. I came to the rescue of one of our girls at the *Tivoli Theatre* in Hull. She was screaming and, rushing into her dressing room, I found her standing naked on one of the chairs, pointing to a rat that had her panties in its mouth. In the corner of my eye I saw a large prop sword so, brandishing it to and fro, I managed to frighten the rat back into its hole. Hearing all this commotion, the other artistes came to investigate and started to cheer me on after seeing me dance with a sword round and round a naked girl on a chair.

Landlady's daughter, Pickup Street, Nelson
First theatrical date after army discharge

My 'Big R'

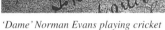

'Dame' Norman Evans playing cricket

Bunny Doyle

Will Murray (Charlie Chaplin discoverer), with our cast from the Blackpool South Pier Show

Act Eight

SHOWTIME

Engagements followed in Ayr, Southport, Preston and Lewisham before I joined the production of Jack Taylor's *Aladdin* pantomime at Morecombe. The cast included Jimmy Clithero, Bert Errol, Peggy Stamula, Jeannette Haley, Billy Scott Coomber, Collinson and Breen, Ralph Wilkinson, Karina Vadio and Hertz and whistler Albert Whelan. Under 'specialities' appeared RONALDE. Jack Taylor had booked TWO whistlers.

We met the first time at a Rotary Luncheon with Jack Taylor announcing during his speech that he had booked the greatest whistler in the world and looking at Albert Whelan introduced me. It was quite embarrassing but Albert and I did become quite firm friends.

It was understandable that this billing made the public think that I was Albert Whelan's son, again bringing to the fore Jack Taylor's black comedy streak.

Aladdin did well and during its run Mr. Taylor asked me if I would take over from Donald Peers in *Stardust*. Donald had been a good third top of the bill on the Moss Empire circuit but with his continuous singing of 'By a Babbling Brook' on his BBC radio series he had become a number one attraction and as his contract ended decided to leave the show. I joined the cast of *Stardust*, acting the scenes 'my way' and together with my whistling and singing spot the audience showed their appreciation with a big hand, hence upsetting a few of the cast, who kept on reminding me how 'Donald always did it!', singing from one side of the stage and his leading lady from the other side. I preferred her next to me, I felt it was more natural.

Stardust went on and on, but I didn't want to stagnate nor enter a new production Jack Taylor wanted to bring to Blackpool. So I wrote him a letter stating that, if I was to stay on, I wanted larger billing and an increase in my salary. Mr. Taylor came to see me backstage and wanted to know why I needed more money as I was so young.

'Look' he said, pointing to the upper circle, 'see that limeboy up there? you're earning three times the amount he is getting, and he is married!'

I was sorry for the limeboy, but I had to look ahead and get my name on the top of the bill and the only way to do that was to increase my salary. I told him that as he was changing the title of the show I was due for a new contract and I would sign, if I received a higher salary and bigger billing.

Again he asked me what a 'kid' like me would do with all that money?

Finally he gave in, I got my desired billing and salary and he did not call me a kid any more.

We toured *Stardust* all over the country with Albert Burdon, Karina, Freda Barrie, Spence (a master in voice throwing) and Davies, Ina Claire, Vadio and Hertz and Jimmy Clitheroe. Jimmy, only half my size, but very lovable, would often sit on my knee in my dressing room, just like a child. For his skin, like a baby's, he had a special ration book, allowing him to buy Pears soap.

In one of the scenes, called 'Piano-Lid Reflections', I made my debut as a 'piano player', portraying an old man, appearing to sit in front of a huge piano behind a gauze cloth, while the old man's memories in vision were acted out behind him. The actual sound came from the pianist in the orchestra pit. I received terrific write-ups in the newspapers, not only as a whistler and singer but also as an accomplished pianist, giving me quite some problems if the cast was invited out to a party, and I was expected to sit down and play.

I left *Stardust* during May 1944 and rejoined Steffani who, with me in partnership, was presenting a revue called *Showtime* with comic Roy Lester, Jack Cranston, Peggy Stamula, Petro and Petrova, Bert Collins, Jones and Thomas, the Ten Tiller Girls and featuring 32 Silver Songsters.

More and more I took over the running of the show as well as performing in it. We were quite a Company to shift every Sunday from town to town and open again on Mondays. Many times British Rail gave us the use of a reserved railway carriage extra to our 30-foot booked truck accommodating our scenery and costumes but failing that we did have many ways of trying to make ourselves comfortable. Some of us held a key to lock and unlock railway carriage doors, others collected old reservation labels so they could exchange them in the provided frames and then of course there was me with my whistle. Or one of our acts would powder his face white, so if anyone did venture into 'our' compartment, the comic sitting next to the 'patient' would inform the intruder that he was taking him to the Hospital for Tropical Diseases.

Stemming from bygone times, when artistes were called thieves and vagabonds and theatre owners were not to be trusted, it was the custom that performers were paid in cash on the night and this tradition is still upheld, one does usually get paid at the end of the week on weekly engagements although some performers demand to be paid even before the show like Harry Belafonte at the *Opera House* Blackpool. Impresario Harold Fielding did not like that at all.

After the last show on Saturday nights I would often walk back to the digs with my pockets full of cash; I wouldn't dare do that now. Having to deal with the money side of the business did give me an insight into some artistes' problems and recalling my mother's teaching of 'waste not want not' made me realise that my way of putting away a certain amount of my salary each week into a savings account was not such a bad idea. After paying out on a Saturday night, I found that on Monday some of the artistes were already asking for a sub. Where had it all gone?

One particular artiste would receive around £50. Well, there were bets on horses, cards, the inevitable drink and women. One has to understand that a tradesman's wages at that time were around £7 a week.

Frank Ruebins of Feldman's Music Publishers told me that 'Chorlene', another great whistler, feigning to be asleep in a park scene was often so drunk that he actually did fall asleep and it needed the stage manager to shout:

'Chorlene! Chorlene! Wake up, you are on!', all heard by the audience.

I tried to be firm with Claude Lester who sadly was drinking his money away as fast as he got it and if he did not manage to get a sub he would revert to busking, entertain the queues outside the theatre he was later to perform in. There had been talk that at another theatre he had been locked into the dressingroom to keep him sober until his performance, but when they opened the door they found him paralytic. A stagehand had brought a bottle into the theatre and Claude, with his straw through the keyhole, had drunk the lot.

Comic Harry Tate too had his drinking problems and his son and stage partner Ronnie would often have to try and rescue a gag because Harry, befuddled, would tell the tagline first. At the *Hippodrome* Dudley his bar bill was close to what I paid him.

Comedian Jimmy James didn't drink but loved backing horses, unfortunately the bookmaker nearly always came out better from the deal. Jimmy often used Roy Castle in his act. Roy could play virtually every musical instrument one can think of and dance. Roy also wrote a Christmas song which I later recorded.

Robert Newton, another heavy drinker acting in a murder scene with Marie Clare would get so carried away that she had to hold a large hatpin in readiness to stick into him if he overacted in 'strangling' her.

With the stage and management side of running the show I did not forget my own performances. I was forever trying to improve my whistling, yodelling and singing. My write-ups did not just hail me as a whistler who puts the birds (the feathered kind, naturally) to shame, but also as a singer. Of course the showgirls helped as well trying to look after me. One day, watching me put on my make-up from my matchbox, one of the Tiller girls told me, that as I had 'wickedly long eyelashes' I should try and curl them up. This I did. With soap. Unfortunately the powerful limes shining on my face melted the soap, running straight into my eyes and making me shed floods of tears. The sympathetic audience applauded like mad for this 'sad whistling lad'.

There was another 'sad' instance. One night 13-year-old Songster Charles 'Insper' Ford from Wales nearly choked during his rendering of Mozart's 'Wither Vanished'. The audience loved him when the tears were running down his face; tears were running down the faces of mothers in the audience too. After the performance Steffani asked what had happened.

'My chewing gum slipped down my throat' he replied.

The war was still going on; no family was untouched. Mine, too, had its share of sorrow, but much of it brought about by my father's second wife. She was the exact opposite to Mother, chain smoking and drinking. Father had been warned before their marriage about her debts and bad habits by many well-meaning neighbours but to no avail. Although she looked after us children, she always needed more and more money for her needs.

Whenever I came home for the odd day my former schoolmates told me that Father's and my suits went into the pawnshop on Monday and out again on Friday. One day I had to break my railway journey between theatres as I needed my black evening outfit for a special finale Steffani had incorporated in this particular show. I arrived home, unexpectedly, to collect the suit. It wasn't there. I was told that I must have forgotten to pack the suit at my last lodgings!

After hesitantly writing to the digs the answer came back, very quick and very short: 'No.'

I never did manage to get the suit back and my stamp collection, guitar and beloved Meccano set disappeared as well.

Quite early during the war the council moved my family from 126 Downham Road, Islington to 102 Falkland Road, Hornsey because of a large bomb crater near our home all surrounding houses had been declared unfit for habitation. I did not like to go and visit the new home because there was no bed for me. Unbeknown to the council, my stepmother had rented out the top rooms of the house to a family for extra money. After my family had been in this house for two years on Christmas Eve the bailiff arrived and ordered us out of the house. My father had always thought that my stepmother had paid the rent but no, she had falsified the signatures in the rent book for a complete year. Neighbours and shopowners became weary of her dealings and it came quite as a relief when another bomb took the roof off the house and they were relocated once more, to 50 Woodberry Avenue, Winchmore Hill. Here I bought a large wooden trunk with a padlock and from then on all my belongings were locked up while I was away.

It was inevitable to sometimes catch a cold through travelling on draughty trains, staying in unheated digs and being in constant contact with so many people. So how did I celebrate my 21st birthday? In bed! With a high fever and sweat pouring off me. The landlady kept on changing my bedlinen. I must have fallen into some sort of delirium when suddenly I woke up, feeling something very cold on my forehead. Then I heard a female voice say:

'Oh my, you are hot, poor love!'

This voice did not sound like the doctor's but I really did not have the energy to open my eyes and see who it was. Rather, I let myself enjoy her soothing my forehead with one hand while the other rested on my wrist, no doubt feeling for my pulse. Gradually I became more and more relaxed, when slowly she started to draw back the sheets and, lying down beside me, took me in her arms and began to cuddle and then comfort me. I did not resist, I just let it be. Then it happened, I had lost my virginity.

Well, as the song goes:

'I'm twenty-one today, I'm twenty-one today, I've got the key to the door, never been 21 before,

Father says I can do as I like, so shout hip hip hurrah

Sing a song in the garden of life, if you only gather a thistle

Sing a song as you travel along and if you can just whistle.'

Steffani and I decided to produce a pantomime, *Cinderella*, with me playing the role of Dandini, breaking with tradition, as this part was always performed by a girl. To put this show on was costly, so I had to withdraw £1000 of my National War Savings Bonds. I did that while appearing in Liverpool and there caught up with Lieutenant Norman B. Shalders RNVR, who was working on the National Savings Committee for the Admiralty, but known of course to me by his theatrical name, Paul Beverley.

The pantomime opened at the *Empire* Kingston in December 1944 and ran for four weeks. Cinderella was played by Pauline Clare, Eileen Murphy was Prince Charming, Clapham and Dwyer portrayed the Ugly Sisters, Bunny Baron the role of Buttons, Darroll Richards was Baron Hardup, the Borstal Boys played the Brokers Men and Margaret Gill the Fairy Godmother. Josephine Martin, Harry Arnold, Stanley Bounds, 12 De Vere Girls and 12 Millie Jackson Girls and the Silver Songsters completed the cast. In the newspaper the following day the pantomime received a fantastic write up:

"The brightness and cheerfulness are its outstanding characteristics and can be commended for the fact that it follows very closely the traditional storyline, hence making it especially attractive to the children, but with the cleverly interwoven modern style of entertainment cannot fail to please old and young alike."

My own review showed that the audience did not just accept me as a whistler but also enthusiastically applauded my acting.

I enjoyed the 'acting' part very much, although I experienced a slight problem in that the wig I was supposed to wear did not fit - my head was too big – so I had to powder my own black hair snow white for every performance.

We took the pantomime for a further two weeks to the *Royal* Merthyr and the *Empire* Oldham. Every show was booked out, my war bonds had multiplied and I was firmly established with Steffani in an associated company that launched a new show, *Happytime*, at the *Hippodrome* Accrington in February 1945. This production, with Wally Wood, Jimmy Leslie, Josephine Martin, Reg Marte, Darroll Richards, Max and Mary, Margaret Thompson, Campbell and Rogers, the Jackson Lovelies and King of the Gypsies, Petrulengo with his daughter Princess Lavanya, was toured separately by our musical director.

Petrulengo's act included the telling of your horoscope as well as the performing of a Romany Wedding with all its genuine rituals and colourful costumes, incorporating the cutting of the wrists and binding them with a silken cord, the jump over a blazing fire and finally the 'chumdevar', the Gypsy Wedding Kiss.

Steffani, the Silver Songsters and I continued to perform in Variety – every week another town, another theatre. In one place the landlady's daughter, who seemed a little naive, kept taking some of Steffani's beloved chocolate cake from the cupboard in his bedroom, so he decided that something had to be done about it. The comic of our show had the idea of purchasing some De Witts pills and told Steffani to push them deep into the cake. Mission accomplished the two of them went off to the theatre. When they returned that night, first Steffani and then the comic gingerly made their way upstairs to the bedroom. After closing the door they took one dive across the room to the cupboard. And, yes, there it was, or better, there it was not, a good portion of the cake had gone.

Next morning, the landlady's daughter brought their breakfast.

'You don't look at all well!' said the comic.

'No,' she answered, 'I do feel proper poorly!'

'What's up?'

'Oh dear' she sighed, 'I can't tell you, its private'.

'Come on, you can tell Uncle Joe,' the comic urged.

She paused, then, taking a deep breath, uttered:

'You see, its me water, when I looked into me pot this morning, its gone all greeeen!'

With that Steffani and his partner in crime knew that the pills had done their proclaimed job, but still the pair had not quite finished with their quest.

The same evening the comic crept upstairs into her room and poured a tin of Enos Liver Salts into her pot under the bed. Soon after she went to her room one mighty scream could be heard, her door flew open and out she came, running, adorned in her white long nightgown, furiously gesticulating and yelling:

'Me gawd, oh me gawd, me water, it's boiled over!'

Britain was the home of variety theatres. I never played the *Shoreditch*, the *Angel* or *Hoxton* although I did perform with some of the greats like G.H. Elliott, Norman Long, Marie Kendal, Will Fife, Hetty King, Talbort O'Farrell and Nellie Wallace. In those days a variety show was put together with 12 acts and later reduced to ten and during the war very often to six, each doing two spots. The first act on the bill, generally a dancing duo, opened the show and again was first on after the interval. The second top of the variety bill usually closed the first half and the main star attraction dominated the second half, with only one closing act to follow. This running order gave the audience the cue to up and go the moment the closing act made its entrance. This exodus must have given a shattering feeling to the artiste on stage, an undeserved experience for a well-rehearsed act; to me, it was a waste.

I suggested that the Songsters, the star attraction, should move to the last spot of the show. This surprised Steffani - it wouldn't have looked good if patrons were seen to walk out on them - so I said:

'I'll take the gamble and close the show myself'.

The audience, apart from the few who always do get itchy feet, sat in their seats and listened to the end of my performance, they did not want to miss my rendering of the 'Monastery Garden' which I kept on purpose as my last number. I continued with this running order on our variety bills with so much success, that soon the Moss and Stoll theatres adopted it as well.

A second film offer to play a young monk, singing Handel's 'Largo' in Latin for a film called *What Do We Do Now?* was put to me during June 1945. After the film's release, director John Baxter took the scene showing me and made a short of it. He also told me that my voice had something that should be trained:

'You have a young Gigli voice, look after it'.

A few years later Gigli himself surprised me by visiting the *Empire Theatre* Edinburgh where I appeared and was very complimentary to me.

I took Baxter's advice and over a two-year period trained with singing Master Lawrence Leonard of Steinway Hall, who had sung with Caruso and what a joy it was to meet bubbly Evelyn Laye who was also taking lessons although she had been a star for the past ten years. I had first seen her as Prince Charming at the *Hippodrome* Birmingham and when I told her about my desire to visit America, she warned me how hard it would be to crack 'that nut'.

Yes, the war was over and I took part in a 'V-Show', Victory Cavalcade, that had been organised for the benefit of the many servicemen and women. It also featured Elsie and Doris Waters, Jean Kent, Cyril Fletcher, Steffani and his Songsters, Al Roxy, Percy

Rich and Eva, Reg Bolton, The Bon Tons, George Mackenzie and boxer Jimmy Wilde.

One of auntie Nan's job was to do the weekly shopping for all the Songsters food, which was quite a formidable task and for this she was in charge of their ration books. She soon found out that at the end of the week butchers often had some meat left over they could not sell to their normal customers. But to theatricals it was all right because they were gone next day. When we returned to a certain town again and she revisited that butcher he didn't want to know her. She was most upset when she found out that Elsie and Doris Waters had shopped him to the authorities when they had found out that he had supplied us with more than we were permitted to have. Have you ever tried to feed 21 growing lads?

All during the rest of the year my date book was full. Some towns do remain firmly imprinted on my mind due to various incidents of both a mysterious and amusing nature. Appearing at the *Hippodrome* Salford, whistling 'Birdsong at Eventide', I suddenly heard what sounded like an agonising shriek accompanied by some sort of commotion from the audience. At the end of my performance I asked the stage manager if he knew anything about this hubbub? And he quietly explained that apparently a chap sitting in the front row of the balcony had a visit from the theatre's resident black cat. She had walked along the rim of the balcony, as usual, eyeing every patron and chose his lap as her seat for the duration of the show. Everything went well until I appeared on the scene, giving my birdcalls. The cat's sensual instinct was immediately aroused and with it sank her extended sharp claws into the poor man's private parts.

Not quite sure that I'd heard correctly I asked:

'Into his what?'

'Into his balls!' the stage manager shouted, and there I was thinking that black cats bring you luck.

Mrs. Sprigs (Spriggy), a friendly landlady and also a renowned spiritualist ran the digs in Peterborough. One day whilst listening to her chatter she suddenly stopped, her body became rigid and staring at me, she said:

'Your face has changed, you're dressed in a naval uniform. Do you know anybody in the Navy?'

I replied with a hesitant 'No' while my mind started to work and then it suddenly came to me, Paul Beverley.

Spriggy carried on talking, describing his features to me – 'a strong square chin, sparkling eyes and dark hair'.

The next day at the theatre I received a call from Hyman Zahl informing me that Lieut. N.B Shalders R.N.V.R., theatrically known as Paul Beverley and my discoverer had been lost at sea, presumed dead.

When I told Spriggy the sad news she replied with:

'He is there, he is there, he is guiding you'.

1946 arrived with no let-up in my bookings or in my performances at charity shows in hospitals or at high society dinners given in aid of a particular organisation. These functions were often organised under the chairmanship of well known names, such as Lady Waddilove, The Countess of Middleton, Mrs. Mark Ostra or the wealthy socialite Viscountess Ann Rothermere, who would write to me on Dorchester notepaper and always sign herself as Ann. She introduced me to Ian Fleming, creator of James Bond at one of their fund-raising evenings at the *Coliseum* on 19 February that boasted a very impressive list of entertainers: Henry Hall, Jack Buchanan, Albert Whelan, Randolph Sutton, Lilian Keyes, Reub Silver, Marion Day - and yours truly.

Other venues included the *Savoy, Mayfair, Dorchester*, the *Grosvenor House* Hotel and many private residences with Ambrose, Carol Gibbons and Henry Hall. Once I was offered a key to a certain apartment, another time I was told to use a special staircase to reach a certain boudoir. I never took up any of these well meaning offers having been warned by Jimmy Messini of Harry Roy's Band to be careful as these Ladies had it in their power to destroy you as they did Jack Doyle, the great Irish boxer. It was quite unbelievable that little me, who came from a background of seldom having two halfpennies to rub together, was mingling with the Upper Crust where money played no role.

On Sunday, 3 March I appeared at yet another *Victory Cavalcade* show, this time at the *Royal Albert Hall* in London, bringing back quite a few memories of when I performed there first on 28 September 1935 at a Concert called *Children's Jubilee Celebration*.

This, my second appearance produced by Ian Johnson had a tremendous cast: Gwen Catley with Ivor Newton, Mark Hambourg, Jack Train, Carmen del Rio and Donald Edge, Delya, Naughton and Gold, Tommy Handley and Clarence Wright, Guy Mitchell, Nervo and Knox, Petula Clark, Eddie Ready and Joy, Ethel Revnell, Troise and his Mandoliers, The Ballet Divertissement, The Massed Bands of the Brigade of Guards, The Bands of the Grenadier, Coldstream, Scots, Irish and Welsh Guards, The Drums and Pipers of the Scots Guards, Charles Shadwell and his Concert Orchestra, The Alexander Choir, Steffani's Silver Songsters and Ronalde.

Truly a night to remember quickly followed by another event when during an overnight stay in Beccles I saw my dream car: a white Rolls Royce.

'That's the car I'd like!'

Unbeknown to me, Nick knew her owner, Frank Lavelle the dentist and asked him if he wanted to sell his car, having heard rumours that Frank wanted to return to his beloved Ireland. We arrived at the golf course and sure enough, there stood the white 1938 Jack Barclay coachwork on a 1926 Chassis 22-25 HP Rolls Royce Convertible with a note pinned to the steering wheel:

'If you want it you can buy it!' I bought it.

I had obtained my driving licence earlier that year and so was ready to settle myself behind the wheel and drive off. But I had not reckoned with Steffani, who obviously did not trust my road sense and told me in no uncertain terms to

'Move over son, I'll do the driving!'

Sunday journeys became a new experience, sitting in my own car and being chauffeur driven by Steffani. Gradually he allowed the 'Whistling Kid' to take the wheel but only on quiet country roads, in towns I was given strict instructions never to touch the car, let alone drive it.

Disobeying this rule did get me into trouble quite a few times. I remember the Dudley *Hippodrome* where the stage manager, seeing me in the Rolls outside the theatre, went and told Steffani that:

'One of the kids is messing about with your car!'

and was totally surprised when Steffani informed him that the 'kid' was Ronalde, the star attraction in his theatre and the owner of the Rolls.

The Rolls had a gate change gearbox and needed the driver to double declutch. Both the gear lever and the handbrake were operated from the right of the driver's seat on the floor. A petrol gauge lever, situated on the steering wheel column, allowed you to conserve fuel on long distance drives and as England was still petrol rationed, a very welcome device. Again, having been warned not to take the car onto the road I still proceeded and drove on a very busy Monday morning right into the centre of Liverpool. At the *Adelphi* Hotel the car stopped. A policeman on traffic duty frantically waved me on, hooters and horns were blasting everywhere when two other policemen arrived on the scene ordering me to move on. Shamefacedly I had to tell them that I could not move the car.

A fellow on a motorbike pulled up exclaiming:

'Surely not a Rolls!'

He leaned over and through my open window touched the petrol gauge lever, pressed the start-button, and would you believe it, the engine started. One of the policemen asked if the car was 'really yours?' and a lorry driver, sitting high in his cabin, shouted:

'They'll let anybody drive them these days!'

It was most important in every town and city to quickly find the best laundry and Liverpool was no different. All went well, except one of Steffani's shirts kept coming back with the collar button still missing. He returned the shirt again and to emphasise the missing button he took the lid of a Cherry Blossom boot polish tin, punched two holes into it and sewn it to where the missing button should have been replaced. The following day the shirt arrived back, beautifully laundered with a little note:

'We hope we did right, we made the buttonhole fit your 'tin button'!'

*Famous BBC comedians
Clapham & Dwyer as Ugly Sisters*

*Darroll Richards,
often understudy
to Richard Tauber*

Warren Dean Girls

G.H. Elliott

Harry Tate

'Insper' Charles Ford without his chewing gum

Randolph Suttou

Scenes from 'Showtime'

Scene in the film 'What Do We Do Now?'

Act Nine

SWITZERLAND

With the war over travelling on the continent was a reality again. This enabled us to attend a yodelling festival held in Lucerne, Switzerland.

After our sea journey to Calais, we travelled by rail on to Basel where we couldn't believe our eyes - they had everything: food, drinks, chocolates and one could actually buy everything! You could see that Switzerland had not experienced any war rationing, we were served two eggs each and ham for our breakfast.

In Lucerne we boarded the steamer on Lake Lucerne, to bring us to the Park Hotel in Vitznau where, from our economy priced Garret room (Britain permitted a meagre £78 yearly for overseas travel) we had a breathtaking view of all the majestic mountains surrounding us.

My mind was never far away from the real purpose of my journey: yodelling! I watched a typical Swiss festival and parade, everyone dressed in their different national costumes, dancing and yodelling to the music of the various bands. So many different yodels! I had never realised how many variations actually existed; I listened and listened and learned, so eager to practice what I'd heard, we booked a cable-car ride up a nearby peak. There I found that the surrounding mountains threw their eerie echo of my practicing yodels back at me. This realisation was of tremendous benefit to many of my future yodelling songs, giving them that extra Swiss touch.

The weather started to deteriorate rapidly so we hurried to the cable-car station to get off the mountain. Only after a hefty push by the attendant did the cab start its descent into the valley, too late for Steffani to get out again after taking one look down the steep mountain. We were swaying to and fro in the heavy wind, I was petrified and holding on to the rails praying every minute. I was glad when I stood on terra firma again.

Back at the hotel we were asked if we'd heard anything unusual in the mountains? A shepherd must have been in distress because seemingly he tried to alert the villagers with his yodelling and some sort of whistling!

It soon became known that I was an artiste and with Steffani at the piano gave a few songs after dinner. Next day we were offered a suite, free of charge, as long as I entertained the guests each night.

In 1993 it was reported that the Swiss Government forbade whistling in the mountains, as it would scare the mountain goats who are the suppliers of the famous chamois leather.

Switzerland did give my yodelling more quality and depth, so much so, that when we were home again, I wrote the lyrics and Steffani the music of 'My Little Swiss Maid' and later 'Lady of Lake Lucerne'.

Again my date book was full for all of 1946. I remember at the *Empire* Oldham we had a Lady Fire Eater act booked, Donna Delbert. The bill also included Chasadey & Dawn, Claude Lester, the Sterlings, Danny Gray, The Four Graham Bros. (one had been a Songster), Jackson & Brown, the Songsters and myself. Due to the shortage of dressing rooms, Donna had to dress with the Dancing Troupe Girls.

To have a lot of girls in one hot and stuffy room, with one wash basin, applying make-up and all sorts of other things dancers have to do, it was not surprising that the headgirl complained that her girls did not like the looks Donna (older than them) gave them while they were in their birthday suits. I could do nothing to change the situation but had a talk with Donna. What a sad story it was. Her husband, an American in the USA Air Force had been killed and she had to work and bring up their little son.

A month later came the bombshell. Donna was *resting* as they say in the theatre when you have a week out at her Brixton digs, when she was visited by the USA Military Police who had acted on a tip off.

They found her, dressed as usual in her long trousers and colourful shirt, lounging with her feet up, a pint of beer in one hand and a pipe in the other.

The story made headlines in the *News of the World* when our Lady Fire Eater was sent to prison and we heard, wrote the book 'Through a Man's Eye'.

Donna Delbert was not only an Army deserter, she was also a man.

At the *Empire* Shepherds Bush I appeared on the Variety bill of 'Cheeky Chappy' Max Miller. He would always have someone in his shows he knew would attract the crowds, somebody on their way to stardom, this time it was me.

As his home was in Brighton he used to catch the 5 o'clock train and arrive at the *Empire* in time for his star closing spot at the end of the second half of the first house.

Second house he would alter the running order with him closing the first half – my spot – so he could catch the last train to Brighton, an hours journey away and I would fill his star spot at the end of the Show whilst he was already at home.

Max was a keen bird watcher, the feathered kind, so we arranged to meet at a bird sanctuary. I arrived early in my Rolls and sat waiting until I saw Max on a bicycle, puffing and blowing, coming up the hill. Over tea he told me that he was teaching his budgie to talk and to ring a little bell. One ring for water, two for food. One night Max was woken up with three rings. After rushing downstairs to see what's up he asked the bird why he rang three times?

'It's once for water and twice for food!'

'Yes' said the budgie, 'I want a pot'.

'Do it on the floor' answered Max.

'That may be alright for you' said the budgie but 'I need a pot'.

I began to receive many letters from Fans and it soon became obvious to me that if I would only be given a few radio shots I would quickly become 'Top of the Bill' material. My agent did his utmost but could not gain me entry into the BBC. So I approached Phil Brown, hoping that he could change the situation. Before setting up his own radio agency, Phil had been a BBC producer, so I thought that he would be the right person and suddenly, there it was: a BBC date for Sunday, 8 December 1946, on *Variety Band Box* with Tessie O'Shea, Ivor Moreton and Dave Kaye, Derek Roy, Reginald Gibbs, Valerie and Dey, The Three Imps and Billy Ternent and his Orchestra. On 12 January 1947 I did a second show including Jack Warner, Maudie Edwards, Mario Lorenzi, Frankie Howerd, The Two Rascals and Maria Var.

This was also the year when the final curtain came down on an act that had truly glorified the stage for over 12 years and had ingratiated itself with the theatre public and won applause second to none: *Steffani's 21 Silver Songsters.*

The decision came after Steffani could not take any more harassment from the weekly visits by the Health and Welfare Inspectors who made demands the way the boys should be looked after on and off stage, often way beyond comprehension of theatre life. Some theatres only had five dressing rooms. The Health Officer would measure the room and decide that four of them would have to go to the 21 boys. He took no interest that there were also other acts on the bill, male and female who now would have to share ONE dressing room.

Digs accommodation was also looked at. No more three or even five boys in one double bed as it happened in Aldershot because the town was full of Canadian troops waiting to be posted overseas or bathrooms doubling as bedrooms.

'The war is over now' the Welfare Officer voiced.

'Yes' said Steffani, 'the Show is over now too!'

The Songsters gave us many performers, Ken Morris, Peter Purvis, John Ramsay, Les Roy, the Cox Twins, Conrad Chambers, Leo Yarr, Vincent O'Hagan (Kentones), Graham (Warren, Latonia, Sparks), John Jackson, many theatre managers and me.

Steffani returned to East Anglia to become a politician whilst I continued retreading the same theatres, working with Joe Crastonian, who showed me how to make tiny sequins for costumes out of empty food tins, Victor Seaforth, Allan Melville, Hal Monty, Caryll and Mundy, Hatton & Manners, Jimmy James, Maurice Colleano, Ford and Sheen, Sam Linfield, Max Wall and Robb Wilton. But there was a difference. The two radio spots had an effect on my stage act – now I received applause just for announcing my next song, because they had been heard on the radio. Yet I did not seem able to get onto the next rung of the ladder to fame.

Leslie Holmes, one of the Two Leslies, a star act, said to me, 'Ronnie, you go too well, you unbalance the bill, Stars don't like supporting acts doing better than themselves'.

Feeling very down in the dumps I looked through my scrapbook and realised that I had been a professional entertainer for the past ten years, had played every theatre up and down the country and, in spite of my success on stage and with the press, I still could not get into the BBC for a weekly radio series, which was the only way to become a top attraction. Phil Brown had obtained radio spots in the *Variety Band Box* but not in the important *Sharman's Music Hall*. He had tried all his radio contacts, but could not get the BBC interested, they felt that I was unsuitable for a weekly series but alright for individual spots. One producer said that my whistling was too toppy another wanted me only to sing and yodel.

Then I found that Moss Empires and Stolls would not book me because I had turned down the *Prince of Wales Theatre* for *Strike a New Note* show. My world appeared to fall apart. My dream of becoming a top star was surely over.

But this despondency was interrupted, when the Swiss jeweller from whom I had bought a watch in Lucerne, phoned to say he was coming to London for a visit. This brought back memories of my whistling and yodelling at the *Park Hotel* in Vitznau, where an American family staying there assured me that there was no one like me in America. They told me that I should go to the USA.

'Yes! Why not?' I started talking to myself.

'Get your skates on, Ron, go and do it!'

I went to London's American Embassy to ask what to do about obtaining a visa and was greeted quite tersely with the order to 'Sit down over there!' where hundreds of people were already anxiously waiting for an interview. I waited and waited until the American official proclaimed, 'We are closing for the day, come back tomorrow!' Next day I was back, very early, and so, it seemed, was everybody else. I was called just before 5pm, only to be told that I needed a confirmatory letter from my theatrical agent stating that I was going to go to America to obtain future theatre work contracts. My patience was near breaking point – I'd wasted two days and was no further forward, but I knew I had to get that letter.

A week at London's *Eastham Palace* was to prove important to me. It marked the beginning of an association between me and a member of the Hyman Zahl Agency, Cyril Berlin. Many years later Cyril told me that he had become intrigued by the name Ronalde, as it was for ever being heard at the Zahl Agency through phone calls from Steffani explaining that I should be among the top attractions on the British variety stage. Cyril's wish to see me perform had become so great that he got into his car and caught my act during first house.

Apparently he approached Hyman Zahl next day at the office and told him that he agreed with what he had heard about Ronnie Ronalde:

'One day he'll be one of our biggest stars!'

'All right, all right, if you want to take him over, its all right by me!'

So from that day on until he died in 1988, Cyril became my agent. I was his first star, and others followed: Lonnie Donegan, Reg Varney, Roy Castle, Jeannie Carson, Diana Dors, Shani Wallis, Arthur Askey, Des O'Connor, Micky and Griff. Cyril also arranged the Beatles to tour Australia. He became the only agent to be honoured for his work in Australia by His Excellency, Douglas McLelland, and the first honorary Life President of the Entertainment Agents Association.

I returned to the American Embassy with my agent's letter, a banker's reference that I had sufficient funds for a stay of six weeks and return ticket. Eventually I was given a six weeks entry visa with the proviso that I would not be able to work. If I did obtain US theatre contracts, I would have to return to Britain and re-apply for a work visa. Also they would have to see proof of the American entertainment contracts with a written application for permission to work and an American agent's letter of confirmation.

Now on to the next hurdle – an allocation of US dollars from my own bank account with Barclays. This brought more problems due to the fact that if I were not to work, I would be rated as being on holiday. I had already used the yearly allowance of £78 in Switzerland and so had to write to the governmental currency division, requesting that, as I was going to America to obtain future contracts, would they grant me extra dollars. On 8 April 1947 I received a special allowance of £285, which had to last for six weeks and pay for everything. Five years of war had made Britain a poor country, yet big American acts were coming over to play the London *Palladium*, with no opposition from our Variety Artistes Federation (VAF), and were paid in their own currency and at salaries British acts had never even dreamed of. The American acts also got top billing.

There was also the matter of pride. I had to practically beg at the American Embassy for a US visa, when their theatre acts were arriving in Britain with little or no fuss at all, they did not have to join the VAF to be able to work, they took all their money out again and sometimes demanded to be paid in America before they even left for Britain. Yet we, British artistes, had to fight to obtain permission to change a few Pounds of our own hard-earned money into dollars that we could, with luck, turn into more dollars for Britain.

This made me more determined than ever before to cross the Atlantic and if the worst came to the worst I could always sell my diamond ring. I looked at it on my little finger and felt reassured. Yes! that should fetch a few dollars.

I had bought the ring in Rotherham after a jeweller's visit to the Theatre Greenroom. The bright sparkle of the ring he was wearing caught my eye. Seeing my interest, he slipped it on my finger just before my entrance onto the stage where the lights made it dazzle even more. Coming off stage I looked for the jeweller, alas he had gone home somewhat happy. There was nothing else I could do but to take the ring with me back to my digs.

While undressing I was thinking where I should hide the ring during the night? I had seen that the landlady's eagle eyes had noticed the sparkle.

'I know, I'll place it under my mattress!' and knelt down beside my bed, lifted the mattress with one hand and tried to place the ring with the other under it.

At that precise moment the landlady opened my bedroom door:

'What time would you like your tea tomorrow?' and seeing me kneeling in front of the bed added:

'You'll find it in the cupboard under the washstand! I don't like the pee-pot under the bed because the fumes rust the bedsprings.'

With relief I returned the ring next day to its rightful owner who had wondered where he had left it.

I wanted to go to America but the thought of having to endure a 17-hour flight over the Atlantic absolutely terrified me. There was only one alternative. I had to go by ship. But when? All passages were fully booked for months ahead. Eventually a travel agent secured the last ticket for me on the Queen Elizabeth, a state cabin.

I could have done without that extra expense when help arrived in the form of a letter from the owner of the Government requisitioned house my family was living in, asking my father if he would like to buy it for £500. Well, thanks to my whistle, I was the only member of the family who had anything near that amount. After a complicated series of transactions, involving the Derequisition Offices, the local Council and the War Damages Officer, I owned my own house for £350, which shortly after I sold for £2200, thus enabling me to book the state cabin and I also had sufficient money for the down payment on a far larger house, Oak Lodge in Enfield, which would accommodate me, all the family and with room to spare. How my mother would have loved this spacious house and garden.

Producer Joy Russel of the BBC *Variety Band Box*, on hearing that I was going to New York, immediately offered me another radio spot which unfortunately I could not accept any more, but BBC Phillip Shearer did wish me well over the radio in my new venture.

When Steffani decided that he would like to see the States too, I was delighted to say yes.

'I'll be your manager,' he beamed.

'Well, I can't pay you,' I replied, 'but you can share my state cabin'.

Troise & his Mandaliers

Oak Lodge

Saying a prayer on the Swiss mountain

Hilda Mundy

Billy Cargyll

Act Ten

AMERICA

The *Queen Elizabeth* looked vast and as I stepped onto the gangway I felt very proud that I'd got so far. If only my mother could see me now. But where was Steffani? I had lost him already and we were only just beginning the journey! He had started doing his job. He had met Frank Betts from the *Kings Features News Syndicate* and he must have impressed him because after I performed on board at a concert in aid of the seamen, he told Steffani that he had won a few dollars: he had put his money on Ronalde to receive the most applause.

When we arrived in New York, with the ship's horn blasting every few minutes, people poured onto the docks, including the press, who came in force to gather stories and pictures of the famous embarking from the *Queen Elizabeth*. Steffani told them that he had a story about the greatest whistler in the world. One of the pressmen looked at him and, chewing his gum, drawled, 'So what!' We were learning already that America would indeed be a hard nut to crack.

We had pre-booked our rooms at a hotel in West 49th Street, just off Broadway and soon realised that the many American hotels we had seen in films most certainly did not portray reality, but there was nothing we could do to change the situation as we needed to conserve every dollar. The hotel had no dining room as we were used to – you had to tip the porter to bring you sandwiches from the nearest drug store.

Before leaving England I was given a letter of introduction by Harold Ramsey, the famous Canadian organist, to Gus Eysel, the Head of the *Radio City Music Hall* in New York. Wee Georgie Wood had also given me a warning:

'Always remember Ron, everyone has influence until they use it!'

Eysel made us welcome in his office in the Rockefeller Building and arranged for us to see senior producer Leon Leonidoff of *RCMH* who, after hearing me, quite categorically proclaimed:

'I couldn't have you with my Symphony Orchestra of 90 musicians, you'll go out of tune like that mouth-organ player.'

The conductor had apparently broken his baton and after the mouth organ player's performance thrown it onto the stage.

All Steffani's pleading was to no avail – the producer had said no.

My dreams were shattered. I left the theatre fighting back the tears; the door to Broadway had been slammed into my face before I'd even started. Because of this setback, we moved to the cheaper Van Cortland Hotel, an old theatrical haunt where Al Jolson (my idol) had stayed in his early days. Perhaps this was a good omen? We were offered a room on the first floor, with its window opening out onto the tin rooftop of the storey below, and enclosed by two other walls of this triangular building. A fire escape coming down one side of the building was used daily by about 50 cats, which were regularly called to get their tit bits by a crazy woman living on the top floor. Frequently a porter used to climb onto this roof and sweep up all the empty cans, bottles and rubbish that had come hurtling down from the various windows, landing with a crash on this tin roof, or on one of the cats who then would let out one mighty screech, making us jump off the bed. Then the music started. Everyone was tuning up on their different instruments and, with all the open windows facing into this airshaft, there was no air-conditioning, the echo bouncing off its walls did not sound anything like a Glen Miller Band.

Steffani and I managed to put up with these living conditions for a couple of days but when a can thrown down the shaft ricocheted into our room, we'd had enough. As luck would have it, a top floor apartment had just become available and even had a piano in it, although, ironically, when I lay in bed I could see the *RCMH* lights flashing, on and off, on and off, all night, as though they were teasing me –

'America has beaten you! America has beaten you!' – until, exhausted, I fell asleep.

The days slipped by and so did our dollars. We were in dire need of a haircut but could not afford a New York barber so I went to Woolworth, purchased a hairdressing set and from then on, cut our own hair. We also rationed our food living on tea and biscuits during the day and for the evening, having purchased a little burner heated up canned food in our bedroom. We further supplemented our diet with iced water and broken slices of bread at *Childs* or *Whelans* on Broadway. Both items were free as long as you bought something to eat at their counters. So one of us would sit at the table and eat and drink the free offerings while the other one looked at the food along the counter as if trying to choose. Then we changed places. We always managed not to buy anything.

Finally, Steffani had enough:

'Tonight, we will go and eat.'

What had happened? While I had been thinking about selling my diamond ring, he had gone out and done exactly that with his ring. I did not know what to say.

It was still early and wanting to draw out the anticipation of a good meal as long as possible, we walked into a men's outfitters store, to browse. Steffani, purely by way of conversation, related my story to its Jewish proprietor, a Mr. Jaysel.

'Do you mean that nobody in this city will listen to what you do? Then the heck

I will!... Let's hear you, kid!'

I started with all the different bird whistles and ended my little performance with a few bars of the 'Anniversary Song'. Shop assistants and customers alike stood there looking at me in disbelief – how could something so powerful come out of one so little? Mr. Jaysel was so astounded that he went to the phone and rang a friend who happened to be an agent. Within 24 hours this agent had contacted the Eddie Smith Agency who, in turn, booked me into the *Jamaica Theatre* at Long Island for three nights. As the agent handed me the contract he warned me,

'This is where they'll make or break you!'

Well, they didn't break me – they rebooked me for another week. The theatre manager told Steffani that when I walked onto his stage, announcing that I would sing 'A Nightingale sang at Berkeley Square' with my English accent and wearing that English suit, he expected to hear all sorts of bird and cat calls from his audience. But it didn't happen. There was just one small piece of advice: because I was so young, I should wear sportier looking clothes. And 'by the way', he added, 'the directors who syndicated Frank Sinatra will be in next house'.

Next show and the audience kept on applauding, it was difficult to leave the stage. The directors were in the wings and after my performance asked Steffani to make an appointment with them which he did.

It felt great getting up in the morning and having some Dollars in my pocket, ordering a full breakfast of ham and eggs. Broadway had taken on a different dimension. My steps had acquired a sort of spring and I held my head high. Especially when we passed *Lindsy's* on Broadway where a couple of days previously myself and Steffani together with another three British artistes, Wee Georgie Wood, Ernest Shannon the impressionist and Serge Ganju (who in time was to run Cliff Richard) had entered this hallowed restaurant and ordered one strawberry shortcake with five plates and five spoons. Upon taking our order the Irish waiter asked if we wanted five glasses of water too?

'Yes please' we all voiced in unison.

It is a fact that anything can happen in America. I was privileged to meet the great music man, Duke Ellington, who played some of my music and stood over me on a rostrum, conducting. He suggested that I should go and see his agent, the William Morris Office, one of the largest in New York, and most powerful in the world. Steffani took his advice and phoned for an appointment.

'Yes, 10 o'clock tomorrow, and do bring your music!'

A secretary took us to one of the many auditioning rooms, which slowly began to fill with different Morris Office agents. By the time I was asked to whistle I felt thoroughly sick.

'Okay Steffani, let's hear him then'!

I stood there, in my Swiss suit, Steffani started to play the 'Tritsch Tratsch Polka' and I began to whistle. Our second number, a yodelling song, was interrupted by one of the agents, who asked us to stop while he phoned. A few minutes later the London representative of the Morris Office joined us.

'Listen to this! He'll kill them at the London *Palladium*!' The agent wrote down some details and then asked if I was French or Swiss.

'No, English,' replied Steffani.

'Does Val Parnell of Moss Empires and the London *Palladium* know him?'

'Yes,' replied Steffani and then it dawned on us – they wanted to send me to the London *Palladium*!

'Now Steffie, if we changed Ronnie's name and put him into different clothes, do you think Parnell would know him then?'

'I'm afraid so.'

A look of dismay appeared on their faces; the audition ended. Again I'd managed to go so far and again the door stayed firmly shut.

The following day Steffani kept his appointment with the syndicate directors. They would back me for a yearly sum of $50,000 but first I would have to sign a long-term contract, containing many clauses. They were to have full jurisdiction over what I did and when, conform and perform when told to. They would pay to dress, photograph and publicise me through their own press agent. They would take care of all accommodation and transport, both for performances and private; even a yearly private trip back to England was thrown in.

What could I say? To be presented with such an offer after such a short stay in America was quite an achievement for a British artiste.

'I'm sorry,' I said to Steffani, 'but I really can't be tied down like that.'

I wasn't prepared to have someone else rule my life. Although I was grateful to Steffani, I asked him to inform the syndicate of my decision.

That evening we were taken out by Sam and Mary Eisner, relations of Cyril Berlin and a long friendship was formed.

Eddie Smith had managed to book me for a week at the *Gaiety Theatre* in Montreal. What would Canada bring? I opened on Monday 19 May 1947 and the next day the *Montreal Daily Star* wrote of '*a young chap with a nice stage presence who gives a marvellous exhibition of whistling and singing. His yodelling is good and he sings... very well, but it is his clear, birdlike whistling that amazes one... This is his first appearance on this continent but he should make quite a hit over here.*

Atlantic City followed, with an appearance at the *Steel Pier*, deputising for Connie Boswell, hosted by Dean Martin. This show was a buster for me; people kept stopping me in the street, wanting to know how I did that whistle. Atlantic City will always stay in my mind. We were sitting on the hotel terrace, overlooking the beach and drinking coffee. As it looked so inviting Steffani decided to go for a swim.

Suddenly I heard someone say:

'Gee, there's a guy out there trying to commit suicide!'

The absence of people in the water should have made us realise the danger – Steffani's few feeble swimming strokes were no match for the severe undercurrents beneath the calm of the water's surface. The Coast Guard got the 'crazy Englishman' out.

Back in New York Eddie Smith had been busy on my behalf. After keeping my promise and reappearing at the *Jamaica*, I was booked for a week in Philadelphia at the *Court Square Theatre* Springfield, Massachusetts.

And my name? Top of the bill.

We returned to Toronto, this time to appear at the *Casino*. As Steffani and I walked towards the theatre I saw the billing: top star – Harry Conley, second - Sylvia Starr, and where was I? Among many others was the name, 'Rinaldo' – was that supposed to be me?

When my music started I walked onto the stage and whistled the 'French Can Can' and put all my inner fury into every note to vent my anger. After this initial outburst I sang and yodelled through my act. By that time I felt the audience's reaction and realised that they would not stop clapping so I quickly left the stage after the first curtain.

'Now follow that!' I said to myself.

The star, Harry Conley, couldn't start his performance because the audience kept on shouting for encores. Arriving at the theatre next night, what did we see? There it was, my name all in lights: 'The Sensational Ronalde'. I really could not have asked for more.

The *Toronto Globe and Mail*, dated 2 July 1947 carried a long feature by Roly Young, which included these words: *unless I am greatly mistaken, when Ronalde strikes Broadway he's going to make theatrical history. What that lad could do at, say the Paramount, with a big band behind him, would really give the folks back home in Islington something to cheer about. Look out Bing and Frankie, a real singer is coming to town ... and don't forget the name... RONALDE!'*

Back in New York I was confronted with two developments. The first was an appearance at the *Grand Hotel* in Glenville; the second was something I had feared was coming: my visa had run out and the USA Immigration quite firmly reminded me that I was working illegally in their country. Another point raised was the AGVA, the USA Entertainments Union. Had I asked for their permission to work? We hastily went to the AGVA head office to sort out this oversight, naturally we were both thinking of returning to America.

It was not only a matter of paying your fees and joining the union, it was more a matter of being accepted by them. As America at that time had literally a million singers, I had to get in with my whistle. Joining the union was very costly: one year's dues was a calculated percentage of my few weeks' fees multiplied by 52 weeks, plus a $50 entrance fee. This nearly broke me – surely American artistes did not have to pay that much in Britain? Emigration ordered me to leave the USA.

Steffani, who had trained as a boy cadet at Cramwell always had a love for planes and so had booked us to fly back to Britain on a 'Stratocruiser', which took nearly as long as the ship, having to stop and refuel in Newfoundland and Shannon. As a matter of fact it was such an adventure that one was given a certificate, the *Winged Order of the Pond-Hoppers*, signed by the captain and affixed with the seal of the *Empyrean Emperor Phoebus Apollo*, to prove that one had flown the Atlantic and lived to tell the tale. A most outstanding feature of the plane was the club lounge below the plane, equipped with piano, phonograph and bar in its belly, reached via a spiral staircase and enclosed by large windows where one could watch the world fly by.

On board RMS 'Queen Elizabeth'

Steel Pier, Atlantic City

Special friends, Sam & Mary Eisner

Radio City

Casino Toronto

Act Eleven

BACK IN ENGLAND

Following my homecoming my father immediately told me that he was no longer happy working at the Standard Telephone Co. after bragging so much about me. I should retire him, so at the age of 50, with my help, although on hindsight I really should have waited, he did.

Val Parnell of Moss Empires and Prince Littler's Stolls Theatres offered me nothing – it was as though they wished to dispel my American triumph and I'm sure they wouldn't believe that I nearly appeared at their London *Palladium*, of course, with an American salary. What do you do when you get offers from the worlds greatest American entertainment agency, which sees you as a 'wow' at the *Palladium*, yet those in charge of booking artistes into the *Palladium* could not or would not see it?

During my absence Phil Brown had extensive meetings with various BBC producers and the secretary of the Variety Artistes Federation, Harry Marlowe, with regard to a Royal Command Performance; in fact Marlowe himself received many letters asking that I be included.

August 1947 was halfway through and I had performed in only two concerts, Llandudno and Colwyn Bay. It was a worrying time, with the family now dependent on me. Suddenly I received an urgent message asking me to deputise for Jack and Daphne Barker in a *Variety Band Box* radio show the very next evening. Payment at the BBC was small, because of its monopoly in the broadcasting world; although a potential 12 million people were listening, I received 12 guineas, with a further three guineas for a replay and six guineas if the programme would be played overseas. It was an income. The stronger Musicians Union could command more recognition, but our Variety Artistes Federation still had a long way to go.

On 1 September 1947 I took part in my first TV programme from the *Alexandra Palace* in London, the *Television Personality Parade*, starring Gracie Fields. It was not so long ago since I had first appeared with her as a Songster in Glasgow. She had come into our dressing room, perched on a chair and chatted in the inimitable way that had endeared her to the hearts of people around the world. When she left, she remarked, 'I'd like you all to be successful and reach the top of the ladder, but it's the top you'll have to worry about. Remember lads, you're on the way up and I'm on the way down.' I had also worked quite often with Gracie's brother, comedian Tommy Fields, who was full of warmth and charm and became a very good friend.

My second TV appearance was in Richard Hearne's *Variety*, with Linda Gray, Eva May Wong, Boyer and Ravel, Saveen and Hamilton Conrad and the orchestra directed by Eric Robinson. This completely new medium was very exciting, and everyone was still in the learning stages. The actual TV screens were very small, so the performers' movements were restricted, otherwise they would be shown on screen with half their heads missing. The viewing audience was not large as only a few people could afford television sets. Programmes were only shown in the evenings, starting with the news around 6 o'clock, and of course all was in black and white.

So radio was still number one in people's homes and my next two *Variety Band Box* programmes with Cavan O'Connor, Morton Fraser, Michael Howard, Peter Brough, Archie Andrews, Primo Scala, Janet Davies, Klara Katz and Benny Hill received excellent listening figures.

This period saw a change the way agents worked. With the growth of TV, a new breed was emerging, bringing with them ethics from the American entertainment world. The Grades' agency, in their wisdom, went fully into association with television, but many other British agents either gave up or joined with other agents to make their organisations larger. Hyman Zahl's office became part of Harry Foster's agency, although this alliance later became their downfall. Foster's, founded in 1880, stated categorically that it wanted to remain an agency for theatres only. But, by being associated with Hyman Zahl, Harry Foster had to change a little because Hyman had taken on new young blood, he had not only me but also many young up and coming pop groups on his books. Since Hyman was such a live wire, he needed someone to sort his business deals out, this person was Cyril Berlin.

Hyman was on the phone:

'Ronnie, Moss Empires are in deep trouble!'

They had booked Laurel and Hardy in a variety bill at the *Finsbury Park Empire* and the opening night was a disaster. Could I go on tonight, just before Laurel and Hardy, to give their act a kick up the backside? I went quiet. Why was it that I was only good when there was a problem, but never good enough for my own sake?

'Do it, Ronnie, please do it,' Hymie panted down the phone.

'It's an opportunity, Ronnie, take it!'

I suppose it could be fun working with Laurel and Hardy! 'Okay, I'll do it.'

There was no time for rehearsal. Unbilled and unheralded, I went on first house. Poor Laurel and Hardy had a difficult time following my act. Second house and the Moss Empire management had changed the programme: they presented me after the comedians, in the star spot. I went even better and had the audience in such a happy mood that when I was singing 'Sweet Sixteen' they were up on stage singing with me.

This was unbelievable in a theatre at that time. Newspaperman Jack Oliphant witnessed the scene and wrote the story up to sell it to the Fleet Street papers only to see his scoop collapse when one of the newspaper editors phoned Moss Empire to ask for confirmation but they strenuously denied that the incident had happened. When my agent asked Moss's booking manager, Cissie William and Ted Gallop why, he was told that they could not have it known that their theatres were out of control with uninvited audiences having access to the stage, it could keep people away.

So, no write-up, but by the next night I had two policemen standing either side of the stage to stop anyone coming up to me during my act. Cissie William told me to stay in the show for the week, and the policemen stayed too. Some time later, when two fans went up on stage during Frankie Lane's and Danny Kaye's performances to ask for an autograph, it became headline news, as though it were a new phenomenon.

These were my first five working days for Moss Empire for a year. Despite the appreciative reviews at the end of the week I was meagerly paid. Hyman, too, was disappointed with the Moss Empire management. They had paid huge amounts to Laurel and Hardy, who could not hold the top spot, and gave little appreciation to me. I was happy though with the impact I'd made and became friendly with the famous duo and even tried to teach Oliver to whistle. We all had a great laugh when Oliver tried to get his fingers, the size of bananas, into his mouth. He did give me a little china blackbird ornament, which I still have.

America was again pre-eminent in my mind. I needed pushing and that wasn't going to happen in Britain. In a disheartened mood, I took out my American files and forms to apply for a re-entry working visa when the doorbell rang; it was the postman needing a signature on an American stamped letter.

Eddie Smith, my New York agent, was asking me to return as soon as possible as he had some shows lined up for me. One was to be with Roy Rodgers and his horse Trigger at the *Worcester Municipal Auditorium*, Minneapolis, another with Charlie Barnett and his orchestra, and there were various other dates to be confirmed once I was back in the USA again. There I stood, holding the letter I needed to obtain a working visa.

Steffani got the ball rolling and booked our passage on the *Queen Elizabeth*, again state cabin. When the tickets arrived they showed celebrity rates, and would we perform again?

I still had one more show to do before I left, at the *Palace* in Blackpool also featuring Jimmy Edwards giving one of his Navy Mixture lectures.

Cambridge educated Jimmy Edwards asked me if I knew about the Oozalum bird and could I imitate their call? I looked at Percy Edwards who was also there as he was far more knowledgeable about birds than me, he was a true ornithologist. Percy hesitated with his answer so I asked Jimmy if the bird whistles or shrieks? And in asking him I instinctively knew that something funny was coming.

'Well' said Jimmy, 'the Oozalum bird lives by the sea, feeds on shore life and is a truly majestic whistler. The bird has been known to stick his head in the sand and whistle through the hole of the afternoon.

In the local *Evening Gazette* the next day was the verdict of the show:

'Ronalde has a singing, whistling and yodelling voice as engaging as his personality, so that it was not surprising, that last night's audiences refused, for minutes on end, to let him go.'

But the British theatre bookers let me go, back to America on 11 October 1947.

PLEASURE GARDENS THEATRE

FOLKESTONE. LESSEES—PARK THEATRICAL PRODUCTIONS LTD. LICENSEE AND MANAGER—JACK PERSICH 'Phone : FOLK. 3227.

| 6-15 | TWICE NIGHTLY (FOR GOOD FRIDAY SEE PANEL ON LEFT) | 8-20 |

FROM MONDAY, MARCH 31ST, 1947

VARIETY'S GREATEST EMOTIONAL EXPERIENCE

STEFFANI
AND HIS FAMOUS SILVER SONGSTERS
THE ACT WHICH GLORIFIES THE STAGE
THEIR MELODIES SO RADIANTLY RENDERED AND VOICES SO BEAUTIFULLY BLENDED

THE VOICE OF THE WHISTLER

RONALDE
STAR OF B.B.C.'s "VARIETY BANDBOX" FAME

GOOD FRIDAY NIGHT AT 7-30
(ONE PERFORMANCE)
Prices of Reserved Seats
1/9, 2/6, 3/6 & 4/6
"HARMONY IN EXCELSIS"
Grand Musical Programme
Including
THE SILVER SONGSTERS
RONALDE
PATRICIA ROSSBOROUGH
KEITH WILLIAMS
LEN TREVOR, Etc., Etc.

TAYLOR & GRAY FALLING FOR YOU
KIZMI & KAREN TAPS IN TEMPO
KEITH WILLIAMS THE MAN ABOUT TOWN
IN A MONASTERY GARDEN | YOUTH STEPS OUT
LEN TREVOR AND HIS ORCHESTRA
In a Grand Military Fantasia founded on the world famous Song 'The Trumpeter'
THE EMINENT RADIO PIANISTE
PATRICIA ROSSBOROUGH
VIDE PRESS—"With the delicacy of touch for which she is so famed—and the lady herself so eloquently expressive"

BOX OFFICE OPEN 10 A.M. TO 8 P.M.
Parkes & Mainwarings Ltd., Printers, Birmingham 4 and London W.1.

Salute the Heroes of the Battle of Britain!

GRAND
ALL-STAR CONCERT
Sunday, September 21st, 1947
(Battle of Britain Sunday)
at 6.30 p.m.
Hermitage Cinema Hitchin
By kind Permission of the Directors
In aid of The Royal Air Force Benevolent Fund. The Royal Air Force Ass. Fund(Hitchin & Henlow Branch)

The Voice of the Whistler
Ronalde
The celebrated Star direct from his American Tour

PETER BROUGH
and ARCHIE ANDREWS
The Famous Ventriloquist of Stage and Broadcasting Fame

Special visit of the celebrated Stage, Screen and Radio Stars
Forsythe, Seamon & Farrell
The Celebrated Comedy Stars

MARIO (Harp) LORENZI
Radio's Maestro of the Harp

London's Highlight
TRISS HENDERSON
Star of Piccadilly Hayride

The World Famous
THE DAGENHAM GIRL PIPERS

JACK SALISBURY
The Celebrated Broadcasting Violinist

KATHLEEN LEEDS
The Brilliant Young Soprano

CARMEN HARE
Queen of the Accordian and Star Accompanist

DICK HENDERSON Jun.
Master of Ceremonies

TICKETS: Front Balcony, Numbered and Reserved 10/6. Centre Balcony 5/-. Rear Balcony, 2/6. Very Front Stalls 2/6. Front Stalls 7/6.
Rear Stalls 5/-.
All Seats to be obtained from Box-Office, Hermitage Cinema, Hitchin. Phone 525.
THIS SHOW PRODUCED FOR THE ROYAL AIR FORCE ASS. (HITCHIN, HENLOW & DISTRICT BRANCH) BY TED. ANDERSON, HITCHIN PHONE HITCHIN 383
Borecroft Press, Ltd., Hitchin.

Tommy Fields

Act Twelve

RADIO CITY MUSIC HALL

On board the *Queen Elizabeth* were many theatrical celebrities: Wee Georgie Wood, Scots comedian Harry Gordon, Harold Smart, Mrs. Leslie Howard, Ben Henry, who helped to make George Formby so much money in films after John Blakeley made him in his first film, Googie Whithers, Dame Myra Hess, George Dormonde, William Primrose, one of the world's greatest Cellists and France's Edith Piaf with her Compagnons Chanson. I enjoyed listening to her, she appeared so sad although I did make her laugh when I tried to imitate a French sounding Cuckoo which by far was not as good as Noel Agnew, my friend and lawyer in New Zealand, who gives a superb impression of a gargling Frenchman.

All the artistes entertained the passengers on board for the benefit of the seamen's charity and the 'Celebrity Show', compered by Georgie Wood, was voted the best concert ever seen on the ship.

The sea journey had been calm but when we should have arrived in New York we couldn't find it. And neither could the Harbour master find us!

To quote the *Daily Mail* 17 October 1947:

I can't find the QE. A man spent an hour today looking for the world's biggest ship, then came back in his launch and reported: Sorry, but I couldn't see a trace of her. He was the harbour pilot sent to bring the QE into dock, but for all the bulk of her 83 000 tons, she was well hidden in the fog which surrounded New York harbour today. Visibility was Zero. When the fog lifted the Cunarder had missed the tide, so she joined a queue of 19 ships and docked 12 hours late.

We were welcomed by Welsh Welter Weight Boxing Champion Jack Daniels and his wife Beaulah whom we'd befriended during my previous visit whilst appearing in Philadelphia where after my performance I met Al Jolson who said 'you have a good whistle Sonny Boy!'.

Once back in the same hotel suite at the Van Cortland, I was not given a chance to relax but within three days started work at the *Valley Arena* in Holyoke where I was accompanied by Tony Pastor and his orchestra and a concert at the *Grand Street Boys*. Then I travelled for the first time on a Greyhound bus to appear at the *Penn Theatre* at Wilkes-Barre. It was strange, but for American audiences it was my singing voice, more than my whistling, that made an impact. The manager of the *Penn Theatre* told Steffani that he had never heard a singer get such applause and showed him a copy of a letter he had written to their head office stating that Ronalde was better and more popular than Tony Martin or John Boles.

Back in New York, the second most important agency in the USA, the Music Co-operation of America, who booked American star attractions into the London *Casino* presented by Bernard Delfont, rang to suggest that this would be a good venue for me.

Did Delfont know me?

Of course he knew me. Both Steffani and I were dumbfounded. There we were, in America for the second time within a year, and for the second time I was offered a booking for one of the top theatres in my home city, where they did not want to know me even though I had been invited to the home of Moss Empire's Director Mark Ostra as I was assisting his wife at Charity functions. Their Surrey home was a sumptuous place with a Butler and two huge Great Danes who greeted you.

This was proving the point that you can have a God given talent the public recognises but the powers that hold the strings of the entertainment world do not help talented, young performers. At times I felt quite frustrated but I had to continue the fight.

We barely had time for a change of clothes before we were sent back to Canada to the *Gayety* in Montreal. Impressionist Tony Francis, of the BBC's Tommy Handley *ITMA Show* was touring Canada and came to see me. The following appeared in *The Performer* on 6 November 1947:

Generous tribute to Ronalde's success in Canada comes in the guise of a letter to hand from Tony Francis,. . . he was totally unprepared for the 'terrific ovation' accorded Ronalde, who was compelled to give encore after encore, at the close of which a member of the audience stood up and asked the packed house to stand in tribute to this artiste.

Bookings were coming in so quickly that Eddie Smith warned me to be careful about accepting offers from the *Lowe State Theatre* on Broadway as this could conflict with possible dates at the *Roxy* or the *Paramount*, both on Broadway. After a concert at the *Waldorf Astoria,* attended by the Mayor of New York and many United Nations dignitaries, we were off to the *Victoria* Theatre in Bayonne and to the *Schubert* Theatre at New Haven, Connecticut. I was getting quite used to the various theatre managers coming backstage and complimenting me on my voice. Wee Georgie Wood kept on saying that I should say yes to the big boys who wanted to syndicate me. Mr. Nichol, a friend of Georgie's, suggested I should change my name; he wanted me to meet Paul Whiteman, the great bandleader, and make a test for him. In my diary I wrote: 'What a crazy world this is'. The following day I returned to Canada, but this time to Toronto's *Casino* with the *Globe* and *Mail* writing: *...easily the tops in any singing act to play this town...*

During my week in Toronto I was invited to be a guest on many radio shows and was overwhelmed by the warmth of DJ Lee Hamilton. Not at all like the BBC! The CBS suggested that I should emigrate to Canada. They would provide me with a house if I would work for them; they did not want to lose me to America.

As I continued touring I found I was being rebooked in all the theatres I had played before, although this was a compliment it was not getting me into the top New York venues. I had received an invitation to audition for the next show at the legit *Munroe* Theatre on Broadway which I declined, I did not wish to audition. Incidentally nor did Rex Harrison, for the role as Dr. Dolittle he sent a photo of himself showing his virility instead and Shelly Winters deposited her *Oscar* she'd just won in a shopping bag on the director's desk.

Was the syndicate working behind the scenes to press me to accept their offer? There was a lot of anti-British feeling too because of the Palestinian problem. This became obvious when I was introduced as an English artiste to an entirely Jewish audience at a holiday resort in the Catskill Mountains, although after I had sung an Al Jolson song they soon showed their appreciation.

On 29 November, Sam Wasserman presented a show at the *Worcester Municipal Auditorium*. The host of the evening was Garry Morton and on the same bill were Connie Boswell, the one and only Roy Rogers with his famous horse called Trigger and yours truly. I did cause a little upset with Trigger because my whistling on stage affected his waterworks whilst he and Roy Rogers were waiting to follow my act. It certainly was not funny for the stagehands to do the mopping up.

Years later I told that story on a radio interview in New Zealand with Brian Edwards when as a result I received an interesting fanletter:

Funny about Roy Roger's Trigger as he was and still is my favourite Cowboy as I am an Ex-Jockey. I could just picture Trigger doing that as when a horse wins a race we would take him to the swab box and start shaking up the straw and WHISTLE for a urine sample. Think of it with all the races around today. YOU (Ronnie) could make a fortune. Ten races a day – ten winners at let's say $10 a race – the mind boggles. Ha! Ha! Russel Sutherland.

That whistling can arouse sensuality and sexuality in humans I was aware of, so really it should not have come as a surprise that it has the same effect on animals as proven a few times during my career.

I returned to New York where *Capitol's* Joe Matthew took me to the *Paramount* to see Frankie Laine and the Vaughn Monroe Band. Listening to Vaughn singing his signature tune did thrill me but looking in a competitive manner at Frankie Laine perform, I knew the time had come to do something drastic, so I went to see the Eddie Smith Agency and told them, that if they couldn't book me into a Broadway theatre, then they needn't bother to phone.

They didn't bother to phone.

For three weeks I was kicking my heels, with no work except appearances at the odd function. The money was running low and it was close to Christmas. At night, from across the street, the *RCMH* lights continued to flash on and off, on and off. What were they trying to tell me?

Twelve days to Christmas. It was snowing and everywhere we looked trees were decorated with tinsel and coloured lights. After listening to the carol singers

'Silent Night' we ended up in a coffee shop feeling so homesick that Steffani suggested we should return to England. Back at the hotel a message was awaiting us :

'Please call *Radio City*!'

It must be a joke. Steffani fumbled for his inevitable cigarette before picking up the receiver and dialled.

'*Radio City* here!'

Another joke?

And then Steffani slowly began to smile. He was put through to Leon Leonidoff's office. Could he please bring the boy whistler to him as soon as possible?

Could he indeed! You never saw two people get back into their overcoats so quickly and rush across the street to the door of the *RCMH*, only to be informed that we were at the stage door. The office doors were on the next street.

Nik Daks, the Deputy Producer, was waiting to take us to Leonidoff's office and there they all sat: MD Alexander Smallens, Lyricist Al Stillman, (who wrote 'I Believe') Russell Markert, who directed the Rockettes, Organist Richard [Dick] Leibert, Ballet Expert Marc Platt, Stage Operations man John Jackson, Costume Designer Frank Spencer and of course Producer Leon Leonidoff. (I believe he had Russian ancestors).

'Rrronalde,' he asked, 'pleeese do vat you did zee last time!'

After 'Sanctuary of the Heart' I heard Leonidoff, beaming all over his face, exclaim, 'Isn't hee vooonderfuuul? Didn't I teeel you?'

It had been seven months, a return journey to England, sheer luck that we were in New York in the same hotel suite as before, and there I stood in front of the man who had not wanted to know me and now, suddenly, was hailing me as 'vooonderfuuul'.

The show executives envisaged a production centred around Switzerland so Steffani went straight into playing 'My Little Swiss Maid' and I sang and yodelled the song.

'He yodels tuuuu!?'

That afternoon I walked out of America's number one show place with a contract starting 8 January 1948 for the usual length of three weeks. What a Christmas! What a New Year! Telegrams were sent to Father and to Hyman Zahl's office and rehearsals began, with the 90-strong orchestra. There were also fittings for my costume and I had to learn a dance routine with the showgirls. I must say I liked that, and even my friends told me that they never knew I was so versatile.

I was a hit and I felt a hit. The American write-ups were fantastic and the show ran for a record eight weeks.

Don Iddons Diary: Success notes... Note him for stardom.

Roly Young: ...great source of gratitude to me, as I've thought all along that this lad from England could hit the top spots...

but amongst many more it was the *Collie Knox* New York column in the British *Daily Mail* that pleased me most, because it was telling the British show business fraternity that Ronnie Ronalde had proved his worth.

The 'Rockettes', *Radio City Hall's* own show girl dancers are world class and brought the audience to instant applause the moment their dance routine called for their famous kick-up of their long and shapely legs in unison. The girls number 90 which is a lot of woman to be working with but made life easier back stage as it was hard going – four and five shows a day, seven days a week. Everybody else had their stand-ins for their days off, and the orchestra had different conductors, among them Alex Smallen and

Charles Previn (Andre Previn's uncle), but nobody else could do my act so I worked every day. I was thankful when the Management put a bed into my dressingroom so I could really rest between shows. Steffani, on his return from Canada, saw the bed and laughed.

'So it has started!'

'What's started' I asked!

'Well, when I left the wardrobe mistress told me the girls were taking bets who'll have you first!'

'Now you tell me!'

RCMH, one of the most famous theatres in the world was a truly amazing place to work in with its 6200 seats. The stage measured 144 feet wide and 67 feet deep with a 43 foot revolving stage, there were hydraulic stage elevators, a travelling bandwagon for the orchestra and the contour curtain was the largest in the world containing more than 2000 yards of golden antique hammered satin and weighed three tons. The Wurlitzer Organ comprised of 1000 wood and metal pipes ranging in size from a telephone pole to smaller than a peashooter.

One more accolade came my way while I was at *Radio City:* I was invited to appear at the annual *King Features Syndicate* (owned by the powerful Hearst newspaper group) *Banshees* held at the *Waldorf Astoria* on 22 January.

As *The Performer* wrote, *these annual functions are much coveted by stage and film personalities all over the USA... It is interesting to note that among the artistes who have appeared at various Banshees before attaining international fame are Frank Sinatra and Edgar Bergen. Ronalde's invitation came after the Vice President, Bradley Kelly, had witnessed his performance at Radio City at the conclusion of which Ronalde and Steffani were the guests at a private Luncheon given by the Vice President...*

which took place at the exclusive Toot Shoors. Sinatra sat on the next table and was pushed in the back by Brad Kelley who shouted:

'Hi Frank I'd like to introduce you to a real singer and don't forget the name!'

Gene Tunney, Bradley Kelly & Bugs Bunny at the Banshees

Canadian DJ, Lee Hamilton

Departing on the 'Queen Mary'

Dick Leibert

Al Wilson of the Eddie Smith Agency,
New York

Beccles Boxing Club

On stage at Radio City, New York

Act Thirteen

DECCA RECORDINGS

After my hectic weeks at *Radio City* Steffani and I looked forward to a restful five-day sea journey back to Britain on the *Queen Mary*. Wee Georgie Wood and Hyman Zahl had decided to travel with us. I was a little worried about Hyman. Owing to an unfortunate mishap during his childhood, he had to wear very thick glasses. He was a very lovable man and so true to his Jewish faith. During the last few days in New York, Hyman, for convenience, brought all his suitcases to us for storage. But that was not all. Every day he came to our suite, bringing more items to be packed. He had to buy a present for everybody in his family and friends in the theatre business in an England still suffering after the wartime, and to make things easier, he bought everything in dozens. The mountain grew larger: silk stockings, tinned fruit, salamis, coffee, tea, costume jewellery, packets of jello which he thought was jelly but only later found out was jam, biscuits – you name it, he'd bought it.

Hymie was in a mess, so Steffani went out, bought a wooden crate and after carefully packing everything, hammered the lid down with nails and forbade Hymie to bring more presents.

Also on board were Charles Tucker, Tommy Trinder's agent as well as Julie Andrew's parents, Ted and Barbara Andrews and again a ship's concert had been organised.

One could pay the customs officer on board ship in advance on the purchases to be declared in Britain, so Steffani and I went along and paid our dues. Hymie did not. He said that, as he was always putting on charity shows in Southampton for various legal bodies, someone was going to meet him; he had told them that he was travelling with me. When we arrived in Southampton, an official came up to me.

'Mr. Ronnie Ronalde?'

'Yes.'

'I'll arrange all the baggage transfer onto the train for you. Please follow me!'

What service! But where was Hymie?

'Don't worry,' said Steffani, 'he must have met somebody and is probably talking business.'

After a speedy and uneventful debarkation Steffani and I sat down in our reserved compartment and the train pulled out. When we reached London and were organising our taxi, we heard my name come over the railway station's tannoy system.

'Would Mr. Ronalde please proceed to the stationmaster's office where an urgent message awaits him?'

We looked at each other. Now what?

In the office I was put through to Customs in Southampton to a tearful Hymie. Apparently nobody had met him off the ship, so seeing all that luggage Customs had pulled him aside and opened up the lot, including the tightly packed wooden crate with the result that they charged him the earth on duty which he couldn't pay as he had no pounds on him. Would we please bale him out and also send help to put all the things back into his cases? He couldn't manage it and nobody would help him!

I didn't know whether to laugh or cry. I could well imagine him, sitting there like a hen, guarding all the goodies and feeling utterly dejected. I called his brother, Sonny, who immediately dropped everything and raced down to Southampton to help not before reminding me that my first date was the *Metropolitan* Edgware Road in London which had been pre-booked before my departure to America and when Steffani saw that I had been billed among the small acts he went crazy.

'What have we come back for? What are they trying to do to you, son?'

'Don't lose your cool Steff, as I'm such a small act I'm sure I won't be missed.'

I didn't appear, proving yet again that a small act on a small salary gets a small billing. I had to get my weekly salary up and with that in mind phoned my agent and told him that from now on I wanted £100 per week, bearing in mind that unknown American acts were getting far more than that at the London *Palladium*, which the American Morris Agency had only recently offered me.

Yet Moss Empires and Stolls Theatres offered me £75 but would not increase to £100. The result? I was left for weeks without work.

I had a further two dates. During May a TV show called *Haven't a Clue*, hosted by Michael Miles and featuring Evelyn McCabe and Dawn de Ray, for which I received 12 guineas, and in June the *Empire* Sunderland where I appeared with Chefalo, the Two Leslies, Renee Houston and Donald Stewart. The reviews said I stole the show. On to Leeds, and again I was to be found amongst the Wines and Spirits, as was Bill Kerr. But John White, of the *Leeds News,* mentioned only Ronalde in his write-up.

By now I had changed my appearance. Gone was the evening suit and in its place I wore a bright yellow jacket, a yellow and brown tie and off-white trousers. The Americans told me to loosen up and brighten up, and the newspaper write-ups seemed to prove them right like the

Evening Post: *...Biggest applause goes inexplicably to the yellow jacket....*

Out of the blue, Impresario Harold Fielding offered two concerts in the Isle of Wight for £26 each at *Shanklin's* Theatre and the *Pavilion* in Sandown. These two appearances were the beginning of many future concerts and pantomimes offered by him. Then a deal came from the Stolls Theatres: six weeks' work, but for only £70 a week. I thought it over for some days, my position not made any easier with all my home expenses, mortgage and Father's wages, so I finally gave in. That was the last we heard.

No bookings came but my guardian angel did. Cyril Berlin phoned and kept repeating over and over again:

'I've got your 100 pounds! I've got your 100 pounds!' Independent theatre owner, Bill Bastiman, from the *Empire Theatre* in Middlesborough, would pay my first £100. I had broken the barrier. Middlesborough was a record week, with police at the stage door every night. Over the years I went back many times and always for £100, even when I was earning £1000 per week.

In the middle of all this came a letter from Florence Leddington, chief booker for Consolidated Theatres, warning me that they were going to sue me for not having appeared at their *Metropolitan Theatre*. Steffani was called to their offices and told of the punishment they had in store for us. They were not suing but they wished me to play in *all* their theatres and they would pay me, yes, wait for it, £100 per week. In no time at all Miss Williams, of Moss Empire, offered me £100 too. It gave me great satisfaction to have risen from 15/- playing the very small *Argyle Theatre* Birkenhead in 1938, (perhaps one of the most famous Music Halls before it was demolished and where the Songsters had to stand three deep to fit all onto the stage) to £100 per week in 1948, appearing in all the Moss Empire Theatres.

Although Phil Brown had not succeeded in securing a weekly radio series, he did manage to come up with a Decca recording contract and two *Variety Bandbox* radio spots during June and July. The *Weekly Sporting Review* hailed me *whistling virtuoso and a singer whose quality has been compared with Crosby and Sinatra...* I needed police protection from admirers after the broadcast. And the *Musical Express* said that '*Apart from his phenomenal whistling there are few people in this country who can put over a corny song like Ronalde. He deserves more support from the BBC.*'

There it was, press backing for the fact that the *BBC* should support me.

The press was running hot with accolades but still I had to fight to get myself up the ladder, it seemed that merit and talent did not matter, I needed a lot of luck in some quarter, somewhere.

The Decca contract for two double sided 10 inch records, recorded on 9 June 1948, Brixton Road, London SW9, was at the agreed fee of £31 plus on halfpenny Royalties, except any sales in the USA, Canada or South America.

Phil Brown advised to sign on the dotted line, otherwise I wouldn't be making any records at all and I needed them. When we were travelling through America and Canada, we had to shop-record some of my whistling, so that Steffani could let agents hear what I could do. Then they inevitably requested to hear the singing discs, which really surprised us, especially as America had so many of their own singers. Would the AGVA Union have given me permission to enter America as a singer? I doubt it, they listed around a million singers themselves.

I had to decide on the song titles for the two records and came up with 'Birdsong at Eventide', 'Down in the Forest', 'When You are in Love' and 'Somewhere Beyond the Stars'. Robert Farnon arranged the scores and conducted his orchestra. I wanted to whistle two songs and sing two songs and had rehearsed with Steffani accordingly. After my first singing run through Decca's Harry Sarton came out of his recording box and said:

'It sounds all right, but there'll be NO singing on the record!'

These terse words left me speechless. How could I make him change his mind? How could I tell him of all the Americans and Canadians wanting to hear me sing? How could I tell him of all the singing encores requested in the British theatres? How could I tell him of all the letters I received from the young girl fans, asking where they could obtain my singing records?

Frustrated, I whistled the songs, which turned out to be some of my best ever whistling records, still being re-released in the Nineties.

Tatler Record of the week by *Robert Tredinnik*:

If the ordinary song is really successful it must flow with ease, both lyrically and musically. Therefore when you hear a song being whistled in the street you may be sure it possesses those ingredients and that the composer and the publisher are saying to themselves that they have a hit on their hands. But it is not everyone who can whistle, and I suggest that the whistling of Ronalde will be the envy of all those who may aspire to that particular form or art... Not only can he whistle a tune, but he is able to hold the interest of his listeners in whatever he does.

This write-up helped to ease the pain though later this negative decision by Harry Sarton would prove his biggest mistake as Decca's recording manager, when EMI's Norman Newell contracted me to sing 'If I Were a Blackbird', which became a million seller. In the Eighties 'Birdsong at Eventide' was used in *The Singing Detective* TV series and featured on cassettes and CD, becoming top sellers.

Harry Sarton can rest in peace.

The *Palace* Chelsea and the *Empire* Glasgow with Hal Monty, Renee Houston and Donald Stewart brought revues:

Sound: Larry Stave's Diary:*...he rocked'em with one of the most polished solo acts I've seen in many moons....*

The Bulletin, Glasgow Evening News and *Scots Pictorial: ...the audience whistled at the whistler...stood on their feet and applauded until Ronalde returned for a third encore... most popular act to appear at the Empire for some time...*

Someone up there in the BBC must be reading the papers too; would all these accolades bring an invitation to appear in the Royal Command Performance?

During the week at the *Palace* Chelsea a cable arrived:

WANT YOU TO STAR WITH OLSEN & JOHNSON – GRANDSTAND TORONTO – 2 WEEKS – OPENING AUGUST 27 – FOR CANADIAN NATIONAL EXHIBITION.

But Cyril Berlin had to cable back:

'RONALDE COMMITTED TO THEATRE ENGAGEMENTS. UNABLE TO ACCEPT.'

Cyril received another cable: 'IMPERATIVE YOU ACCEPT THIS BOOKING – DON'T LET US DOWN – Signed WILLIAM MORRIS AGENCY – NEW YORK'.

What should we do? Cyril, working overtime, managed to postpone all the UK theatre bookings that had suddenly started to come in. He achieved this in stressing the point that the US dollars I would earn would benefit Britain.

On Saturday night we finished in Glasgow, on Sunday I performed at *Butlin's* in Ayre, then took the overnight sleeper down to London and home, packed my cases and caught the plane, a Constellation, leaving that night to fly via New York to Toronto.

In the Forties if one went on a plane journey it was normal to take out an Insurance Policy just in case one didn't make it, the airports even had machines especially for this purpose.

The flights across the pond to America were often quite empty and one could safely rely on finding three empty seats for a sleep. So after we were going a few hours the steward told me that there is another entertainer at the rear of the plane and would welcome a little conversation. It was none other than James Stewart. We talked a lot and in retrospect I believe he chatted to me because I was a musical entertainer on stage and he was about to film the Glenn Miller Story and wanted to get the feel of the live stage entertainer into his film acting.

James Stewart did get awards for the film but sadly the story Stewart didn't know was that Glenn Miller did not die in a plane going to France but in a house of ill repute in the red light district of Paris where he had a heart attack and died in the arms of a prostitute.

Bill Bastiman – my first £100 man

Norman Newell & Teddy Holmes

Act Fourteen

CANADA

The Grandstand was a mammoth 25,000-seat amphitheatre. I had arrived very late in the evening, everybody seemed very tired, especially me having travelled for the last three days non-stop, the producer with Ole Olsen and Chic Johnson, the stars of the show, welcomed me most warmly but expected a rehearsal there and then. My music was given to the conductor, and away we went - except that he was playing his way and I was whistling my way.

'Hold it, hold it!' he shouted up to me. 'It's Strauss's 'Tritsch Tratsch', and that's how it's played – slower!'

'But I'm whistling it the tempo I want to do it in, and that's faster!' I shouted back.

'Who's this?' asked the conductor, looking at the producer and pointing the baton at me, 'I don't want this!'

'Okay, okay, let's take 15 minutes' called the producer.

Steffani came over to me with a steaming cup of coffee and told me to steady on, 'it'll be all right after a good night's sleep'.

The break over, the musicians reassembled and the conductor looking up at me said: 'Okay Ronnie, how do you want it?'

He appeared to be a changed man. Already then the drug world was showing its power although Ollie Olsen did apologize for the conductor, he told me later, he was more worried about me splitting my lip with all the effort I seemed to put into my performance.

Next day *Laffacade* opened, with the Grandstand packed to the brim, including Lord and Lady Louis Mountbatten with Canadian Prime Minister Drew seated in the royal box. The stage, 450 feet wide and 150 feet deep, was lit by hundreds of floods and spots and 15 microphones were used. Most of the scenery, 100 feet in length and up to 70 feet high and far too heavy to carry, glided along on railway tracks. I had to make my entrance from behind a *swan* flat, otherwise it would have taken me too long to reach centre stage for the beginning of my act.

The cast numbered well over 300 and the magnificence of the whole spectacle could only be topped by the actual entrance of Olsen and Johnson from a helicopter landing centre stage. Actually it was only Ole Olsen who arrived in the chopper as Chic did not like flying. They put a look alike Johnson doll next to Ole in the helicopter and when it landed Chic would appear from behind a large set piece and join him on stage.

Laffacade was a complete sell-out right to the last night. The management were even selling the steps with cushions to make sitting more comfortable.

The *Globe and Mail*, 28 August 1948:

…big hit was the singing and whistling of Ronalde…

So much money was made that the Canadian government actually questioned the wisdom of it all in Parliament, as Olsen and Johnson, who were on a high percentage of the takings, took most of the money out of Canada after they paid me my little bit.

As there was no show on Sunday, Ole asked me to be at the wharf at 7am. A lovely little boat took us very quickly, surprise, surprise, to a waiting seaplane which flew us in no time to a fishing lodge situated on one of the thousand lakes, for a spot of fishing in this grandeur of Canadian scenery. I can't remember if we actually caught any fish but I do remember a fantastic lunch at the Lodge, fish of course.

Another time he drove me in his open convertible Cadillac to the *Brant Inn* for a midnight radio interview. I dearly paid for this trip with a tremendous cold and became so feverish that Steffani had to wrap me in blankets for next day's ride to the Grandstand. Eventually we had to call a doctor who proceeded to give me a penicillin injection in my bare behind, but when I saw the needle I shrank away.

'Are you coming to me or am I coming to you?' he quietly asked.

Olsen and Johnson introduced me to the Variety Club. Ole, who was a tireless worker for the cause invited me to take part in an '*Across America Radio Variety Club Appeal*' which went on for 24 hours and quickly passed $1 million. I whistled over the air and the listeners with Bert Larr's guidance paid $500 for each song.

I became a member of the London Variety Club Tent 36, then Guernsey's Tent 55 followed by Tent 68 in New Zealand where in 1994, with my stage-friend Max Bygraves, I was proud to meet Catherine Variety Sheridan, who, in 1928, was the abandoned baby found crying on an empty theatre seat and adopted by big hearted USA show business personalities; thus the Variety Club, now the world's greatest children's charity, had been formed.

The Canadian Broadcasting Corporation invited me to be guest on six of their radio programmes before I took a break at Niagara Falls, which are, as my New Zealand accountant and friend Pam Fauvel says, 'quite awesome'.

That's when I saw my name in a music shop:

'Imported: LONDON RECORDS: 'Down in the Forest' and 'Birdsong at Eventide'. Ronnie Ronalde whistling, 75c plus tax' and I wasn't getting a ha'penny of it!

A week later I was back with Olsen and Johnson in *Laffacade* in Minneapolis, followed by Chicago's *Palmer House*, another huge complex with many different rooms where

I was offered a 40-week season by the Morris Office. Ole Olsen wanted me to carry on touring with them for a further six months, to California, in another mammoth production of *Hellzapoppin*, with the possibility of the show being filmed, but both offers I declined. I was getting homesick and wanted to get back to England – perhaps now I would be offered a Royal Command Performance?

No sooner had I landed in Britain a cable arrived from Sol Shapiro of the William Morris Agency in New York:

'WANT YOU TO RETURN FOR NEXT PRODUCTION. Leonidoff, RCMH. It really was an ultimatum, I had to accept. The show was to open on 7 October 1948 so I had to turn around and go back to New York to appear for the next five weeks in a production called the *Golden Harvest*, in which I was featured as *Ronnie Ronalde*. For the second time within a year I was working in this world-famous Broadway theatre, and once again the American producers had changed a part of me - this time my name from 'Ronalde' to 'Ronnie Ronalde'. I liked it.

The Van Cortland Hotel was our home again and theatre friends often came to visit. One day we heard a faint knock on the door and when Steffani opened it we found Wee Georgie Wood leaning against the doorframe, dishevelled and obviously in great pain.

'My God! What's happened?'

'I've been trodden on!' whimpered Georgie. 'Help me, Steffi!'

Apparently he had been knocked off the pavement by some 6-foot plus person and, as he was lying in the gutter, another man had stepped on his arm and broken it. Steffani took him to the French Hospital and when they both returned Georgie looked like a mummy ready to be shipped back to the British Museum.

One evening we were invited to the Birthday Party of Bradly Kelly's wife's at the *Stork Club* where we sat with world boxing heavy weight Gene Tunney, Isadore Freleng creator of Daffy-Duck, Tweety-Bird, the inventor of Bugs Bunny and Hal Foster with his Prince Valiant puppet. Our table was decorated with the club's bird emblem, a white stork adorned with a black top hat, standing on one leg and the other clasping a small vase carrying an orchid. I liked this novelty.

As we were waiting for our cars outside the *Stork Club* Entrance, Bugs Bunny put something into my hand with the words:

'Keep this birdie safe Ronnie, it kind'a got lost!'

Looking at this stork on my desk in New Zealand, brings back so many great memories of New York, like George Libby, a representative of Lou Walters, wanting me to work for a season at the Latin Quarter; a Mr. Schreiber, who wanted to feature me in a water show (how do you whistle under water?); Harold Dobrow of the Morris Office, who took me to the top of the RCA Building for a CBS broadcast in honour of Damon Runyon; Mr. Brough, of the *Daily Mail* who came for an interview back in Chicago where I worked alongside the great Yiddisher Momma, Sophie Tucker, at the *Chez Paree*. I never forget her sitting in the foyer after the show, selling and signing her records, counting every Dollar as though her life depended on it.

I was getting tired and becoming more and more vulnerable to the affections shown to me by the many beautiful dancers, the Rockettes and singers of *Radio City*. A day didn't seem to go by without my receiving some cakes, or even love notes. Steffani greatly approved of the first, but otherwise kept a strict rein on my movements, as drugs had already penetrated the entertainment world, to help reduce the pressure under which some of us had to work, four sometimes five shows a day, every day for weeks on end.

After the last show of another season at *Radio City* we threw the cases into a cab to catch the last plane out of New York, we wanted to get back home to Britain where, for the first few days, I felt completely drained of energy.

Gradually I began to sort through the accumulated mail and was touched by all the interest shown by the public, some of whom suggested opening a fan club.

Entrance by helicopter

Waiting for the conductor to return

Ollie Olsen & Chic Johnson

Act Fifteen

COLUMBIA RECORDS

Early in 1949 I was offered a *Variety Band Box* radio show with Frankie Howerd, Avril Angers and Tony Hancock. The BBC requested five minutes of material for a fee of 15 guineas. Hal Bevin orchestrated my music for five Pounds 10 shillings only to be told that 'Sweet Sixteen' was unsuitable as an American artiste was to perform this song during the same week. On hearing this Steffani sarcastically asked the BBC producer if we now had to submit my songs to the Americans first for clearance on British Broadcasting.

For *Workers Playtime* I was given 6 minutes airtime. This was followed by a TV show called *Rooftop Rendezvous*, produced by Richard Afton.

Phil Brown had arranged a meeting with David Miller of the BBC at the *Aeolian Hall* and although the talk was very pleasant, the situation with regard to a radio series remained the same.

Nothing.

Unhappy about this state of affairs, Steffani and I had already engaged a publicity manager, Rosa Heppner, who was willing to act as our press representative. We thought that her knowledge - she was also working for Delfont – would help me to be heard and read about in the right quarters at a fee of £800 per year and rising. Phil and I mutually agreed to end our association.

With hardly any bookings in hand, out of the blue I received a letter from the Al Wilson Agency in New York, asking me to come back to the United States to star again with Olsen & Johnson. America had again shown its appreciation of my talent, but I felt that somehow I had to break through in Britain and another absence would not help, so I decided to stick it out at home.

I had one more engagement at *Empire* Finsbury Park before I went for a week to *Olympia* in Dublin with Victor Seaforth and Foster and Clark.

Steffani had opened an office in my London house where Cyril came for a meeting and brought out a list he had prepared, showing all that I had achieved during my years in the theatre. My 1945 Blackpool season alone, he said, should have won me a Royal Command Performance, and if that was not enough, surely all my American success during 1948 ought to have brought forth some sort of recognition.

Discontent seemed to be ripe and not only in me. Animosity was growing in Britain within the public who by now had noticed that you could hear an American's recording weeks before he was due to appear at a London *Palladium* Show. The BBC would free airtime and allocate slots for the convenience of American singers who, more often than not, were quite unknown in Britain to the detriment of the British recording artiste trying to have his new song heard by the listeners. Even the press began to notice these discrepancies.

Gradually my date book started to look up. I was getting top billing in many theatres, my weekly salary had gone up to £150 and my write-ups in the newspapers were nothing but complimentary – and not for my whistling alone, but also for my singing and yodelling. Somehow I had to make more records.

There is no way I can record all the newspaper write-ups I received from the British press in those early months of 1949: I was *the Whistling Troubadour; truly deserving the reception he received; takes his place at the top of the bill; his voice earned him several curtain calls; when you get a new juvenile lead he can often sing and look good, but it's seldom that this quality is allied with the appeal of a Jimmy Cagney.* More often than not, though, I was called *The Voice of a Whistler.*

Over the years the song 'If I Were a Blackbird' seemed to be liked by the audiences, especially if I played a theatre where many of the patrons were Irish, thus bringing back to them a little bit of Ireland with one of their very old folk songs.

I was at the *Metropolitan* Edgeware Road, when Florence Leddington, from the Syndicate Theatre Group, rang and asked me to double the *Empress* Brixton, where the British version of Olsen & Johnson's Hellzapoppin had failed to start its run, because all the scenery and costumes had gone to Sheffield instead. There I had a visit from Norman Newell of Columbia Records. He wanted me to sign a contract with Columbia and begin making records immediately. What had happened?

Norman told me that, by chance, he was in a pub on Sunday night, when suddenly the whole room, which was full of very noisy Irish drinkers, became absolutely hushed when my 'If I Were a Blackbird' came over the radio. If somebody can do that, quieten an audience from near deafening to where you can hear a pin drop, surely that must be hit material.

After banging my head time and time against a brick wall, trying for a whole frustrating year to convince Harry Sarton to record more of my songs, within a month I had recorded four new songs with Columbia, not just whistling, but singing too. Around 200 more records followed over the years, singing, yodelling and whistling. All my life I have maintained that my mother and Paul Beverley have kept a very close eye on my well-being, so quietly I thanked them both.

Before we could record 'If I Were a Blackbird', Norman flew to Ireland as the rights of the song belonged to Delia Murphy and ask her permission for using the music.

Years later I met Delia Murphy and she gave me a big kiss. Inadvertently I had helped to make her a considerable amount of royalties. I had been taught the original melody of the old folk song but for the recording I was asked to use her version. With hindsight I should have stuck with the original.

I seemed to have broken the ice with regard to recordings but I still wasn't offered a radio show of my own, although I was included in another *Workers' Playtime,* a TV show called *Caribbean Carnival* and made a once only appearance in John Sharman's *Music Hall* programme. I think someone must have pressured John Sharman, as Peter Sellers was also booked. Peter was really before his time; his completely new kind of comedy impressions struggled to get laughs in front of a North of England theatre audience. He did eventually get into the BBC where he quickly started to earn recognition and by the time I booked him on one of my variety bills at the Chiswick *Empire*, he had become aloof. I vividly remember arriving on the Monday morning in my Mark 7 black Bentley wearing a sand-coloured cashmere overcoat with a brown velvet collar. Next day Peter arrived, parked a Mark 7 Bentley next to mine and was dressed in a carbon copy of my overcoat, only he had gone one better with adding a fawn coloured bowler hat.

Weekly Theatre appearances were still my bread and butter and I continued to work all over England.

W.B.Stevenson heralded my appearance at the *Empire* Nottingham in the *Nottingham Journal* with 'ANOTHER STAR FROM AMERICA'. The article went on: *Yet another American variety star will be billed in Nottingham next week. He is youthful looking Ronnie Ronalde...*

A similar episode happened at the *Empire* Edinburgh. The newspaper reporter asked me from where I originated, so of course my answer was London. *'London, Ontario?'* she asked.

'No,' I said, 'London, England'

'Oh', and with that she closed her notebook, got up and left.

At the same theatre, while I was having a pee backstage, three musicians came into the toilet and I happened to remark that the weather was jolly cold. 'You just wait till you've been over here for some time, you'll soon get used to it'. They, too, thought that I was American. Why was it, that having been elevated to 'American' status in the eyes of the British press I still was not given any airtime over the radio, or a spot at the *Palladium*?

I had to carry on with a smile, especially as my first Columbia record was now on sale in the shops. Would the records make a difference? Well, they did insofar as you could suddenly buy the Decca ones as well.

Cyril made an appointment with Michael Standing, Head of Variety for BBC Radio, to have a round table discussion, as he said, and try to secure my own radio programme. In the meantime I kept up with my schedule of appearing in different theatres working with Jimmy James, Reg Bolton, Ford & Sheen and Johnny Lockwood as well as various radio broadcasts, *Workers Playtime* also featuring Bob Monkhouse, *Variety Fanfare, Variety Bandbox, Housewives' Choice,* and *A Date with Betty,* featuring Betty Driver (Coronation Street). By now my weekly salary had risen to £175 and for Sunday Concerts I received £75. September 18 I took part in an all-star concert for the Jewish Ex-Servicemen's Association at the *London Casino* with Derek Roy, Sam Costa,

Max Bacon, Mark Hambourg, Heddle Nash and Margaret Eaves.

Christmas arrived early for me with a phone call from Cyril. The meeting with Michael Standing had been fruitful and,

'Guess what, Ronnie? You've been given a spot on December 17th to take part in the *Music Hall* programme, with Walter Jackson, Jimmy Wheeler, Claude Cavalotti, Max Bacon, Anne Shelton, Cyril Fletcher and Ted Ray acting as MC.'

Did I know that John Sharman, BBC's *Music Hall* producer, had left and Michael North had taken over?

Ah, now I knew why I got the spot. Furthermore, this programme was to be repeated on 21 December. But that was not all.

I had been offered one radio programme on my own. The BBC consented to feature me in a 20-minute programme of my own during the Christmas holiday peak period 27 December 1949 titled:

Ronnie Ronalde, The Voice of Variety, with the BBC Orchestra conducted by Rae Jenkins, introduced by Franklin Engelmann.

When the press heard of my impending programme they wrote:

A MILESTONE. His many friends in the profession will be interested and glad to learn that Ronnie Ronalde has just been given his first 20 minute radio programme.

After 13 years trying to establish myself I saw the year of 1949 out with my own Radio programme.

Christmas is the time to give some thought not only to your own circle of family and friends but also to those who, during their lifetime, have tried to give pleasure to others. I'm talking about the Variety Artistes Benevolent Fund home, Brinsworth House in Twickenham, Middlesex, which looks after so many artistes of yesteryear. On 20 December, Wilfred Pickles hosted a Christmas party for them, which included Vera Lynn, Hal Monty, Leslie Strange, Fred Brezin and Les Diagoras and me.

An hour of this revelry was broadcast on TV and so that the residents of Brinsworth House could watch themselves on screen, Harry Lewis and Vera Lynn organised the purchase of televisions; I helped towards the cost.

PALACE

Manager - HARRY CUNNINGHAM. **HUDDERSFIELD.** Telephone No. 1263

6·30 | MONDAY, MARCH 14th, 1949
TWICE NIGHTLY | **8·30**

SPECIAL PERSONAL VISIT
★ OF THE SENSATIONAL RADIO STAR ★

DIRECT FROM

HIS TREMENDOUS SUCCESSES AT THE
RADIO CITY MUSIC HALL - NEW YORK

RONALDE

★ THE VOICE OF THE WHISTLER ★

NEATEST OF THE NEAT
BUNTY
ST. CLARE

REXANOS
COMEDY ACROBATS

COMEDY ON A BAR
GEORGE
AUGUSTE

Yorkshire's Gift to Variety
**WALTER
NIBLO**

BARNEY
POWELL
XYLOPHONE
XTRAORDINARY

**YALE &
DIANE**
Youth in the Balance

"HAPPY-GO-LUCKY"
JACKLEY & JEE

W. E. Berry, Ltd., Nesfield Printing Works, Bradford.

Workers' Playtime

125

Act Sixteen

EASTER PARADE

Upon opening the *Blackpool Evening Gazette* on 3 January I realised that 1950 was probably going to be a little different from past years. The paper said:

..to eclipse both these artistes (Jean Cavall and Winifred Atwell) however, came Ronnie Ronalde a young man whose singing, whistling and yodelling voice is now a well established stage, radio and gramophone feature.

Another recording session with Norman Newell was a must.

I was booked to appear at *Empire* Hackney with Gladys Hay, Syd and Max Harrison, Winifred Atwell, Bill Kerr, Nat Hope and Doreen Ray when I received a cable asking me to appear in the *Easter Parade* show at *Radio City Music Hall*, beginning 16 March.

Now what? After the success of my Christmas radio show, the BBC had given me another 20-minute programme *Eastertime* 23 March. So Cyril had to tell them to cancel it, because of an offer from America for yet another season, my third which I had to accept because it meant that my income for the next few weeks was secure. The BBC did not like that at all. I had thrown the cat among the pigeons. They wanted me and I had said NO!

The outcome of all this?

Cyril came away from the meeting still with my Easter programme, but to be pre-recorded, *and* with a six-week radio series of my own to start after my return from America. What a turn around!

Before my departure I was also invited onto *Workers' Playtime*, *Variety Band Box* and the *Palace* Leicester, where I headed the bill with Avril Angers, Sirdani and Slim Rhyder, and the *Tivoli* Hull with Ossie Noble and Freddie Sales where the *Daily Mail* reported:

"Five times Ronnie Ronalde had to reappear before the footlights at the Tivoli last night to give encores"

As a performer one is often approached by people who wish to be part of all the glitter and lights. I was not surprised when at the *Palace*, Leicester the Stagedoor-keeper brought a card that simply read: 'Lord Viscount'. Yes, that's what it said! In he came, strikingly handsome with a very self-possessed manner and shook my hand. He told me that he was living in Leicester and that another person was wrongfully in the possession of the title and he was awaiting the ruling of the Courts to proclaim him the rightful heir. Having given me this explanation he asked if I could introduce him to our nice dancing girls as he was in need of company for the week.

'I am afraid you've come to the wrong place, our girls have their own companions.'

Steffani had his story checked out and found that the real Lord Viscount was an officer in one of the Guards regiments and not the person who had called. We were pleased that he didn't get anywhere with our girls. Years later I saw in the press a photograph of a man sentenced to death for sexually violating and hideously murdering women. It was none other than this very 'Lord Viscount', only his name was George Neville Heath and in South Africa, so Moira Lister told me, he was known under the name of George Armstrong.

After the show's last night Bill Kerr offered to drive me home to Enfield as it was already well past midnight. It had taken rather longer than expected to pack everything up and say good by to the girls.

The roads were quite deserted so Bill stepped on it with the result that he didn't quite manage one of the bends but did manage to get through a, thank God, open farm gate, coming to a screeching halt in front of the Manor house.

'Gee, I'm sorry mate'.

'Don't worry, just get the hell out of here!'

I'd noticed lights in the house coming on. I must admit I never saw anybody back a car through a pair of gates that fast than Bill.

The newspapers wrote that *Ronnie Ronalde makes show business history when he opens in two different shows on the same night – and on different sides of the Atlantic...*

On 23 March I opened at *Radio City* and at the same time *Ronnie Ronalde, the Voice of Variety* was heard over the radio in England and Ted Ray said during his *Rays a Laugh* programme:

'There's a clever boy!'

Halfway through the run of the show Leonidoff invited me up to the private living rooms of the famous Rockefeller family and introduced me to young Nelson who had seen the show and I felt quite proud that he asked to see me – after all, this was New York's Royalty!

One of the numbers I sang and yodelled was a little Swiss folk tune. One night I received a message that a lady from Switzerland wished to see me. Entering my dressing room she hesitated, gazed wistfully at me and repeated:

'No, it is not him! No, it is not him!'

Eventually she told me that her son used to sing and yodel that very song. He had disappeared at the age of 14 and she thought that at last she had found him. Next day a posy of Edelweiss arrived for me.

Whistle Series: Young Ronnie Ronalde, the whistling singer, hardly had time to return from a successful visit to New York's Radio City Music Hall when the BBC pounced on him and signed him up for an eight weeks' series at a peak listening hour... from July 6 ...John Gay's Showdown column and *Barry Baron's* with ...*he is our own Ronnie Ronalde...* had said it all.

Immediately after my return from America I recorded another four songs with Columbia, including 'Sweet Sixteen' which had become my signature tune and played by the orchestras as my tab music.

I still had theatre commitments to fulfil working with, amongst others, Max Wall, Lizbeth Webb, Peter Sellers, Johnny Lawson Trio and Sandy Lane, and attend record signing sessions in shops before my radio series began.

But fame and money, my weekly salary had increased from £175 to £250, were not the only things that had grown – so had the number of fan letters. They came and they came, not just to me, but to the BBC as well. I had to give some thought of organising a special club that could deal with and answer all this correspondence.

While I was on radio I did not neglect my theatre audience and carried on performing. The newspaper articles became bolder, describing some of the scenes that were taking place ... *the female element in one audience was said to whoop with delight! ...even after conceding six merited encores, he had patrons clamouring for more... the teenagers yelled for more...*

My records, no doubt helped by all the airtime given over the radio, were beginning to sell at tremendous speed, but it was still a surprise when Emery Pearce of the *Daily Herald* announced in his *I Hear That* column *that Ronnie Ronalde... has sold more records in the last month in America than Frankie Sinatra.*

My first own radio series was coming to an end. The BBC was getting huge requests to play my records and inquiries about when my next series would start. Norman Newell, looking at some cards for the BBC Housewife's Choice programme said he was amazed to see that practically every other request was for Ronnie Ronalde.

Radio City Music Hall 'Easter Show'

Jack Daley   *Henry Hall*

Programme

PAUL FENOULHET
and his AUGMENTED ORCHESTRA

Britain's Phenomenal New Radio, Stage
and Columbia Recording Star,
RONNIE RONALDE
"The Voice of Variety."

Official Accompanist:
JENNIE SIMPSON

JAMES JOHNSTON
The Celebrated Tenor.

1—

"Tunes From the Films" .... (arr. Paul Fenoulhet)
"Air (for the G. String) .... J. S. Bach (arr. Paul Fenoulhet)
"Two Symphonic Rhapsodies" .... (Eric Coates)
   "I Pitch My Lonely Caravan."
   "Bird Songs at Eventide" and "I Heard You Singing."
ORCHESTRA

2—

JAMES JOHNSTON

3—

"The Three Bears" .... (Eric Coates)
"Sapphires and Sables" .... (Peter Yorke)
ORCHESTRA

4—

JAMES JOHNSTON

5—

"Great Day" .... (Vincent Youmans)
"Opus One" .... (Sy. Oliver)
"Etude for Saxes" .... (Stan. Kenton)
"Disc Jockey Jump" .... (Gene Krupa)
"Moonlight Serenade" .... (arr. Glen Miller)
"Mingled Tunes" .... (arr. Paul Fenoulhet)
ORCHESTRA—DANCE BAND SECTION

6—

RONNIE RONALDE
Radio's "Voice of Variety" in Selections from his Repertoire,
including
"In a Monastery Garden," "The Tristch Trastch Polka," "Down
in the Glen," "The Windmill Song," "If I were a Blackbird,"
"Just a Rose in a Garden of Weeds," etc., etc.
(Ronnie Ronalde appears by kind permission of Henry Hall.)

"GOD SAVE THE KING"

SUNDAY NEXT, September 10th, at 8 p.m.: POPULAR CONCERT—
PAUL FENOULHET
and his AUGMENTED ORCHESTRA
Admission Prices 2/- to 5/-

ALLAN JONES
Hollywood's Famous Singing
Star.

DOREEN LUNDY
The Singing Star from "Sweet
Serenade."

129

Act Seventeen

HEAR MY SONG

My next theatre engagement from the 21 August was the *Palace* Blackpool where I had been given second top, at £200 for the week and Josef Locke appeared at the *Grand*. He was a larger than life character and did many naughty things, but all was forgiven the moment he began to sing. Wherever he went the theatres were packed and in Blackpool he was the toast of the town.

On Monday morning, during band call, rumours began to fly.

'Have you heard?'

'Heard what?'

'Josef Locke is off, ill, at the *Grand*!'

'Oh no,' I remember thinking, when my thoughts were interrupted by a hand on my shoulder. A message from Mrs. Williams the head booking chief of the Blackpool Tower Company, I was not to leave the *Palace* until she had spoken to me.

I started to worry - had there been an accident? It was not long before she arrived, making it known officially that Josef was ill and told me that I was to take over his star spot at the *Grand*.

'But what about here, at the *Palace*?' I managed to stammer.

I was to do both with a car to drive me back and forth between the two theatres.

Suddenly I felt that I had all the cares of the world and if that was not enough, Mrs. Williams continued:

'Henry Hall is flying up from London, Ronnie, so don't let me down. By the way, your band call is at three this afternoon, all the musicians have been called.'

She smiled at last, and just before leaving reminded me that Josef's spot was down for 30 minutes, so will I make sure and have enough material to keep to that time!

I sat down and, looking into my dressing table mirror, saw a face staring back at me I didn't know, it looked sick, and boy, did I feel sick – stage fright had truly got hold of me.

At 6.45pm I opened first house in my own act at the *Palace,* singing, whistling and yodelling seven songs. Then I was hurriedly pushed into the waiting car and ferried across to the *Grand's* stage door, where the under manager stood waiting. He ushered me onto the side of the stage assuring me that I had plenty of time. This, of course, was the wrong thing to say - it sounded like a death sentence. I stood there, literally shaking.

The moment the last act had finished, the front of house manager, with a note in his hand, made his entrance onto the stage.

Another few minutes of waiting, while he told a hushed audience that, owing to illness, their idol, Josef Locke, would not be singing for them tonight, but Ronnie Ronalde would take his place. That's when I could not contain myself any longer – I threw up right there and then, I was as sick as a dog.

Then I heard: 'So please, give a warm welcome to Ronnie Ronalde!'

One could sense the disappointment running through the audience and when my music started, with a slight push and a 'You're on, Ronnie' from the manager, I was facing an audience of 1600 patrons, and they were silent.

I whistled Pipes of Pan, which brought some warm applause. I followed this with the Whistler and His Dog and Tritsch Tratsch Polka and then sang Sorrento. By this time I knew I was winning them over, there were shouts for more and I overstayed my 30 minutes.

When I walked off stage I was greeted by all the stage hands applauding me too. This, I felt, was a compliment indeed.

There wasn't much time to wallow in success I had to get back to the *Palace* for my performance in the second house and then, once more, I was hurried to the *Grand,* again to take Josef's place.

During supper that night in one of Blackpool's restaurants, where many of the theatricals used to meet after the shows, the story making the rounds was, that while poor Joe was ill in bed with a sore throat, a Josef Locke lookalike had been spotted at the Newcastle races. And we all knew that Joe did like the horses!

Next day newspapers reported: *Two First Nights kept Ronnie on the Hop... Ronnie hustles – 28 songs at two first nights... Ronnie Ronalde captures Blackpool...* and the *Wizard of Whistles...*

There is one notice I'd like to re-print in more detail:

August 22 *Evening Gazette: One of Variety's brightest Stars: What's wrong with Variety? People are constantly asking me. After last night's show at the Theatre I'd reply: Nothing. This bill, that spotlights singer, whistler and yodeller Ronnie Ronalde is quite one of the most enjoyable to hit Blackpool. Ronalde scored the sort of success that a lot of artists dream about but never realise. Curtain after curtain a packed house recalled him; recalled him so often that ultimately he was singing before the big drop curtain that generally means the end of a performance but in this case merely heralded more insistent demands for encores. Ronnie is one of Variety's brightest stars, and besides being a most talented one is also one of its most generous.*

Henry Hall, witnessing the audience's reaction to my performance made me replace

Joe for three weeks to give the great man plenty of time to get well. This one night and its success encouraged Cyril to respond to Henry Hall's offer with a request to upgrade my salary. He agreed; at £350 per week, I had gone up another step on the ladder.

A week later Jack Taylor, who had fought me tooth and nail when I wanted a rise in my salary, stopped me in the street. He told me that he knew how much Henry Hall was paying me, he would double it to £700 if I'd play his theatre in Blackpool the next summer season.

There are times when fortune's favours come so fast that they are almost bewildering. Having achieved some success on both sides of the Atlantic and then to suddenly achieve such a degree of fame was something neither Steffani nor I had contemplated. I'll always be grateful to Josef and when I heard him sing 'Oh Danny Boy' to Princess Diane at the age of 75 at the Royal Premier of his film 'Hear My Song' it brought a lump to my throat.

No better act could have followed this standing ovation but the one by Michael Aspel who, clutching his 'Red Book' went up to Joe and simply announced:

'Josef Locke – This Is Your Life'.

The BBC had another contract waiting for me, a further series called *Song-Time*, to be broadcast on Sundays at 6.30pm. They wanted to produce this new show in a big way and with an audience, so the 1200-seat *Poplar Town Hall* was chosen as the venue.

Meanwhile the newspapers were showering me with compliments. In the *Sunday Pictorial* Paul Boyle reported that at 27 I was making about £15,000 a year and drawing 5000 letters a week.

'For doing what?

...For putting new sentiment into the songs that people have always loved – the old ballads, the favourite snatches of opera. And for perfecting the accomplishment that every errand boy envies – a whistle like a thrush and a liquid yodel...

Yes, by December 1950 my salary had risen to £500 guaranteed plus a percentage.

In the *Daily Graphic* I was honoured another accolade by Jonah Barrington who wrote:

'To be frank, I am not entirely au fait with the work of Mr. Ronnie Ronalde. I know him as a versatile singer in his own series 'The Voice of Variety'. But (if last week's ballot box is any gauge) you listeners have already spotted him as an obvious heir to the Donald Peers throne. In fact your vote conclusively proves him the most popular radio light singer of the moment. Runners up were Lester Ferguson, Lee Lawrence, Josef Locke.'

In a second article he noted:

Now here is an interesting ballot result - not so much for who is up top among the six most popular radio stars, but for who isn't. Wilfred Pickles of course walks away with it, that was only to be expected - but the runners up are rich in surprise. Here is the Daily Graphic Top Six: (1) Wilfred Pickles; (2) Ronnie Ronalde; (3) Ted Ray; (4) Richard Dimbleby; (5) Kay Hammond; (6) Ethel Revnell and Joy Nichols, (7) Jimmy Edwards, (8) Vanessa Lee and Peter Brough, (9) Webster Booth and Ralph Whiteman, (10) Julie Andrews, (11) Max Bygraves

And Esther Farmer from *Housewife's Choice* radio programme sent a letter:

I am sincerely glad to hear of Ronnie's repeated success. The next place should be 'The Palladium' because I feel he is a great deal bigger than most of the Acts they put on...

In the course of my career I became acquainted with many journalists. I am sure many artistes can tell stories about interviews, some good, some bad and some quite hilarious. I would like to tell of one incident here. Logan Gourlay, the writer of the *Show Business* column in the *Sunday Express*, was a very influential journalist so I thought it would be courteous and invite him for some lunch, especially as he had written a nice article about me recently. The date and place were fixed, the *Renomme* Restaurant, off Leicester Square. After we had been shown to our table, the waiter brought us two menus each to browse through. I thought one was for food, the other for wine, but, to my amazement, I found that one was a record list, all tabulated so that you could choose a song for the management to play.

Not wanting to waste any time selecting a particular song I casually said 'Monastery Garden' and carried on talking to Logan Gourlay. That's when the *Renomme* boss came to our table and, after ceremoniously putting on white gloves, picked up the disc, placed it onto the turntable of his record player, which stood on a rubber mat to stop any vibration, and said to us, in his broken English,

'With Rrronnie Rrronalde, evvvery morrning I getta uppa.'

It turned out that at six in the mornings his alarm went off and automatically my record played. He had to wake up with the 'birds' from the 'Monastery Garden'– he could not live in London without 'zee' birds singing.

'There's no need to go to those lengths, Ronnie,' said Logan.

'I can assure you that I've never been in this restaurant before,' was my answer.

Upon hearing who I was, *Renomme's* boss could not do enough and I returned to his restaurant many times.

With Christmas only a few weeks away it was necessary to organise our next recording session with Norman Newell for the disc to be in the shops in good time for the festive season. For 'X-Mas in the Village' Steffani had chosen a combination of well known Christmas melodies and carols.

The *Columbia Record Guide* described it:

Here is something of an innovation in Christmas releases – a famous star of radio and records teamed with about eight schoolchildren for an unsophisticated but nevertheless enchanting rendering of seasonal song favourites.

Because so many children were taking part in the recording the producer Norman Newell, engineer George Martin, and other culprits hit upon the idea of having it 'snow'. So while we were all merrily singing 'I'm dreaming of a white Christmas' they opened a previously hidden box above our heads and down came the studio snow, covering everything and everybody, much to the delight of all our singing guests.

There were many more theatre engagements before 1950 was over, Isle of Man, *Olympia* Dublin, (*...a warm reception, one of the loudest heard in this theatre for a long time...*) and Gordon Irving after my performance at the *Empire* Glasgow wrote:

...Glasgow is admittedly one of the toughest theatrical nuts to crack, but I have to report to you the unqualified success of Ronnie Ronalde who topped the Empire....

and the *Evening Chronicle* wrote of my appearance at the *Palace* Manchester with Max Bacon, Harry Worth and Vic and Joe Crastonian:

...is the answer to America's invasion of British Music Hall and the girls where enthralled...

I had also been invited to take part at a Sunday Concert for the *Caxton Convalescent*

Home by the *London Newspaper Printers,* thought as one of the best concerts of the autumn season and included Tommy Trinder, Spike Milligan, Donald Peers, Bob Andrews and many others.

A write-up by James Mack put the seal on the past year's efforts:

'I was delighted with the inclusion of a Ronnie Ronalde Programme lasting three quarters of an hour on the evening of Christmas Day. This singer and siffleur (french for the art of whistling) has an unusual good choice of songs, and he has an unerring instinct for bringing the right ones into his programme. [It] was a perfect choice for Christmas, and 'The Voice of Variety' put it over the air faultlessly.'

What would 1951 have in store for me? Perhaps a BBC *Desert Island Disc* interview? a BBC *Old Tyme Music Hall* spot? the London *Palladium*? or even a *Royal Command Performance*?

The year opened with my third BBC radio series, but they didn't allow me to speak because my voice was not 'Oxford or Cambridge' trained – in short, it was 'common!' So Jean Metcalfe was chosen to do all the talking for my six-week series.

(The Tommy Steele nor the Beatles talk was on the scene then).

Producer Glyn Jones told me of the opposition he'd received from the powers above about my talk so he tried to give me some 'Oxford' lessons, but I was not having any of it. I knew that my speech was well received on stage and in my hospital request programme, indeed I had been told that my voice was soothing to many patients. I really didn't have an accent; travelling up and down the country with the Songsters had knocked all pronunciation peculiarities out of me. I had become posh for Islington, but obviously not posh enough for the BBC. On the one hand the BBC had given me a series, but on the other hand they had taken it away from me. A similar situation happened when Wilfred Pickles took over the BBC news reading for a while – his Yorkshire voice made headlines.

In spite of all this, my series became popular nationwide, and so many letters were received not only at my agent's office, but also at the BBC, so they asked me to refrain from mentioning Southern Ireland in my *'Hospital Corner'* spot, as they couldn't cope any longer with the onslaught without engaging extra staff so Steffani arranged for the letters to be redirected to Oaklodge where they arrived in sacks. He emptied them onto the floor, thousands of them – I could not believe it. Each letter was opened, read and put into order to answer. Some were purely congratulatory, others wanted to know more about my records, theatrical engagements, my private life, and then there were the ones begging for help of one sort or another.

The letters also told me that a fan club had been formed in Scotland. The *Glasgow Sunday Mail* reported that *'the forming of fan clubs in honour of a favourite stage personality ...in the last few months has grown to immense proportions. It is an interesting form of hero-worship. Some call it 'plain daft'. Others see in them the signs of a genuine interest in live theatre.'*

The Ronnie Ronalde Fan Club was launched by 17-year-old Betty Baillie. Soon there were 12 more fan clubs in existence and the number was growing. President Peggy Hardwick from Nottingham later married a 'Bates' and moved to New Zealand and Dorothy Hardy still writes to me regularly. That month also heralded the first publication of the Ronnie Ronalde *Voice of Variety News,* which contained information about my future engagements and answered many of the individual questions I'd received in letters.

Eventually we printed 55,000 copies twice yearly. Roneo devised a set up for my home and we had to put a complete room aside to accommodate the filing cabinets, printing and franking machines. It was quite an industry keeping all the photographs, badges and certificates in order, and sending out the post and print matter to the different club presidents, so I engaged a secretary, Christine Eldrett. I also received many letters from overseas when my radio programmes were repeated by the BBC World Service from Bush House and my records were played by *Radio Luxembourg* over the European wavelengths and by a Mr. Merkelbach of the AVRO Hilversum in Holland and in Denmark through Mr. Blicher-Hansen. EMI had released my discs in Britain and in some 25 countries worldwide.

Josef Locke

Act Eighteen

AMERICAN INFLUENCE

The *Birmingham Post* reported:

There is always the danger that radio reputations will wilt under the footlights, but admirers of Ronnie Ronalde need have no fear that their idol becomes tarnished in changed surroundings. At Birmingham Hippodrome last night this smiling young man of cherubic countenance strode through his repertoire of whistle and song with charm and convincing success which can only enhance his popularity.

And the *Birmingham Mail*:

Ronnie Ronalde, radios singing and whistling star, differs from some other artists in the same field in that his 'bobby-soxing' admirers are not confined to autograph hunting young ladies of fifteen and sixteen. Grey hairs and middle aged spread were no bar to starry-eyed wonder among, for instance, the older women in his audience at the Birmingham Hippodrome last night. And the long drawn 'oo's' of delight which greeted his announcement of each and every song came quite as much from the over-fifties as the under-twenties. That's of course how it should be. Why should all the teenagers have the fun? In any case there is no need to apologise for wanting to hear - and go on hearing - this likable young man with his natural gift of song to which is added such remarkable skill as a whistler. Anyone who has splutteringly tried to whistle in the dark to keep his courage up will envy the mellifluous Mr. Ronalde.

Radio exposure had brought my songs into many people's homes, proving the point, that if British artistes were given the same treatment over the airwaves as the Americans, we too could fill the theatres. Around this time the Variety Artists Federation was experiencing a considerable amount of discontent because of the infiltration of American entertainers, often not of star quality, who were pushing British artistes out of Moss Empire and Stoll theatres.

The BBC record programmes could also be blamed, as they had not followed up an official circular advising them to include more British music in their programmes.

But how many have taken note? asked the *Daily Mirror. Of course there are exceptions …Donald Peers, Gracie Fields, Ronnie Ronalde and a few more are always helpful to British songwriters. So are some of the bands, Jack Simpson, Billy Cotton, Henry Hall in particular. But there is even opposition within the BBC themselves to new British tunes. I know of one Variety Producer who refused to allow one British song on the air this week – because it's unknown! …. So, if any of you feel like writing songs for a living – forget it. The outlook is so bleak that one large publishing house has refused to print any new British ballads because they cannot get any broadcasts. Others have just closed down.*

Everything seemed to be American. The world-renowned BBC was a satellite of the American entertainment industry. My EMI record hit in Britain and the Empire 'If I Were a Blackbird' could not be released in the USA, because America's Capital Records had asked Bing Crosby to record it. I had never heard Bing whistle a blackbird, and so his version of the song was not a hit, but the situation proved, once again, the power the American recording companies held over the British organisations.

Disc jockeys, too, were pressurised and lavishly entertained by these overseas business companies and so of course started to enjoy their new status. There was talk that you did not just send your new record release to the DJ hoping for air time on his programme, but also a new HMV record player. All these little thoughtful extras could be achieved by scattering the almighty dollar like confetti. The British were left behind – they did not have the dollars and they were not used to this type of dealing.

Theatrical artistes, once the backbone of the entertainment world in Britain, were suddenly finding themselves short of dates. Talk circulated freely of how the agent of a work-needy artiste sitting in front of his desk would vacate his office for a few moments, leaving his desk drawer conveniently open. When the agent returned and noticed some cash in there, the artiste would be given a theatre booking. A story told against himself by an artiste who became an agent, Johnnie Riscoe, went as follows:

One day Johnnie was out walking near the Consolidated Theatre Booking Department, carrying two large shopping bags.

What's in the bags?' shouted Jimmy Wheeler from the other side of the street.

Johnnie yelled back, 'This one's for the Metropolitan', lifting the right arm holding one bag, 'and that's for the Chelsea *Palace*', raising the left arm holding the other bag.

One of the chief culprits in booking American acts into London was Val Parnell of the *Palladium*. During the early 1930s the General Theatres Corporation had merged with the Moss Theatres Circuit. George Black was in overall charge with Val Parnell the general manager and Cissie Williams the chief booker of this vast empire of theatres all over Britain. All three of them wielded tremendous power, especially George Black, who became one of the most influential personalities in show business. A shrewd businessman, but always a gentleman, he gave many up and coming British artistes the opportunity to show their art in his theatres, but all this changed when he died in 1945. Although Cissie Williams carried on as the chief booker for the Moss Circuit and General Theatres Corporation, Val Parnell took over the running of the Moss Empires and under his leadership, many changes started to take place. He separated the cinema from the theatre circuit hence many places of work for variety artistes were lost, but Moss Empires still evolved as the biggest circuit, above the Stoll and other individually owned theatres in the country, inclusive of its flagship, the *Palladium*.

Another change, which had an even bigger impact on the variety act scene, was Val Parnell's 'importing' of American 'talent' into his newly upgraded *Palladium* Theatre and paying salaries that till then had been quite unheard of. One of those acts was Danny Kaye, who, in his earlier years, had been booked into a London Club that proved to be a disaster for him and so naturally he was somewhat worried, to put it mildly, about appearing again in front of a *Palladium* audience. Shaking with fear on the opening night, he admitted his anxiety to the audience who appreciated his openness and so turned his performance into a sensational success. On the last week of his engagement Cissie Williams took me along to one of the matinees, to, quote her words:

'to see a man work, who can do nothing, but does it well, and this could help you to become even better as you are talented'.

Unfortunately I was not to see Danny at his best, as he seemed to be thrown off his balance by an American woman in the audience, shouting to him that she came from the same place where he was born. Danny was lost. He always rehearsed every line and every movement right down to detail and was not an impromptu performer.

Cissie Williams was quite disappointed – 'Ronnie, I should bring Danny Kaye to see you work!'

The American artistes might have had their following at London's *Palladium* but when they went on tour around Britain the public didn't always appreciate the American style of entertaining, or the rise in the price of tickets, so when the following week a British variety bill was once more offered it had to be very good to entice the audiences back again.

After appearing on radio in *Henry Hall's Guest Night* I travelled to Liverpool for my next show. During rehearsal on the Monday morning Steffani realised that I would have to work all week without the house tabs as they had been taken down and sent to the cleaners in readiness for the following week's show with, guess who? Danny Kaye! No way was I going to work using only the front runners, as suggested by the management. That would affect my performance before my British public, who had paid their hard earned money to book the theatre out. This was not fair to them or to me. I told the stage manager that unless the house tabs were back for the night's show I would not be appearing. Within half an hour a message was brought to me; Val Parnell had conferred with the manager and my house tabs would be up. And Val Parnell was driving up from London to see me.

A few hours later Val Parnell did walk into my No.1 dressing room at the *Empire*, confirming that the house tabs were back up and asked me why I caused so much trouble? That, I said, was not my intention, but I was making sure that I get fair treatment in my country so that I could present my performance to my audience in a way I felt they deserved. The Liverpool papers wrote:

…Full House… Ronnie Ronalde now one of the highest paid Music Hall Artists in the country, whose gramophone records top those of Frank Sinatra appears at the Empire… no difficulty capturing the audience.

I also advised him that I was not happy with the broken down chairs I had to sit on, unlike American performers, for whom the Moss management always hired new furniture for the duration of their stay. Looking back through my diaries which included all the good as well as the bad things which happened during my stays in America I noted, that British artistes in America did not receive preferential treatment above their own. I had also noticed that many of their Variety Theatres were quite dilapidated, no way did they come up to the standard of our Moss or Stoll theatres. Yet when Frank Sinatra who had just done the worst business in history at the *Capitol* Theatre in New York with *Never again Sinatra* written in the papers, coupled with his disastrous tour of Scandinavia and our own Bristol *Hippodrome* as well as Mickey Rooney having played to small houses at the London *Palladium* so much so that he tried everything to cut his contract short, Val Parnell would smarten up their dressing rooms and lay a red carpet from their room right onto the stage.

Of course they jumped at Val Parnell's offer to appear in Britain and his ability to ensure that their records were given all the air time available One way or another, the British public could not escape American singers, songs and faces. It was not until many years later that the Beatles made the real reverse breakthrough. Hallelujah!

Many Americans claimed that, even with the high salary Val Parnell paid them, they could have earned more back in the USA. They might have, if they could have found work, but in Britain they saved on their income tax and increased their record sales. All in all not such a bad deal for them.

We British artistes made do, but then I suppose you could say that's what made us.

Many Theatres had a dressing room on stage which was often used by the star comic who had many costume changes. This particular comic arrived at the *Garrick* Southport only to find this room full with all the cleaned tabs in readiness for the following weeks show, staring an American.

'Well' he said; 'If tabs are in No.1 dressingroom you'd better put them on t'night!'

He did not appear that night, neither did the tabs.

My little controversy with Parnell paid off. Arriving for Monday morning Band call at the *Empire* Sheffield the following week my No.1 dressingroom had new curtains and chairs.

Mind you, I did fill the theatres for him and approaches were made, in Liverpool and Sheffield, that I should seriously consider playing two weeks in every town rather than the conventional one week.

Sheffield Telegraph: *When the first house spilt from the Sheffield Empire last night small boys were whistling and yodelling... who sets the vogue now in singing, whistling and yodelling...*

Newcastle Fan Club – James Croudance

Betty Bailey, Glasgow Fan Club

Mile End Road

Leeds Fan Club

Veronica Bond

140

Act Nineteen

GREAT YARMOUTH, BRITANNIA

Cyril needed me in London. So many bookings were coming in that I had to decide what I wanted to take. Surely not the *Palladium* or the Royal Command Performance? No! After having swallowed my disappointment at not finding the two most coveted dates among the offerings, I settled down to make decisions.

A BBC radio programme for 26 weeks, with a further offer of a five-year contract! How many years had it taken to get just a one off programme, and now this!

The following is best described by John Gay's *Showdown* column:

Kid-glove BBC. There's a new spirit abroad at the BBC. The old take-it-or-leave-it attitude towards artistes – the 'its an honour to broadcast' outlook is fast giving way to a more realistic view, spurred on no doubt by the 'captures' of established players and programmes by commercial radio. No doubt the competition is beginning to bite. In those bad old complacent days the height of ambition for any artiste was a 13-week series. If he got a second or third series he was a top-liner. What's happening today? A few weeks ago I told you the Corporation were handing Billy Cotton an 'indefinite' contract. Now their latest plum has been given to a 28 year old Islington lad who made the grade on the stage and air a mere four years ago, Ronnie Ronalde has just been given a five year contract. When the BBC offered Ronnie a 26 week series, he flabbergasted them by saying: 'I'll do 13'. They wanted half an hour time. Ronnie said 'a quarter of an hour'. So they settled for 20 minutes. But an artiste who wants less time on the air is something new in Broadcasting House and I'm not surprised they were shaken.

My contention was that when I was on air I worked full-time and didn't really want to know about variety dates. I like to do one thing at a time – properly. The fourth BBC series of 13 weeks was confirmed, starting on Sunday 13 September 1951, at 1.30pm, peak time. Oh yes, and I received a rise in my salary too – it had gone up to 30 guineas.

After the rest of the dates had been sorted out, I turned my attention to the summer period. Cyril had two offers: one for Blackpool with Jack Taylor for 20 weeks at £700 per week, and the second from impresario Tom Arnold, who wanted me to appear at the *Britannia Theatre* in Great Yarmouth for their 12-week summer season at £400 per week. He could not pay any more, as his theatre had never gone beyond £1600 takings per week, even when Frankie Howerd was its star.

What should I do? It had to be Yarmouth. The thought of spending some time on my beloved boat on the River Waveney in Beccles only a few miles from Yarmouth made the decision quite easy. I regarded Beccles as my home, having spent so much time there during the war years and it was Steffani's hometown. Eventually a compromise was reached between Tom Arnold and Cyril - I was guaranteed the £400 a week plus 20 percent of the takings, thus also giving me a say as to who else should be on the bill.

Cyril had okayed all the Yarmouth artistes for me: Charles Warren and Jean, Neville Bishop, the Cox Twins, the Miles Twins, Joan Rene, Bert Platt, Pamela de Waal, the Six Starletts and the orchestra was under Hal Bevan's direction. There was only one act he was not quite sure of - would I go and see him and give my opinion? So Steffani and I went to the London *Palladium* where this new comedian had taken over from Ted Ray, who was ill. I liked what I saw, a very smartly dressed artiste, no funny hat but telling clean, humorous, sophisticated stories and a very pleasant voice to listen to. Max Bygraves was his name, and I was only too pleased to have him on my 1951 Great Yarmouth *Ronnie Ronalde Summer Show.*

The scene had been set for a most enjoyable season and I had no doubt that I had made the right decision in not letting money rule my head. Because Yarmouth was a seaside holiday resort, we had to cater for a family audience. Steffani, walking along the seafront, listening to what the public was saying, heard that I was an elderly man, no doubt because I was singing many of the older songs over the radio. This realisation of the public's opinion brought about a change in the way we presented my name on bills. Steffani immediately printed head and shoulder photos of me on double crown billheads and distributed these to all the guest houses, boarding houses, hotels and shops in and around Yarmouth. It most certainly did the trick. Old and young alike, they came, and they came.

Many invitations arrived to open garden fetes, present cups, make speeches, all of them supporting one charity or another. And there was the Miss Yarmouth contest. I let Max Bygraves do the judging, I preferred to stay the presenter of sashes and cheques and kiss the winners. No way was I going to be accused of preferring one girl to another – I was after all still a bachelor.

We also had a Wedding, not an ordinary one, it was Twins marrying Twins. Frank and Fred Cox married Pauline and Estelle Miles, all four were dancers in my Show. The Cox Twins originally started with Steffani in his 'Songsters' act so it was only natural that he was chosen to be their best man and both Max Bygraves and myself acted as witnesses.

For Steffani, drinking tea was a religious ceremony. Although it was a few years after the war Britain still had ration books and allowances for many items were small. Playing Liverpool a few weeks back I had become acquainted with someone who had asked us if we would like some tea. Sure, especially as our tea caddy was nearly empty again. On Saturday night the stage doorkeeper informed us that somebody had left something. 'Well, bring it in!'

'Can't, it's too heavy,' he answered.

Steffani went to investigate but within seconds was back.

'The tea's arrived Ron, two bloody big chests full!'

We were leaving on the midnight train to London. The black market was thriving in Liverpool because it was a port and Lime Street Station was full of police trying to catch wrongdoers. So there we were in the middle of the night telling the porter to be careful with the two chests, making out they held fluorescent stage lighting, praying that we would reach our train without leaving a trail of tea behind. At London's Kings Cross we went through the same procedure. I could already see the newspaper headlines:

'Ronnie Ronalde, caught with thousands of people's tea rations!'

We arrived home at Oak Lodge and stored the two chests in my office. During the Yarmouth summer season Father and the family joined us in Beccles. One day my secretary phoned. She'd gone to my house and as she walked up the drive on one side a large furniture van was driving away on the other side. My front door was wide open – I'd been done. Apparently nothing had been taken but the oak entrance doors were damaged so we came to the conclusion that her arrival may have disturbed them.

'There's one thing I'm puzzled about?'

'What's that, Christine?'

'There's a tea chest on the back porch!'

'Oh, they must have taken some of our stage props we keep in the tea chest in our office'.

'But why is there a message written on it saying, 'Mind the hole, regards John?'

Then I realized that our kind 'tea friend' must have unbeknown to us delivered another chest of tea as a surprise for us.

Towards the end of August Harold Fielding phoned if I would I be available for a Sunday night concert at the *Opera House* Blackpool? I wasn't interested. It would have meant a long car journey from Beccles to Blackpool and back again.

'Ask for £500, they'll never pay that amount for a concert.'

Back came the answer: yes.

So we request two plane fares.

Again, they said yes, I had no alternative but to fly to Blackpool. They wanted to see my drawing power by the Blackpool audience; they had watched the success story of Yarmouth and were already planing next summer's Show in Blackpool. I obliged them with two packed houses.

I was delighted with the Yarmouth result. The Ronnie Ronalde *'Meet the Stars'* show had beaten every record in the pier's history. On the last night the Mayor H.J. Shorten came onto the stage to thank us all, saying that Yarmouth would miss Ronnie Ronalde and Max Bygraves.

There was no time to waste. Another recording of two more discs had been arranged, and with only a few days to spare I had launched my next radio series, and of course the travelling began again with weekly performances and concerts and the by now invariable record signing sessions in the music stores. At the *Granada* Walthamstow 2000 old folks were invited to see my show and at Woolwich nurses brought patients who could walk from a nearby hospital to the theatre but at Tooting I went to *St Benedicts Hospital* to talk to their patients. When the nurses pushed a piano into one of the wards, the look in the patients' eyes made Steffani walk to the piano and I started to whistle. After a few songs I thought I had finished, but no, porters pushed the piano into the next ward and again all eyes were looking at me, waiting.

The end of 1951 was drawing near. 'Fantastic' was the BBC's description of the listeners' reaction to my radio series, which finished at Christmas – and that was a large and unusual word for them. Result: another series of 13 weeks starting April 1952.

I must have endeared myself to some as Jean Butt wrote in her *Gramophone Notes:* *...his whistling is such that I would like to have him in a cage and keep him in my sitting room throughout the year to remind me of the spring! The next best thing is to have him on the gramophone and if you want to hear how sweetly a thrush can sing I advise you to get his record.*

In the festive period, many of us artistes tried to bring Christmas cheer through various concerts for folk who could not come to theatres due to their disabilities. One of those events was held at Kilburn, for the Royal London Society for Teaching the Blind.

I also took part making a *Columbia Cavalcade* record donating the royalties to the Variety Artistes Benevolent Fund with Teddy Johnson, The Beverley Sisters, Steve Conway, Marie Benson and others.

My last radio programme for 1951 was scheduled for 23 December and after completing the show I took the family and drove to Beccles where Steffani already had reserved some rooms for us at the Kings Head Hotel and made arrangements for a large Christmas Eve party, inviting half the town who were all friends and his family. This gathering amounted to a virtually non-stop cabaret until well after Midnight.

But there was a small reason for celebrating. No, I had not been offered the *Palladium*. No, I had not been offered a Royal Command Performance. Yes, my records were selling amongst the top three of the country: Mario Lanza, Bing Crosby and Ronnie Ronalde. And yes, oh yes, I had just been offered Blackpool for the 1952 summer season – 15 weeks at the *Winter Gardens*, staring in George and Alfred Black's show *Happy Landings*, at an all-time record fee for any British artiste: a guaranteed £1000 per week plus 20 percent.

What one does have to take into consideration with regard to the above salary is that at that time the cost of seats at the *Winter Gardens* Blackpool were Stalls 4/-, 6/-, 7/-, Circle 4/6, 7/6 and Balcony 2/6 and 3/6, varying between 12 1/2 pence and 62 1/2 pence in new money.

At the Newcastle *Empire* a variety of seating arrangements and prices were on offer during my appearance in March 1951, ranging from Boxes at 12/- and 18/- to Box Seats at 3/- and 4/6, Fauteuils 4/6, Royal Stalls 3/6, Settees 3/3 and 3/6, Stalls 2/9, Circle 4/-, Upper Circle 1/6 and Balcony at 9d.

Oh yes and programmes were between 2d and 3d.

In Ireland the *Grand Opera House* Belfast during my 1951 February appearance charged £1-10s-0d and £1-0s-0d for a Box, they must have been more affluent.

And to compare with pre-war prices? During 1939 at the *Argylle* Birkenhead one had to fork out between 5d and 2s.6d and if you wanted a Private Box? Well that cost was 3 shillings indeed.

How I wished that my mother could have shared my triumph with me, however Cyril was tickled pink and so, of course, was Steffani.

Tooting Hospital

Cox twins marriage – Max looks on

Christmas Eve party

Sister Vera

Act Twenty

BLACKPOOL

Steffani and I decided to stay a few days on our boat, the Goldfinch, moored on the river Waveney on a grassbank just outside Beccles. It had a piano on board and so was ideal for me to rehearse in peace for my next recording session during January 1952 for Columbia.

It was absolutely bliss to wake up in the mornings, listen to all the birds welcoming the dawn of the new day and hearing Steffani in the galley preparing the breakfast.

With gusto I picked up my knife and fork to commence the task of devouring this innovation of the British palate which no other country in the world can lay claim to, namely British bacon, eggs and mushrooms, all fresh delivered to us by the farmer.

'What's this Steff, my mushrooms are moving!'

'Moving?'

Worms had started to eat their way out of the mushrooms and all Steffani could say was:

'Perhaps I didn't cook the field mushrooms long enough!'

After an early lunch at the nearby Waveny Hotel we returned the same day to London.

'Springtime' was an interesting disc to cut, as by means of multi-track recording one bird whistle was superimposed on another, giving the effect of a chorus of varying birds chirping all at the same time. (How technology has advanced since then) And 'Lo! Hear the Gentle Lark' was by no means an easy task as the music had a range of over two octaves and had only been attempted by coloratura sopranos to record. Lionel Solomon, playing the obligato with his golden flute, accompanied me brilliantly.

With the recordings finished I took part in another *BBC Music Hall* radio programme with Max Miller and for the next four months I was back on the road again. I started my fifth radio series in April, which meant continuous travel to London from the various theatres. I had to think about transport. Having sold my Rolls I was in need of another reliable car. I had been introduced to George Abecassis, the racing driver and a director at H.W. Motors Walton-on-Thames and through him I ordered a new Lagonda, a cream coupe with red leather seating – for the grand price of £3691-23-9d. I felt great but much to Steffani's consternation, as I liked driving fast.

Many of my fans wrote, asking me to include my music in the 'Voice of Variety Newsletter', so we approached Feldman & Co. in London to produce a 'Ronnie Ronalde Album', which included my latest songs, and a short story of my life. This arrangement helped us to keep my biannually newsletter free for all the up-to-date information concerning my different theatre engagements, forthcoming records and behind the scenes chat, which normally would have been difficult to convey to the them unless my secretary had written thousands of individual letters.

After entertaining 400 old folk at the at the annual *Enfield Technical College* party, the *Empire* Finsbury Park was my first week's theatre date for 1952. Joyce Golding, Robert Harbin, the Trio Kalmar, Gold and Cordell, Maurice and May, Godfrey and Kerby, John and Suma Lamonte and, last but not least, Bill Waddington ('Percy Sugden' of Coronation Street) were all with me on the bill. The show was a huge success, and I was very thrilled when I read in the *London Gazette*, that the writer had been quite amazed by the *royal welcome* that the audience gave me, and particularly by the young people, who called for more and more encores.

More theatres followed, each theatre bill not only carrying my name but my head as well and so brought instant recognition by the public. At the *Opera House* in Belfast I was singing a Mario Lanza hit 'It's the Loveliest Night of the Year' and at the other theatre across the street, Mario Lanza himself was appearing. After the shows we met and he remarked that he liked how I sang his song; I wonder how he would have whistled my 'Monastery Garden'!

Glasgow was known by many artistes as the English comics' graveyard. Max Miller, Tommy Trinder and quite a few others never accepted engagements there. I remember Max Wall playing to stony silence and looking off to me, asked, 'Are they all asleep?', and another night he questioned the side he should play to. Des O'Connor, privileged to have the same agent as me, Cyril Berlin, attempted to play the *Empire* Glasgow and went to pieces. Yet for me the Scots audiences were the tops.

My stay in Glasgow was made even more memorable with a letter from one of my fans who had listened to my new BBC radio show the Sunday before.

I was listening to you on the weekend. There was a glass bowl on top of the radio. One of your piercing notes cracked it. The bowl, incidentally, was a quarter-of-an-inch thick. When the press got hold of this story printed:

He has a cracking time on air.

More letters arrived telling me of incidents that had happened when I hit a high note. In one I had sent the goldfish flying as the bowl cracked in half on top of the television and another one wrote:

You have broken my favourite piece of Swedish glass... At the time of your unprovoked attack it was standing on my radio set, harmlessly minding it's own business when you 'smote it hip and thigh' with a particularly piercing top note.

Ramsdon Greig's advice, a critic with the *Scottish Daily Mail* was:
all listeners should remove their spectacles when Ronnie was on the radio or TV.
The cartoonists got hold of these stories too and had quite a field day, advising girls not to wear spectacles when whispering to the boys to play a Ronnie Ronalde record, because when the glasses cracked they wouldn't be able to see what the boys were doing.

They also drew my house in one paper with all its windows shattered.

Cyril became quite worried about these incidents and tried to obtain legal advice to see if anybody could actually take me to court and sue for compensation and, if so, should we take out special insurance?

Mid-June had arrived and with it my first summer season as a £1000 plus star. The lavish scenery of *Happy Landings* promised a successful show, and the holidaymakers of Blackpool were not disappointed. The newspapers had given us the thumbs up and continued to do so all through the season. The other artistes were the Morton Fraser's Harmonica Gang, Freddie Sales, The Salici Puppets, Faye & Tamara, Marion Sanders, Billy McCormack, Doreen Hinton, Kathleen Gray, Annette's 12 Beau Belles and the Eight Hill Billy Happy Hoe-Downers.

The *Empress Ballroom*, next door to the *Winter Garden* Theatre but under the same roof of this vast entertainment complex, had booked different stars for weekends during the summer season, one of them was Danny Kaye, July 17 and 18. On his opening night he could hear me whistling and the response of my more than enthusiastic audience. His manager was sent over to tell us to move the time of my performance so it did not interfere with Mr. Kaye's. Steffani's answer was, that if Mr. Kaye did not like my timing, he could move his.

'You can't expect Mr. Kaye to do that! He is Danny Kaye!'

Steffani's reply was equally concise:

'Surely you can't expect Mr. Ronalde to change! He is Ronnie Ronalde!'

Blackpool was very gratifying for me. Not only did it bring the 'star status' but also the love of the people, and that is really what theatre is all about. You reach out to them with your God-given gift and they repay you with their adulation, although sometimes it can become a little frightening.

During the Fifties the British Press still shied away from printing the news of any occurrence of riots in either a theatre or heaven forbid, on the streets so it made headlines when the *The Performer* on 17 July reported:

We hear from Blackpool that the local police had to be called out on Friday last to control the big crowds that gathered to see Ronnie Ronalde when he made his first appearance of the season at the Music Store of Messrs. Sharples for the purpose of autographing gramophone records and 'Ronnie Ronalde' albums. Traffic was held up, and it was half an hour before normal conditions could be restored... The measure of Ronnie's success in this, his first Blackpool season... can be gathered from the capacity crowds which are now packing the Winter Gardens Pavilion at every performance.

David Southwood invited stars of radio, television, film and stage appearing at different theatres in Blackpool, to join him in the fun and laughter of an informal children's party at the *Jubilee Theatre* which he broadcast over the *BBC on Children's Hour.* Five hundred children turned up, all shouting and cheering. When it was my turn to entertain them I had all the children whistling – it sounded as if an aviary had been let loose. After the show all the kids surged en masse backstage to hunt for autographs, some of them tried to get into the dressing rooms on all fours, through the legs of the stage staff.

And another party was held – the *News Chronicle Stage and Radio* Garden Party at *Stanley Park*, Blackpool acclaimed as the biggest, happiest and jolliest party Blackpool had ever known. Thirty thousand came to that afternoon's event, opened by the Mayor of Blackpool, Counc. Peter Fairhurst and attended not only by nearly 300 leading personalities of stage, screen and radio, but also by a score of North Country mayors and mayoresses wearing their gold chains of office. The people could buy a 72 page souvenir programmes and have them signed by us artistes for 6d a time in the special autograph tent; you did not dare move outside, you just got mobbed.

The only Sunday Concert during that hectic Blackpool season was to the Isle of Man where the newspaper quoted:

Ronnie Ronalde mobbed... at the invitation of Fred Barwell he played a Concert at the Palace Theatre. A packed house roared their approval... a crowd of well over 1000 people waited for him to leave the theatre...and the scene which followed was unprecedented... 'we want Ronnie' they surged and fought to get near him... eventually he reached the Castle Mona Hotel whereupon this great crowd of people stood and sung lustily 'When you were sweet sixteen'...

I had rented a house for my 15-week stay in Blackpool. Since one side of its garden fence bordered onto the South Shore Golf Course I thought I'd give this sport a go. One morning, after crawling through the fence I strolled to the clubhouse and inquired if somebody would give me a few lessons. I was soon on the green with hired clubs and golf pro, Mr. Cox, thoroughly enjoying myself. After one lesson while we were drinking coffee, which he paid for, he asked if I wanted to purchase some second-hand clubs, £1 to £3 a time; over the summer I could acquire a nice set. That was fine by me: I had my lessons, he brought me second-hand clubs and paid for the coffee.

But then this idyllic arrangement was shattered. His daughter had recognised me with him so collected her friends' autograph books and asked her father to have them signed by me.

'My,' he said, 'you are a quiet one, you never told me you were Ronnie Ronalde!'

'You never asked my name!'

From that day on there were no more second-hand clubs, he had put my name down for the best Bobby Locke set available and, oh yes, I had to pay for the coffee from then on.

As in Yarmouth I used a life size cutout of me for publicity, which was put in front of the theatre. Unfortunately this was often taken for 'walks', and after it had been returned by the police once too often, it was chained daily to the theatre entrance. Steffani went to a photo shop on Blackpool's 'Golden Mile' and asked them to put my cutout on display. They did but allowed passers-by to have their picture taken with me, often in compromising positions. Many of my loyal fans didn't take kindly to photos of me standing next to drunken sailors putting their caps on my head or, in one case even holding a chamber pot upside down over me.

I realised that my choirboy image was becoming tarnished when the Lancashire police brought a notice that they had picked up a lady who was working the red light district in Manchester. She was carrying a picture of me being cuddled by her, showing it to potential customers as proof that she gave star service! This had to stop but was easier said than done. The shop would not release my cutout until the end of the summer.

Only after the Blackpool Tower directors threatened not to renew their shop's licence were we reluctantly given our cutout back.

Happy Landings broke all records and because it had been such a very happy summer season I wished to give a personal thank you to the complete cast, and decided to take them all on a mystery tour to the Lake District, stopping at the Windermere Hydro for a champagne Lunch, a trip on the steamer and high tea at the Garnforth Hotel. A perfect ending to a perfect day and a perfect season which was highlighted at the Church of St. Stephen-on-the-Cliffs by the Bishop of Blackburn, Dr. W.M. Askwith during the annual Stage and Screen Service, where, after reading the lesson, I joined the sidesmen in taking the collection.

Not for nothing was Blackpool called the 'Mecca of the North' with all its different shows and golden sands. These are only some of the entertainers who were in Blackpool during the 1952 summer: the Cox Twins with their wives, Ken Morris, Terry Thomas (he got so fed up in listening to my whistling that apparently he introduced a wicked caricature of me into his act), Lester Ferguson, Bob and Alf Pearson, Ben Lyon and Bebe Daniels (with their family were hot favourites over the BBC with their radio show, The Lyons Family; although it was American comedy, the British really took to them), Ted Heath and his band, Al Read, Kenneth Wolfstenholme, Beryl Orde, Lee Lawrence, Semprini, Reginald Dixon, dancing act Robert Drage and Vivienne, (Robert emigrated later on to New Zealand and is often heard on Radio Pacific, reminiscing about British variety), and many, many more.

With the last radio broadcast of the BBC's 'Blackpool Night' series for the year, produced by David Southwood including Jack Warner, Harry Bailey and myself over and with even the famous Blackpool illumination lights switched off, there was only one thing left to do, and that was to lead my audience into singing 'Good Luck, Good Health, God Bless You'.

Goldfinch

My Lagonda

Photo used for my cut-out

Wintergardens, Blackpool

Thankyou tour to the Lake District

Act Twenty-one

MIDDLE EAST

There was no time to give any thought to relaxation. I had been approached by the British War Office to tour the Canal Zone and North Africa over the Christmas period, departing on 14 November and as my records were so much in demand and played in Holland, M. Muriloff had specially come to Britain and invited me to Holland the following March.

I had also recently bought a new home, Croylands in Winchmore Hill, in a road known to me as Millionaires' walk; not till later did I find out its real name, Broadwalk. Other artistes also seemed to favour this neighbourhood: Ted Ray, Suzette Tarri, Tommy Lawton, Walley Barnes, Alfredo Campoli, Cliff Richards and Mike Ryder (Mike Roberson), who lived two houses away from me and also left years later for New Zealand. One of the reasons I bought this home was the fact that my yearly earnings had risen so much that my accountant advised me to invest in a more expensive house, so that the higher mortgage rate could be offset against the percentage I had to pay in tax: a staggering 95 percent.

The BBC, hearing that I would not be available for another series until the following year, made sure that they had a couple of radio recordings in the can. Then, out of the blue a call came from Cyril.

'Ronnie, Val Parnell would like to book you for a show at the London *Palladium*! He's offered you second top but with same size billing as the American comedian Billy De Wolfe and he's prepared to start talking from £1500 per week upwards.'

Ah, that's the catch, the money, I thought.

'What do you think, Ronnie?' Cyril asked.

My reply to Cyril was very clear.

'Tell Mr. Parnell that I would be happy to play the London *Palladium*, but as first top, I do not wish to go second to an American in my own country in my own home town.'

Cyril was actually gleeful with my decision, for it allowed him to say no for the first time, after years of no from Val Parnell's Moss Empire.

They must have read the article in London's *Sunday Express* where it stated under Housewife's' Choice that there were three singers the public could not hear enough of: *Bing Crosby, Vera Lynn and Ronnie Ronalde.*

On 14 November we left England on an extremely cold and uncomfortable Viking aircraft for Malta, where our show was scheduled for the day after our arrival. Cyril together with Major George Brightwell personally saw us off. The party included Gerry Ray, Gwenda Wilkin, Paula Coutts, Nat Hope, Patricia Henry and Harry Jerome. We were met by Major Granado and Miss Gordon and soon realised that we were in a different world when we drank our first cup of tea at the Astra Hotel: tea made with chlorinated semi-salt water! Looking round the breakfast table next morning I could see that everybody was on coffee.

For our first show at the *Australia Hall* the organisers had to find an extra 250 chairs, the demand for tickets was so great. Only once before was the hall so full, when Frankie Howerd headed the bill but his show was free; with ours an admission fee was charged. This was a great start for our following two months of daily appearances in theatres, hospitals, camps, airport hangars, tents and under the sky - in short everywhere there were soldiers, on duty, off duty or sick. We soon left Malta and flew to Tripoli where Major Middleton looked after us. One of the pleasures of being a performer is that, wherever you go worldwide, there is always someone who will take you in hand and point out all the amazing sights of that area and tell you its history. This tour was no exception.

As so many of the camps and town theatres where we performed during the day or at night were positioned within driving distance from the main headquarters, the drivers took the most interesting routes to incorporate a little lightness into what was a very gruelling timetable. I remember visiting Sabbratha's Roman excavations with its amphitheatre and watching the locals working their metal and leather wares in the same way they had done since well before the birth of Christ. Looking up at the shelves full of goods I saw a wooden box full of wool and on it was written, wait for it, 'Yarmouth Bloaters'. We all knew that bloaters kept for a little while, but surely not for over 2000 years?

We were also shown the Tobruk war cemetery, where the eerie sleepy silence brought back memories of my own brother Alf, who was lying in another war grave, in Germany's Black Forest. This very sad and emotional experience made it that much more urgent to bring a little of England to all the troops, specially at Christmas, where many a thought surely must go home to their loved ones.

Very often our company was invited for dinner in the officers' mess. We looked forward to those events as it was amazing how these army cooks managed to put on such good food. It was difficult to comprehend that one was sitting in the middle of the desert with the Royal Hussars and all their regimental silver on display or in use.

During our stay in Benghazi I recorded with Douglas George *Christmas Greetings* at the Forces Broadcasting Station, which were included into the programme 'Calling Home' on Christmas Day. Several camps were too far away to visit, so we arranged that every town with a forces broadcasting station would put a radio programme over the air with the help of their disc jockeys.

At one studio a music manuscript was shown to us which was intended to be the new Libyan National Anthem and I was requested to make it into a disc for submission to King Idris I. This was a challenge indeed to launch this unique song so after a few alterations the recording was sent to the Royal *Palace*. The King did express delight, but what happened to the song I do not know.

We soon came to realise that travelling with show girls on army buses or trucks caused quite a sensation amongst the local fraternity. The all male camps gave us problems too, where should the ladies sleep? Special toilet facilities had to be built and dressingrooms near the stages erected. I remember one camp where one girl came quite shaken out of a makeshift toilet. Apparently, as she was sitting on the plank of wood with its hole in the middle, the bucket underneath started to disappear. It had been a native's job to periodically pull the bucket out through a gap in the wall, empty it and give the hole a good scrub with a brush.

Another incident happened when the girls were using a temporary dressing room built on four posts half a meter off the ground. As one of the girls was bending down to pick up her knickers she realised that the black air holes in the floor were actually rolling eyeballs, belonging to a hoard of natives all clamouring to catch a glimpse of the white naked women.

We were very well looked after, by Mr. McLeach, Col. Stewart and Captain George Lambert, which was not always easy, especially when we were on long journeys and nature called. Truck drivers did not like to stop. Forgotten mines were still lying among discarded vehicles at the roadsides, leftovers from a retreating army where the tribesmen would hide and when the passengers of the truck tried to relieve themselves behind a rusting panzer the locals would relieve the truck of its spare wheels or anything else that could be removed. Harry Worth told me some Arabs flagged his Suez driver down whose car had a flat tyre. As he and his driver were attending to the stricken vehicle, their own car was robbed of its back tyres.

During dinner at the hotel in Fayid Joyce Grenfell, who had just finished her tour, kept us in fits of laughter all evening with her anecdotes. Wherever she went she took a piano. Driving along the desert road her driver had to stop. A car was blocking the road. It was impossible to bypass the halted vehicle as her heavy truck would have got stuck in the sand. After helping the other Arab driver Joyce realised with dismay that her piano had managed to disappear, off the back of her lorry, never to be seen again.

Under the Anglo-Egyptian Treaty of 1936 Great Britain had acquired the right to maintain defence forces in the Suez Canal Zone, and for most of the time after the creation of the State of Israel in Palestine in 1948, the Egyptian Government prohibited the transit of vessels to and from Israel through the canal. This caused unrest along the fertile strip of land bordering the canal with many incidents of sniper shots being fired across the narrow band of water. The worrying part was that their main target were the high-ranking army vehicles in which we were often driven, with me sitting in the seat of one of their top brass, having been given the rank of a brigadier for the duration of the tour. I sank lower and lower into the seat, when I was told that only two weeks before an important army officer had been shot while travelling along that very road. I didn't care any more that this flag-bedecked car was being saluted everywhere it drove, which normally would have been quite fun. I did not relish the thought of playing the part of a sitting duck.

The other great worry was the unrest among the Egyptians themselves, as they repeatedly demanded that Great Britain evacuate the Suez Canal, which actually was to happen. Within one year a treaty was signed and by 1956 all British troops had departed. We had been warned not to do anything that could be held against us politically. We already had tasted one example of the brusqueness of Egyptian officialdom towards us British. When we booked into the hotel, we were ordered to show all passports, and did we have any other papers on us that they should see? We carried on performing between Suez in the south and Port Said in the north, but from that day on I took no more notes in my diary.

With Christmas so near, we also entertained the children of the servicemen who had their families with them, at a special party. The kids joined me singing traditional carols and we succeeded in bringing a feeling of a conventional Christmas to all. I was even presented with a special Christmas gift: my own coat of arms put together by our organiser who was a heraldry expert, Ken Mason.

The further north along the Suez Canal we travelled, the more intense the atmosphere became, with Port Said appearing to be the most hazardous area. One army corporal driving us after a show made a wrong turn, and we were suddenly surrounded by a mob of unfriendly Arabs who shouted and bashed their fists against our car and started to rock the vehicle. The corporal, shouting at us to hold on tight, slammed into reverse gear and, with screeching tyres, sped back the way he'd come, eventually arriving back at the hotel.

Even there it wasn't safe. After hearing shots in the street, I cautiously looked from my hotel window and saw people running in all directions. The communication from the room to the reception wasn't working so I walked down to the hall, where a conglomeration of noisy Egyptian officials and police, hotel guests and British Army personnel had assembled. As the Egyptians looked through our passports, one British Army officer came to me with the advice to quietly get my party together, and would the showgirls, especially the blondes, please cover their heads. We should be ready to leave the hotel at sundown. We should leave our luggage in the rooms so as not to attract attention. We departed through the hotel kitchens into waiting cars and sped to our new destination. Surprisingly the luggage did follow suit.

Our tour along the Suez Canal finished on 10 January and our next port of call was Cyprus. I was tired and just wanted to relax without hearing guns, before returning to Britain, but we soon realised that we had walked into another hotbed of problems. The British stationed in Cyprus, who tried to keep the Russians beyond the Dardanelles, were not liked at all by the Greek Cypriots as they wished to govern Cyprus themselves, but then there were the Turks too, clamouring for their rights. In short, under no circumstances was it safe to venture anywhere without military protection, so we decided to break away from the party and fly to Beirut.

We booked ourselves into the St George Hotel, where the waiters served you wearing white gloves and the food was out of this world. It was nice, too, to have running water at the touch of a tap at any hour of the day or night, not just for one hour, between six and seven, as had been the case during the last weeks.

Beirut was fascinating. Who would have believed that this beautiful city's skyline would be completely altered during the unrest in the later part of the 1970s? How lucky I was to have been able to see all that splendour before it was lost.

The tour had been a challenge for us all: 60 shows in as many days, plus the many radio transmissions, children's parties and all the travelling in between.

Troops relaxing

Croylands Broadwalk

Joyce Grenfell & friend

The cast of the Middle East tour rehearsing

Childrens' Christmas party

*Christmas
in the desert*

Act Twenty-two

HOLLAND

During my absence from England Cyril had been busy writing a lengthy report of my past achievements. I was now in my thirtieth year and 15 of them had been spent in show business. This report was forwarded to Val Parnell – perhaps it would promote an inclusion in a Royal Command Performance? Especially as 1953 was to be the Coronation Year of our young Queen Elizabeth II, but the letter was not even answered.

The BBC expressed the wish for a further 12-week radio series starting in April and with fitting in some more theatre engagements it was soon time to fly to Holland where our welcome at Schipol Airport was fantastic. We were greeted by Mr. Muriloff of *Radio Hilversum,* representatives of Columbia records and of Bovema at Heemsted, Mr. G.M. Oord as well as enthusiastic fans. The press were there in force too and next day the papers carried full-front page photos and long articles, telling the Dutch readers all about my life, before my special guest appearance on AVRO's *Bonte Disdagavondtrein* celebrity radio show.

A record signing session had been arranged in one of Amsterdam's music shops. As I arrived, a large crowd of people was already waiting to be allowed to enter the shop. One young Dutch boy was so thrilled to meet me, that he stood in front of me and started to whistle the 'Tritsch Tratsch Polka'. He really was very good, so I thought I'd have a little bit of fun, and joined in with my whistle. Next day the newspaper remarked about the 'uniek duet'.

That's when the problems started. The crowd outside had become so large that, when they heard me whistle inside the shop, their up till then orderly conduct became disrupted with a sudden surge from the back of the crowd forward towards the shop's entrance doors. Many of the fans spilled from the pavement onto the street and caused quite an obstruction to the busy traffic. It did not take long for the mounted police to arrive and the only way to disperse the masses was for the music shop to close its doors.

But how was I going to get out myself?

The only way was through the back door, along a garden path, and climbing up and over a high wall, hoping I didn't land in one of Amsterdam's famous canals. Unfortunately I split my trousers during this exercise.

The AVRO live show was so successful that a further programme was put in the 'can' and a firm date was signed for me to return within six months. A newspaper article from Breda in Holland, reprinted in Britain's *Sunday Pictorial*, highlighted a familiar problem, under the headline 'BRITISH STARS PLEASE! EUROPE WANTS THEM IN TV LINK.'

For Dutch TV Viewers this is an historic occasion... to see their first BBC TV programme... never before has British show business been promised such a shot in the arm... give us British artists. In Holland alone they know more of our radio stars than their own. Anne Shelton and Ronnie Ronalde are only two of many names that every Dutch listener knows...

Why didn't they shout for Americans? I wonder.

Steffani expressed the wish to spend a few days away from it all – why not on the boat in Beccles? No sooner said than done and I was driving my Lagonda out of the garage. I was already imagining the fish dangling on the end of my rod. After we passed through Newmarket and re-entered the highway, a lorry slowly emerged from a side road. I proceeded to overtake the lorry but surprise, surprise, instead of staying in the left lane, the lorry kept on moving towards the right of the road. I tried to gain speed to get out of the situation but the lorry too increased its speed and it did not take long before we made contact with each other – bash, and bash again. By the third bash we both interlocked and came to a halt.

My car had collided with a truck loaded with coal and the convertible roof was completely smashed in by the weight of the fallen sacks of coal. After all the black dust had settled, Steffani and I heard a panic- stricken voice uttering in a very Irish brogue:

'Are ye all right? Holy Jesus and Mary, I tought I'd killed yer'!

'You nearly did,' I answered in a none too happy voice.

In no time a policeman arrived. He took the driver's statement and it transpired that the lorry belonged to his brother-in-law. He had never driven the truck before and, as he was shorter, he couldn't see out of the side mirror. He'd stopped to see if anything was coming up the road but saw nothing, and anyway he was only going a few yards as he had to turn right at the next turn-off.

'They' – pointing at us – 'must have been travelling bloody fast, officer!'

Then it was my turn. The policeman, after taking one look at my driving licence, tried to scrutinise my face through all the black coal dust.

'You're not him? Are you?' and accompanied this question with a little whistle.

'I'm afraid so, officer'.

As he was writing my name down in his little black book he spelled, 'Ronnie Ronalde'. The Irishman, upon hearing my name crossed himself, calling on all the saints, then got hold of my hand and kept on shaking it.

'Oh, Jesus and Mary, when I tell me mother that I've met yee, she won't believe me! I'm so pleased I've met yee!'

'I wish you hadn't,' I muttered under my breath.

There was no way I could have shifted the car off the road. My beautiful Lagonda was a complete wreck, I couldn't even get back into the driver's seat, the steering wheel had almost embedded itself into the front seat.

Although feeling rather downcast I managed to throw myself into rehearsing new songs for my next recording session and radio series.

Then came a letter from a reader highlighted in an article in *The Performer*:

Although it may seem a bit early, the correspondent wrote, this IS Coronation Year, and plans for the next Royal Variety Show in the autumn will be getting under way before long. There has been a lot of talk about these shows in the past, and you must agree that some artists have tended to be invited to appear too often. I am not in any way disputing their ability, but surely it does seem to defeat the prime object when so few names are given a chance to display what they can do, so instead of having foreign names on the bill this time and those who have appeared more than once in the recent years, let 1953 be a really British effort, with the emphasis on youth and new talent in the foreground. May I go so far as to suggest a few worthy names for inclusion – Ronnie Ronalde, whose talent and personality have won him a place at the top... could the organisers not give each artiste longer, and cut out the crowded atmosphere...

So there it was, another cry for British artistes. I was happy that my theatre audiences were as faithful as ever and that my reviews still included such sentences as...

His teenage fans were in ecstasies, and the patrons of the Empire last night were taken on a magic carpet from the heights of the Swiss mountains to the shades and peace of a bird sanctuary.

Van Oord

The Bentley

Schichtl-Rulyan Marionettes

Act Twenty-three

I BELIEVE

Sidney Vauncez of the *Weekly Sporting Review's Show Business* Section wrote:

'Jack Jackson must have high hopes of 'I Believe' because he has aired the same British disc twice in successive weeks as sung by young David Whitfield... but 'I believe' I have heard another British disc at least as good in Ronnie Ronalde's version on Columbia with Ray Martin's Orchestra and Choir. Now hold on to your hats folks... this isn't the Ronnie you have been accustomed to... This is a more mature Ronnie, with real character in his voice, and plenty of body, almost baritone resonance in his low notes, plus a Caruso-like throb in the upper register. It's a new Ronalde a revelation and a best-seller – that's what I believe!'

The record to which he was referring to was the result of Columbia using, for the first time, a separate soundproof cubicle for the artiste where he could hear the orchestra over headphones and receive his cues through a little window. By today's standards this must sound pretty elementary, but at that time it was quite revolutionary. All the Columbia chiefs, Ray Martin and Norrie Paramour, who had produced the record, were sure it was going to be a *hit*. Oscar Preuss, senior artistes' manager for EMI, one of a handful of men who virtually controlled the fortunes of the breakneck disc business which at that time had a turnover of around £8 million, sent advance copies of my 'I Believe' to the relevant radio programmes and columnists, such as the BBC's *Housewife's Choice* and disc jockeys, such as Jack Jackson.

I was riding on the crest of popularity but have you ever dreamed of being on the top and then woken up and realised that you were actually right at the bottom? The BBC decided to split my 12-week radio series in half, so that, having done the first six programmes, there were now no more until the autumn – no chance of giving my new record the needed air time.

On 24 April that year, *Daily Sketch* writer Ker Robertson wrote a stinging article:

It showed Jack Jackson holding a record with the text: *Change this BBC one-sided record:*

American Patty Page she got 15 minutes... American Doris Day for her quarter of an hour wonderful publicity and American Lena Horne half an hour money-spinning boost for her torch songs...

...I love the United States, he wrote, '...But to be pro-American I do not have to be anti-British. And particularly I object to my own countrymen trying to force America down my throat. And that is exactly what some of the disc-jockeys of the big, bland BBC are doing. The guilty men of the gramophone record turntables pour over the air a stream of discs featuring American bands, singers and instrumentalists. I say it must stop. British artists and musicians are getting a raw deal... Let's look at Jack Jackson who has the peak listening period on Saturdays, on April 4 he played eight records by British artists and 16 by Americans... Every airing of a record by an American artist is cash out of the pocket of a British entertainer... Many of the Palladium starred thousands-of-pounds-a-week imports from the US have been made here by disc jockeys... I extend an invitation to BBC producers and disc-jockeys to line up beside me. If they want to support British goods they will find it easy. If they don't I will label them anti-British. I shall be watching them this weekend.

After this outpouring Ker Robertson received letters by the sackful from the public and from within the business; Troise; Julie Dawn; Norrie Paramour; Ray Martin. The following week he wrote again in the same vein:

Lucky the Englishman who gets a BBC plug... American plugs more blatant than ever... 10 minutes to Joni James... barely known in Britain... but after this BBC airing her fortunes will no doubt look up... The BBC have said in the past that they won't give such time to the Britishers because it would be boosting them for the variety stage.

Naturally he also received letters who agreed with the American influence like the one who implemented that all we British can do is copy the Americans and I received the headlines in the Evening News:

STAR WHO DOES NOT APE AMERICAN CROONERS...for here is a British artist who is quite British...quite a change these days when most of our singers develop American style sobbing or yelling vocal tricks and wave their arms in frenzied rhythm...

Grateful as I was to the press for writing all those favourable comments, it was still hard for me to understand the logic of a man like Jack Jackson, who, when I was 14 had me on his show, watched me climb up the ladder of success and yet never gave my 'I Believe' a spin, although he did play American Frankie Lane's version and David Whitfield's recording was aired a couple of times too.

Because the DJs continuously played American discs, the public bought those recordings and with the record-shops supplying the BBC with their weekly sales-figures, inadvertently helped in pushing the American versions into the Top Ten Hit Parade, which of course the BBC was compelled to play again. Naturally there were always the true hit songs that got through on luck and merit, and in that order, as merit very often had nothing to do with it.

And there was another, more sinister side to it all.

'Money'

A new breed of sharp operators was infiltrating the British music scene with its bounty of dollars. They, on behalf of their artistes would find out which recordshop in London was supplying the BBC with their weekly sales figures and so buy their clients discs in large quantities, again boosting the record.

It was May 1953 and I had been working non stop. Passing Paragon Motors Ltd. during my week at the *Palace* Hull I noticed a black Bentley, all shining and gleaming, so in I went and asked for a trial run. Very curtly I was told that I could not have one. The car is so good, that there is no need for that sort of exercise.

'Are you going to have me or not?' the car seemed to ask.

I bought it, £4600 worth, and was to pick it up on Sunday morning in time for my return journey to London. Excellent. That was until I arrived at the garage and saw my car still in the showroom, standing on a slope, facing an enormous plate glass window that separated it from the main street.

'Will you drive it out onto the road for me please?' I asked the showroom attendant.

'Not likely,' was his answer. 'Here are the keys' and with a nod and a 'Good luck' he disappeared. Gingerly I got into the car, somehow managed to find the right button to press the starter and managed to drive serenely off the ramp, through the sliding doors – not the window – and onto the road, feeling like a millionaire.

After about half an hour's drive, Steffani turned to me and said, 'Let's go to Beccles first, son, I'd like to show them (meaning his family) the car!'

'Okay Steff, I could do with a cup of tea.'

I stopped the car to turn and take a different route, but could I get the reverse gear in? Steffani had to get out of the passenger seat, walk round the car and help me to get the gear lever, which was on the right hand side of the driver seat, into reverse. Eventually we arrived at his sister's home, situated in midst a row of terraced houses. Steffani got out of the Bentley, all gentlemanly like, acknowledging with a slight nod of his head all the net-curtains that had suddenly started to move at the various windows, and entered her house. Refreshed with a cup of tea, we were ready to drive on to London.

This time the same gust of wind must have blown through the street again, so Steffani actually accompanied his slight bow by raising his hand to give the unseen audience a 'Royal wave', much to the distress of his sister. Still smiling and like a ventriloquist he ordered me to:

'Start the car, son!'

I pressed the button. Nothing happened.

I pressed the button again. Nothing happened.

'Will you get this car started!' he managed to hiss between his lips, still smiling to his invisible public.

All decorum had flown out the window by then. I could not get the Bentley to start. It was already past five on Sunday afternoon so we had no option but to leave the car where it was, in front of his sister's house, and book ourselves into a hotel for the night.

Next day we phoned for help and a mechanic soon arrived. What was wrong with my car? Nothing. In my keenness to make a grand exit I had merely drowned the motor.

I told the mechanic that I read the instruction book and could not make head or tail of it.

'Ah' he said, 'if you'd been given the American version you would have understood it but here in England only chauffeurs drive this sort of car.'

Meaning what?

For the next few months I was working every week in theatres, some of the supporting artistes were Dickie Henderson, Nicholas Parsons, Lynne Breton, Freddie Bamberger and Pam, the Schichtl-Rulyan Marionettes, Billy Baxter and Harold Smart. On one free Sunday I made a trip to Blackburn to visit Joan and Brian Hutchinson and my godson, Mark. Realising that I had no present for the baby, I stopped the car in front of a toyshop on top of a hill on the main road leading through Blackburn. As I was paying for the toy I happened to glance out onto the street and saw the tail-end of my Bentley slowly disappearing from view. I never moved so fast in my life. Throwing the teddy at the bewildered shop assistant, I hurtled through the shop-doors and pursued my two-ton car, which by then was gaining on speed rolling down the steep street. Eventually I caught hold of the door handle and managed, still running with the car, to pull up the handbrake and so brought the car to a halt. A little breathless, I returned to the toyshop:

'I would like the teddy bear, please!'

Even as a man I admit to shedding a tear when something sad moves me, but I can also shed a tear over happiness, especially when New Zealand's 'All Black' win or Sir Peter Blake holds the 'America's Cup' triumphantly over his head or as in 1953 Sir Edmund Hillary reached the summit of Mount Everest.

I had been invited to my agents the Foster's office, overlooking Piccadilly Circus, to a select Dom Perignon champagne buffet, especially brought in by Fortnum and Mason by Harry Foster, to watch the Queen's Coronation procession pass by. Steffani, American comedy star Danny Thomas who was appearing at the *Palladium* together with his, and my New York agent Sol Shapiro, my agent Cyril Berlin and last to arrive direct from her French Chateau outside Paris where she gave love and a home to her many adopted children of all races and colours, none other than a truly a great celebrity, Josephine Baker, made up the party. The moment we were introduced she made me feel as if she had adopted me too; motherly warmth oozed from her and as we stood watching the Black Queen of Tonga pass by stealing all the onlookers hearts with her happy joviality and waving to everybody, Josephine squeezed my hand, she was crying with joy.

I was quite surprised when she told me that my record of 'If I were a Blackbird' was often played by her children. Josephine's well-known 'Blackbird Show' was first staged in London in 1921 and featured the 'Bye Bye Blackbird' song I recorded later, in the roaring sixties.

Act Twenty-four

ROYAL COMMAND PERFORMANCE

On 21 September I appeared for the week at the *Hippodrome* Bristol before my scheduled return visit to Holland, when a letter arrived.

Dear Ronnie Ronalde,

We are now compiling the programme for the Command Performance at the Coliseum on Monday evening, November 2nd. I am writing to ask if you would be available on that date and, if so, agreeable to do five minutes in a big production scene we contemplate presenting. As you know, time on these occasions is a very important factor. I should appreciate having a reply at your earliest, after which details could be discussed, as the programme, when decided upon, has to be submitted for the Queen's approval. Best wishes, yours sincerely Harry Marlow.

There it was, the long-awaited pinnacle of any variety artist's career, and I was allocated a five-minute spot to be slotted into a large American show production, Guys and Dolls, which was playing at the London *Coliseum*.

I did console myself that, owing to pressure of the public and press, the *Royal Command Performance* had started to use British Star names, but the irony of it was that each performer would do a minute or two in a scene representing 'past' variety stars. Tessie O'Shea was to represent Florie Ford, Jack Radcliffe imitating Harry Lauder and I was supposed to dress up, act and whistle as Albert Whelan. This way the British press could be informed that a good percentage of all performers taking part were British star names, but they would appear for a mere 25 percent of the show's duration, so giving the big American productions running in London ample opportunity to advertise their stars, and would appear with all their scenery and full cast of the show behind them giving them a (very often much needed) plug.

I was hurt by the menial position I had been allocated in front of my Queen. Steffani did try to console me, but what could I expect having declined to appear at the *Prince of Wales* Theatre previously due to the unfavourable billing and salary offered but still sent the following answer:

Thank you for your letter containing an invitation for me to appear in the Royal Variety Performance on Monday November 2nd and at the moment I am free on that date. If however I am to appear before Her Majesty the Queen, it would be necessary for me to perform three numbers – one singing – one yodelling and one whistling; all of which I desire to present as a Variety artiste, and not as a part of any production scene. With my kind personal regards.

Steffani warned me that if I were to send off my answer in that tone I could be sure to lose the call. But I believe that 'right is right and wrong is wrong' and although feeling heavy in my hand, I posted my reply, unaltered with the result:

...I have further discussed this with the selection committee and in view of the composition of our programme it would be quite impossible for us to arrange anything contrary to the suggestion I put forward in my previous letter. I am sorry about this, but perhaps you know best. Signed Harry Marlow.

I had blown the whistle and, by the looks of it, I should not expect to be included in any future productions either. This most coveted engagement of any British artiste, who for one night gives his or her services for free, not only to perform before the Queen but also to raise money for the benefit of the Variety Artistes Benevolent Fund, was tilted in favour of the Americans, whose expenses no doubt had to be met from the show's takings. Many stories circulated among agents of how difficult it was to try and get their artistes into the show.

We flew to Holland for our second visit and were soon immersed in rehearsals for the next day's radio show also featuring Harry Mooten, Frans du Mee and Kenny Baker. Afterwards an enthusiastic audience had gathered outside the studios following us, all with torchlights, back to the hotel where I met Dutchman Leo Fuld, the composer of 'The Windmill Song', which I had recorded.

Due to my popularity in Holland, a few ladies were out of pocket. *Mynheer Ronalde... A Poor Impression... Posed as Ronnie Ronalde to get Money... Got Money Posing as Radio Star* and so forth.

What had happened? One of the Dutch newspaper articles explained:

A 23 year old Dutchman who obtained money from women by posing as Ronnie Ronalde, British radio's whistling star, was jailed for 18 months in Amsterdam. The court heard how an Amsterdam hawker, speaking in English, accosted women and asked for a loan to pay his hotel bill, as he was temporarily hard up. He persuaded his victim that he was Ronnie Ronalde, and added, 'My cheque from the BBC has not yet come through'. He would say he was in Holland for an engagement in Amsterdam. One woman witness told the court she had lent him about 145 guilders. 'I found him charming,' she said. After the judge had given his verdict for 18 months jail he turned to the victim and said: 'Madam, you should have known that the BBC always pays their cheques!'

Many times reporters will come backstage to interview you. Although you try to conceal personal emotions from them when you are handed a letter, I am sure the *News of the World* reporter who was with me when I opened a particular envelope on 6 October did not expect the outburst that followed and wrote this article accordingly:

I was with Ronnie Ronalde in his Dressing room at Manchester Hippodrome when news came that he had been one of the Stars chosen to appear in the Royal Command Variety performance at the London Coliseum. He was as excited as a school boy, and went on the stage to give even more zest to his performance than usual.

Little whistling Ronnie from Islington had stood his ground and won. I had been given the time to perform before my Queen, three numbers as a single act on stage, alone.

But had I won? 1953 to 1998, 45 years I had never been invited back again. C'est la vie.

A one week's engagement at the *Hippodrome* Derby still had to be fulfilled. This date brought a special request to the fore. Raymond Lane, the theatre manager, had been asked if he could bring a young lad into my dressingroom after the show as my records had given him so much pleasure. When Geoffrey Rainsford of Chadesden was brought in by his aunt, I realised that I was the hero of a five-year-old blind boy. Geoffrey showed great interest in the way I whistled the birds and it did not take him long, after exploring my face with his tiny fingers, to place them into my mouth and I whistled through them, much to the little chap's delight. This touching episode brought back memories of my visit as a Songster to Scandinavia where I had a similar experience. Later, too, I made many visits to different blind schools for instance Perth in Australia with Impresario Roy Watterson, Wellington and Warkworth in New Zealand where in December 1990, I entertained 20 blind teenagers from Los Angeles who were spending their holiday of a lifetime as guests of the Kotuko Foundation and the people of Warkworth in a camp near the sea. Whistling seems to hold a deep fascination for blind people worldwide, judging by the amount of letters and tapes I have to reply to.

Rehearsal day for the Royal Performance had arrived and my allocated time for the orchestra run-through was set for 6pm. I sat in the stalls waiting to be called till 10pm and then told it will be 'later' but it did not materialise until well after midnight. I was the last and even before starting was told that one run-through should suffice; everyone was tired and wanted to go home for a few hours' sleep before next day's dress-rehearsal where again I was left until last and after halfway through my numbers the orchestra was told to finish playing my music, we were holding up the formation rehearsal of the finale walk-on. That's when I realised that I had been scheduled by Alec Shanks, the producer, to come on before the cast of the American Guys and Dolls chorus line. It appeared that my previous controversy with the committee had been conveyed to the producer, it was clear the show's production bosses were presenting me under sufferance.

At this late stage I did not wish to make another issue out of it, so instead I told Steffani to inform the producer that I did not wish to take part in the finale. When Sam Harbour, the theatre manager, heard of my decision, he came backstage to try and talk to me. As it turned out, it had nothing to do with me missing the finale; they were worried about the press getting hold of my decision, the British again having to play second fiddle to the Americans. On leaving my dressing room Sam turned round and said quietly, 'Ronnie, just stay in the wings – for me, please?'.

Three hours before the start of the show and a further three hours to wait before my turn to step onto the stage. There was no way I could sit in a dressing room for that length of time together with a petrified-looking Frankie Howerd and stay composed, so I decided to go for a walk. When I tried to get back into the stage door I found the police had cordoned off all access into the theatre with ropes to control the masses of onlookers who had taken up their positions to watch the arrival of the Queen. I had to virtually whistle myself into the theatre, first of all to get through the crowds and then to gain the attention of a policeman and lastly to convince him of who I was.

Tommy Cooper, also sharing our dressing room, had already put his Fez on and off a dozen times, trying to make everyone laugh but at the same time to hide his own nerves. After several trips to the toilet he had to go yet another time and found the door locked. Nobody was able to move dear Ann Shelton, so after another no-go Tommy came back into the dressing room saying, 'I've done it, I used a lemonade bottle!'

'What did you do with the bottle?' I asked him, thinking that I might need it too.

'I made it disappear, ha ha!'

'Overture and beginners, please!' The tension cannot possibly be described. For 15 solid years I had been on stage almost nonstop, sometimes doing five or six shows a day, but for this one appearance my stomach did not belong to me any more. And then there was the long, long wait as my spot was not until the end of the show.

At last my intro music of 'Sweet Sixteen' was playing. I could see the white cross mark on the stage floor where my microphone should have been positioned but was actually standing far to near the front runner tabs. Another thoughtless action. I will recount in the words of our trade paper, *The Performer*:

As the curtain rose upon the scene for Ronnie Ronalde it swept with it the microphone – an unnerving enough happening for any artiste who must have at once thought: 'Is it still alive?' But the young vocal artiste showed much aplomb as he set the fallen microphone to rights and started in on his first item as though nothing untoward had happened. He demonstrated in no uncertain manner his versatility first with a straight rendering of 'Loveliest Night of the Year', followed by Albert Ketelby's 'In a Monastery Garden', in which his bird whistling was of such quality that when he reached the OP side of the stage (he was one of the very few to utilise the whole frontage of the vast area) Her Majesty and the Duke of Edinburgh leant over the edge of the box in order to see closer how he attained his effects. His final item was a yodelling number, 'Yodelling Waltz' and in this, as with everything else he did, there was the stamp of showmanship and ability that brought its reward...

The Royal Command Performance Finale quickly followed with 110 Australians and New Zealanders performing their special dance routine to wish the Queen well on her forthcoming Commonwealth Tour. As I stood there in the wings watching them, I suddenly found myself being picked up from behind and virtually carried onto the stage to be deposited right in the front line of the middle of the stage by the six foot-plus Canadian Edmund Hockridge; Sam Harbour must have had a hand in this.

Harry Marlow was interviewed after staging his 25th annual Royal Variety Show and asked to reveal some of his fabulous stories in a book about the stars and Royalty, he told how my act led to Prince Philip teaching the Queen to whistle.

'Ronnie Ronalde, the famous whistling star, had just finished his act... when I noticed the Queen turn to the Prince. 'How does he do it?' she seemed to be saying. The Prince grinned and with everyone in the Royal Box watching him, put two fingers to his mouth and puffed his cheeks. Suddenly everyone in the party burst out laughing – as if the Prince's demonstration had been a failure. It probably was, for the energy he was putting into it could have produced a whistle heard throughout the theatre.'

Usually the stars of a Royal Command Performance Show are invited to line up to meet the Queen. This invitation was never extended to me.

The press had their field day with:

'Ronnie's whistle get's the Queen to rise... the Queen left her Royal Seat... the Duke teaches the Queen to whistle...

Barely into the New Year of 1954 and performing at the *Grand Theatre* Southampton the director of the *Daily Express* came backstage to tell me in his very cultured voice that my performance astounded him. I had to tell him that John Barber of his paper had written an article saying that my *'Monastery Garden'* was Variety at its worst. John Barber never wrote about me again.

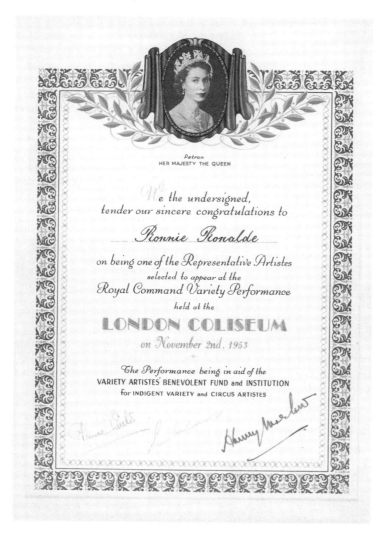

Patron
HER MAJESTY THE QUEEN

We the undersigned,
tender our sincere congratulations to

Ronnie Ronalde

on being one of the Representative Artistes
selected to appear at the
Royal Command Variety Performance
held at the

LONDON COLISEUM

on November 2nd, 1953

The Performance being in aid of the
VARIETY ARTISTES' BENEVOLENT FUND and INSTITUTION
for INDIGENT VARIETY and CIRCUS ARTISTES

Supplement to the Performer November 5th 1953

ROYAL PERFORMANCE
IN AID OF
The Variety Artistes Benevolent Fund

HER MAJESTY
THE QUEEN

ETHEL REVNELL

ANNE SHELTON

EVE BOSWELL

GLORIA NORD

TOMMY COOPER

RONNIE RONALDE

ALFRED MARKS

JIMMY JAMES

MAX BYGRAVES

JACK WARNER

VIVIAN BLAINE

VEIT BETHKE

SHEILA O'NEILL

LIZBETH WEBB

STUBBY KAYE

SAM LEVENE

JOHNNY SILVER

JERRY WAYNE

TOM PEDI

MACKENZIE REID & DOROTHY

ERNEST BUTCHER

JO, JAC and JONI

LEW HERBERT

DANYA & ALVAREZ

HASTINGS GIRLS CHOIR

HENRY COTTON

EDMUND HOCKRIDGE

JOHN TILLER GIRLS

JIMMY EDWARDS

PHILIP GREEN

JOAN DAVIS

HARRY MARLOW   PRINCE LITTLER   SAM HARBOUR

ALEC SHANKS

LONDON COLISEUM 2nd Nov. 1953.

Act Twenty-five

RED TILES

Beccles, Steffani's hometown, had become more and more a haven of sanity for me and gradually my thoughts had turned to buying a house there, much to the delight of Steffani but not of my family. My stepmother preferred the shops where we lived, my sister had a good job in the city and my father assured me, quite strongly, that the beer in Beccles did not taste as good as the one he was used to. But my mind was made up when Steffani's friend, Reg Darby, approached me with the news, that Red Tiles and two Georgian villas, No.15 and 17 Northgate with a garden sloping down to the river Waveney and a boathouse, was coming up for sale. I couldn't say no. It had belonged to a Tea Planter and then to the famous wartime Tedder family.

The next door property belonged to Adrian Bell whose son Martin became a worldwide known BBC News Correspondent. Last time I met him was on a flight from London to Frankfurt, just prior to his being shot on air in the line of duty in Sarajevo.

As we had sold the Goldfinch I needed a new boat – which I ordered at the Olympia boat Show and on my way back home, through the West End of London, I stopped at the red traffic lights when a sudden knock on my car window brought me face to face with a traffic cop on a motorbike who asked me to pull over to the side.

'Certainly, officer,' I answered, fearing the worst, but with great relief soon realised the cause of all this officialdom when I saw one Royal black limousine after another, escorted by police on motorbikes, swishing past me. Immediately I cottoned on and with the advantage of driving a black Bentley quickly manoeuvred myself behind the last car of the Royal procession. I had never been through London so fast, but unfortunately had to turn off at Buckingham *Palace*, I hadn't been invited for tea.

I called my new boat 'Blackbird' after the song that had given me fame.

Again I had become a problem for the BBC. I had become too expensive for them trying to cope with the amount of letters coming in for me so the only way they could stop it was to keep me off air during the whole of 1954. Cyril advised me to consider the offers he kept on receiving from the boys of *Radio Luxembourg*, a commercial radio station. I took Cyril's advice and after a very satisfactory luncheon it was arranged between Geoffrey Everitt, the head of Radio Luxembourg, and myself to go onto his Commercial Radio.

I continued touring the country from Plymouth to Scotland, topping the theatres and supported by many acts like Jimmy Scott, Terry O'Neill, Peggy Haig, the Rexanos, Joe Baker, Jack Douglas, Benson Dulay, Arthur Worsley, Dave King, Janet Brown, the Morton Fraser Harmonica Gang, Bill Waddington, Pharos and Marina, Bobby Wright, an up and coming Bruce Forsyth and gave a spot to Jack Jackson, playing his trumpet.

Slowly it became noticeable that the variety theatres had started their gradual decline. There were many schools of thought as to the reasons for this. Many suffered empty seats through numerous strikes, especially when it effected the adverts in the newspapers or the transport as it did in South Shields, so I would not accept my contracted guaranteed salary. Will and Joe Collins, uncle and father of Joan Collins appreciated that gesture... *I shall not forget your co-operation... yours sincerely Joe.*

But personally I'd always been and still am of the opinion, that the American 'acts' were overplayed and overpaid in our country, leaving little room for other young and upcoming acts to be booked and this meant these performers couldn't grow or be seen by the circuit bookers. Variety surely should have meant what it said, but the vast sums paid to the so-called American stars caused the theatres to cut down on the rest of the artistes and charge higher seat prices which in turn frightened the family audiences away.

Alexander Gray of the *Evening Times* interviewed Lena Horne in Glasgow, a week after my appearance, and asked her*: ...did she think it was giving people value for their money to pay one American star a fortune at the expense of the rest of the bill? Lena's Manager, Ralph Harris exploded: Heck, it cost Lena £9000 the last time she came to Europe. 'Let's be quite clear about this' Gray said. 'Did it cost her £9000 or did she loose £9000? Subtle difference?*

Unfortunately the income tax structure had become complicated and acting on Cyril's advice not to overexpose myself and that of my accountants not to earn more than a certain amount, I had became more and more selective in my work. In my earnings bracket, the Inland Revenue took 19s 6d out of every pound I made. Entertainers are at their peak for only a relatively short period, I was grateful that I'd had a short time with an accountancy firm so that I was aware of the perils that could befall anyone who suddenly earned a huge sum of money and did not grasp its real value.

The American acts in England for a specific time within one tax year were exempt from British taxes, and if they stayed out of America for a certain period they did not have to pay US tax either. Every time I went to work in America, I paid their income tax before I was even permitted to leave their country.

Dickie Henderson had his tax problems too. He was often on my bills and we would share the driving in my Bentley back to London. During these journeys he used to tell me all the gossip, he knew everything about everyone. He also suggested that with my sort of money and it would be tax allowable, I should have my suits and shoes specially made by the best in London. I did take his advice.

He told me how he, Bruce Forsyth and Sean Connory, all dedicated golfers, were in a taxi and running late for Bruce's TV Show so Bruce tapped on the cabbies window and said:

'please hurry, I am Bruce Forsyth of tonight's 'Generation Game' TV Show'

'Oh yes!' answered the unbending driver, *'and I suppose,'* looking at Dickie Henderson in the mirror, *'you are James Bond.'*

'No' answered Dickie, and pointing at Sean said: *'he is James Bond.'*

Dickie Henderson

Red Tiles, Beccles

Blackbird I

A day off

THEATRE ROYAL

Week commencing SUNDAY, 20th   1954.   CONTINUOUS FROM 3 - 11

STAGE:

HE'S HERE
THE VOICE OF VARIETY

RONNIE RONALDE

STAR OF FAMILY FAVOURITES
ORCHESTRA CONDUCTED BY ARTURO STEFFANI

TONY **WALSH** • CHARLES **CAMERELLI** • ERIC **BROOKS**

ALICE DELGARNO • BABS DE MONTE
——— ROYALETTES ———

SCREEN:

AT HIS TOP TOUGH FORM!

ALAN LADD
IN
THE BLUE DAHLIA

WITH
VERONICA LAKE • WILLIAM BENDIX

*Arthur Lucan
& Kitty McShane*

Act Twenty-six

IRELAND

The following write-up made me very happy especially as this tremendous welcome I had received was from the Welsh who know how to sing, all the valleys seem to echo with their voices, and here they gave me so much love.

The South Wales Evening Post:

Seldom can an artiste have received the rapturous reception which greeted vocalist Ronnie Ronalde when he topped the bill at the Swansea Empire last night... completely captured a packed house... After completing his scheduled time he was brought back to sing six encores, and when the audience realised at last that they could get no more out of this versatile performer they stood on their feet to accord him a remarkable ovation...

My tour to Ireland in August 1954 followed and the first port of call was the *Opera House* Belfast and the *Belfast Telegraph* wrote:

Spring is sprung, the grass is riz, I wonder where the boidies is... he sings as we say in Ulster, like a thrush, and never was one of our sayings more apt.

Twice nightly the doors were opened at the *Opera House*. On the bill too were Stan Stennett, Bob Andrews and an Australian, Charles Camilleri. During the day I was 'pass the parcel', moving between tea parties, record signing sessions and openings of something or other. Everything had been organised right down to the last minute by theatre owner George Lodge, with whom I was staying. On the first morning I was introduced to their budgie, Billy. Mrs. Lodge complained that he was so dumb he couldn't 'talk' and they were fed up trying to teach him but as I had to rehearse every morning, the bird was given a daily multi-dose of various bird calls. Imagine my hosts' delight and surprise when, on the Friday night, Billy treated us all to a magnificent display of

'Ronnie Ronalde' whistling, appearing to be a chaffinch one minute and a blackbird another.

The week flew by and I travelled on to Dublin where we played to packed houses at the *Theatre Royal*, again supported by Carnellieri, Tony Walsh, Eric Brooks and Jimmy Campbell.

At the Shelbourne Hotel I had barely unpacked, when the phone rang.

'Why can't people just give me five minutes ', I thought picking up the receiver.

I would have recognised that voice, with its beautiful Irish lilt, anywhere:

'How are you, you bugger, when can I come and pick you up?' It was Frank Lavelle, from whom I'd bought the white Rolls Royce. He wanted to see me and 'show me his beautiful city of Dublin and a bit of the old country too'. Soon I was downstairs, and Frank was pushing me through the hotel doors and onto the street. There it stood, a superb Rolls Royce, I hesitated, and thought to myself, 'My God, you have done well for yourself.'

Frank just looked, saying nothing. Automatically my steps headed towards this masterpiece of British craftsmanship, and with the uniformed hotel porter standing to attention, Frank opened the rear door of the Rolls and I got in. Settled in utter luxury and comfort, I waited for Frank to get into the driver's seat – perhaps he was tipping the porter. The cocktail cabinet all in Mahogany, the hidden table, the radio system, the smell of the leather… where was Frank?

As I leaned forward to look at the porter on the pavement, he was bending down to look at me with a confused and quizzical expression. I turned to look out the other side of the car and there was Frank, across the street, sitting in an old Rover, laughing his head off and waving like mad trying to get my attention. I had to get out of the Rolls, nod to the porter and walk nonchalantly across the street to join my friend as if nothing had happened. Before long we were out of the city and driving leisurely in the country when the car started to slow down, just as we were passing some workmen repairing the road. 'Woman,' said Frank to his wife, 'did you put some petrol in this car?' Before she could reply, the car had come to a complete halt. There we were in the middle of the country, on top of a hill and no petrol. Frank stuck his head out the car window and shouted back to the workmen to ask where the next petrol station would be?

'Half a mile down the hill, over the main road and it'll be just there, on your left!'

'Get out Ron, give us a push!'

And while Frank called on all the saints, I tried my hardest to give the heavy Rover a heave and a push to get it rolling down the hill. If my fans could have seen me I am sure they would have fallen about laughing, as Frank did when I eventually managed to get back into the car for the long ride down the hill.

With cries of 'Have faith, Michael' and 'God be with us', accompanied by frantic hooting of the car horn, Frank tried to warn people to get out of his way. Some did, but two bicycle riders just managed to fall back into the brambles, their response did not sound very saintly. Then came trouble. Ahead of us a farmer was guiding his herd of cows from one field, across the road and into another field. Frank was hooting like mad, his wife was trying to say 'Be sensible, Frank, stop the car', and I was bracing myself in the back in preparation for the inevitable collision. Frank, still hooting and shouting, 'Come on, Michael, have faith, Michael' carried on and somehow managed to pass through the herd without a major disaster. We all relaxed when suddenly we were confronted by the main road ahead of us. Frank, without further ado, simply drove right across the highway, never bothering to look right or left; he had seen the garage on the other side and was heading straight for it. With the last of the car's natural roll he managed to turn into the garage, but not before he had run over the attendant's foot and came to a stop, right in front of the petrol pump.

'Fill her up, me boy.'

I was still fingering the St Christopher, which had been blessed and given to me by a loyal Dublin fan when Frank decided, because it was too early in the afternoon to return to Dublin, we could visit one of Ireland's hidden beauty spots, Glendalough.

Frank's wife told me the fascinating legend of the monk Kevin, seeking refuge from the amorous advances of a chieftain's daughter. He eluded her and built himself a hermitage in a cave on the rocky shores of the lough. The chieftain's daughter learned of his hiding place and one night rowed across the lough, stealing silently into the cave. Kevin awoke and, seeing her there, pushed her into the waters below, where she was drowned. According to the legend, since that time the birds living around the lough never sing. I must admit that standing at the edge of the lough with no bird sounds was quite eerie. As I started to imitate the chaffinch, robin and blackbird whistles, first one cottage door opened and then another. One of the women crossed herself and I saw her looking up into the trees, searching. I whistled, more and more different bird calls. Even Frank had become very serious. The birds started to answer back, until suddenly there was a symphony of birdsong, the birds themselves flying in and out of the trees. All this commotion continued until I stopped my whistling and once again the stillness descended on beautiful Glendalough. That day in Ireland was one that I will never forget.

The welcome I received in both Northern and Southern Ireland was tremendous. Among the many souvenirs I received was a shillelagh, which even now is always somewhere near me in the bedroom. The spirit of the little people with which it is blessed seems to have protected me so far.

After my return to England London's *Melody Maker* wrote:

Manager Paddy Cogan of Dublin's 4000 seater Theatre Royale said: Britain's Stars Are Tops... Two biggest successes? Lita Roza (ex Heath vocalist) and Ronnie Ronalde... the latter packed the house... Ronalde was as big as anything we had this year... just look at the names... Nat King Cole, Frankie Laine, Vivian Blaine, Roy Rogers, Dale Evans and Guy Mitchell... they were greeted by Press Conferences and radio interviews... Ronalde practically 'sneaked' in.

Entertaining fans

Act Twenty-seven

GREAT YARMOUTH, WELLINGTON PIER

We decided to cut down on travelling for a year, so perhaps, we should be looking for something nearer to home? What about Yarmouth for the 1955 summer season? After we approached John Kinnersley, Yarmouth Corporation's Director of Entertainments and Publicity, it was announced that Ronnie Ronalde would present and appear in the 'Ronnie Ronalde Show' for an 18 possibly 19 weeks run.

While these arrangements were being made, J. Burnett, Chairman of EMI Australia and the Australian Impresario Jack Neary came to see me inviting me to tour Australia, and possibly South Africa on the way back, because my records were constantly featured on the radio down under and they had already bought several recorded BBC programmes of my series to take back with them, but I decided to stick with Yarmouth, perhaps I'll go to Australia the following year.

After a Christmas concert in aid of the Beccles Rotary Club charity Fund and a spot in the *Henry Hall's Guest Night* radio show the BBC did offer me four dates during January and February, called *Down Melody Lane.* Had they heard that *Radio Luxembourg* was after me? and then the TV spot on *Saturday Show* when Clifford Davies wrote:

...his highlight was a duet with flautist Lionel Solomon in which he (Ronnie) whistled 'Lo' hear the gentle lark' PAR EXCELLANCE. It was time to prepare for Yarmouth, especially as we wanted to put together a show consisting of three separate programmes that changed every midweek, so holidaymakers could come and see us three times during their customary fortnight's holiday without having to watch a repeat performance. We had signed the Marie De Vere Command Girls and the artists to appear were Grace and Charles Jupp, Mimi Law, The Two Rexanos, Wendy Brandon, Nicky Hilliard,

Audrey Gunner, Eric V. Marsh, Bob Andrews, Helen Turner and Billy Whittaker with musical director Randall T. Topping. I approached the Yarmouth season with tremendous enthusiasm. There was so much at stake. Not just the money side of it but the prestige – and not just my name but also Steffani's, as this was his home ground.

Again I find it easier to copy excerpts from newspapers:

...and even on the first night it moved with a slickness and smoothness that promised a highly successful run... Ronnie Ronalde, the show's star, is probably without peer in this country as a siffleur and yodeller... The 'star' was in fine form and returned time and again in response to hearty applause...Mr. Edgar Barker, the Chairman of the Entertainments and Publicity Committee had every justification in expressing his confidence that the new show will be a 'winner'...

I really could not have asked for more and Steffani was beaming too.

A few days later the papers were reporting that the show was proving to be an even greater success than anticipated. 'House Full' boards are already in evidence, which augurs well for the time when the holiday crowds arrive. And *The Performer* wrote that... *the season has not as yet started, it is playing to capacity business and everything points to a record season. Ronnie himself is a firm favourite as ever.*

At the end of June all Yarmouth shows were to take part in the *BBC Week* on TV at the *Wellington Pier Pavilion* with our orchestra conducted by Randall Topping and Steffani. As well as me, representing the *Wellington Pier*, were the Beverley Sisters from the *Royal Aquarium*, Alice Dells from the Gorleston *Pavilion,* the Two Heinkes from the *Hippodrome Circus* and the Leslie Roberts Girls from the *Windmill*. Tommy Trinder, also from the *Windmill,* compered the show. The next combined show was for 4000 elderly folk from over 100 clubs who took part in the Norfolk Old People's Welfare Summer Rally and in the afternoon an open air show at the *Marina* was put on for them with Neville Bishop and his Wolves, Tommy Trinder and me.

Barely into July, I knew that I had broken all records and a newspaper article in the *Eastern Evening News* confirmed the record takings: *Last week's audiences at the Ronnie Ronalde show broke all records for the Wellington Pier Pavilion . . . In the six days the show was seen by 11,560 people.*

And *The Performer followed this with: Ronnie... has performed the astonishing feat for breaking all records in every summer season which he has played. As one wit puts it, Ronnie spends half his time making records for Columbia and the other half breaking records for theatre managers. Happily, whether making records or breaking 'em Ronnie makes money for all concerned, so everyone is happy...*

A further BBC radio show with the Beverley Sisters, Tommy Trinder, Charlie Chester, Billy Whittaker and me was broadcast from Yarmouth on August Bank Holiday.

It was inevitable, appearing night after night with the De Vere Dancers in my show, that one, Marianne Hatton, standing close to me while we were both waiting in the darkness of the backstage for our entrance, would suddenly slide her hand into mine and hold it, ever so tenderly. That was all I needed, the fire had been lit. Wherever I went, she was there. To prove how attractive she was, she won first the title of 'Miss Yarmouth', then she was chosen 'Miss Personality Girl' of Great Yarmouth and, to crown it all, during the Yarmouth Battle of Britain Week she was chosen as 'Miss Battle of Britain', receiving a sash and cup from Vera Lynn.

I suppose I always had some sort of eye for the girls but never found the time to spend with them, I was always touring. That summer was unique, I was in the same place for 18 weeks. I had a good time, but, because Marianne was so attractive, other men were after her too. After the show finished Marianne returned to London. I did call on her a couple of times but told her that I wanted to break the friendship as I was off on tour again. She threatened to throw herself off London Bridge, but I stuck to my guns; as always, my life was show business first, second and third. Many years later, in Guernsey, she called me from the hospital, to ask if I would come and visit her. I did, for old time sake, and learned that her life had not been very happy

During August a lengthy article appeared in *The Times… Yarmouth is booming and Blackpool better look out… we are catering for the masses… did one realise that the miners are now getting £750 to £1000 a year?…*

Before the season finished an actors thanksgiving service took place at the St James Church in Yarmouth. Tommy Trinder and I read the lessons. Tommy was first and whether it was by sheer accident or mischief, when it came for me to read the lesson I couldn't find the bookmark denoting my passage. There I stood, with the Bible, everybody waiting. Silence. Eventually I found the passage; Tommy remained a picture of innocence throughout.

This was followed by a farewell midnight matinee – over four hours of varied entertainment by artistes from all seven summer shows from Yarmouth and Gorleston including everyone from the Charlie Chester, Tommy Trinder and my show before a capacity audience at the *Wellington Pier*. One of the papers featured a cartoon in which two birds were sitting on a tree branch and one was saying to the other: *Heard my impression of Ronnie Ronalde?* and another paper confirmed that my show had been invited for a second summer season at the Wellington Pier for the following year, 1956.

We took the whole show inland which was a good decision as we broke existing records in both Ipswich and Norwich and so gave the company a further six weeks' work a 24-week summer season altogether. In Ipswich I had previously worked on a show with Paul Raymond, later to become 'King of London's Soho', and Suffolk resident Carl Giles, 'King of the Cartoonists' was often a visitor to the theatre, gathering gossip that he would then turn into his famous cartoons, some of them are owned by Queen Elizabeth II.

Then I had another visitor. Sir Seretse Khama, grandson of King Khama who during the eighteen hundreds curbed an expansion by the Zulu and Ndebele tribesmen and established a fairly unified state. But trouble started when gold was found so the British took the area under suppression. The interesting part was, that Sir Seretse, a keen steward of the theatre was in love with Ruth, a girl from Ipswich. They eventually married and in 1966 when Botswana gained full independence, it was led by their first president, Sir Seretse Khama, until his death in 1980. Unfortunately I never took up his invitation to visit his home in Botswana.

All our scenery, a truckload full of costumes, machinery and lighting equipment from the summer show had to be stored, so for this purpose I had a large store built in the grounds of my Beccles home. We looked upon this not as an expense but as an investment, as we seriously thought we could produce a Yarmouth summer show for quite some years; their last production, Catlin's, had been there for the previous ten years.

Billy Whittaker

Leading lady, Mimi Law

De Vere Girls

Recording with the Beverley Sisters, Tommy Trinder, Billy Whittaker and Charlie Chester

'The Show'

Charles & Jupp

Act Twenty-eight

EAST AFRICA

I had accepted Army Officer G. Brightwell's invitation to entertain the troops in Aden and in and around Nairobi for three weeks.

First I made another Christmas record, appeared at the *Odeon* Plymouth, supported by Norman Vaughan who had the audience in stitches with his imitation of the gimmicks of crooners and on 7 December I stepped on to the BOAC Argonaut at London Airport to fly via Rome, Cairo, Jeddah, Port Sudan and Asmara to Aden, the first stop on my second tour to Africa to try and bring once more a little Christmas Cheer to all our troops so far away from home.

Aden, often called the DA (duck's arse) of the British Empire, the chief port of Yemen near the south entrance of the Red Sea had been the main trade centre of Saudi Arabia since ancient times and really came into its own when the Suez Canal was opened in 1869. Aden had been a Crown colony since 1935 so it was normal for a few troops to be stationed there. Before I left England I was told that Aden was the place to buy anything, so naturally I was quite eager to see what they had to offer. It did not take me long to purchase a fantastic gold Rolex watch for £25 (a similar amount was charged as duty by customs on my re-entry into Britain).

We left Aden for Nairobi, where the New Stanley Hotel was to be our base. Every day we travelled to different outposts, between 80 and a 120 miles over bumpy tracks trying to reach as many stations as possible and bring a couple of hours entertainment to the lads who had been sticking it out for months under quite horrendous conditions. They certainly enjoyed the shows and often came straight from the dense and humid forests in the Aberdare Mountains where they tracked down the Mau Mau gangs, an armed secret terrorist organisation of the Kikuyu tribe revolting against the British rule. The management in the hotel told us not to leave anything in our rooms that could be used as a weapon as the Mau Mau would climb through the window and take it.

We were also told by Helena Sprague, whose job it was to look after us, that under no circumstances should we venture out anywhere after dark without being accompanied by an armed soldier. We already had one hair-raising experience. As we were being driven through the bush one night, the black driver nearly came to a stop. Helena very quickly realised that something was up as the sliding doors of the bus opened, so she hit the driver with the back of her hand and commanded him to 'drive on', at the same time kicking the door shut.

However much one prepares oneself, the unexpected is never far away and when it does come, can be quite terrifying. Many of the 'stages' were only tents or the back of a lorry with other lorries pointing their headlights towards it, so that we, the artistes, could be seen by the troops as the sun would disappear behind the horizon at an alarming speed, throwing everything into darkness.

There I was, standing on the back of a lorry, whistling away, trying to bring to my audience the sounds of a few English birds, when suddenly it happened: I was attacked, from all sides. The noise was indescribable – I feared for my face, my eyes, my hands, and my life! Oh God, was nobody going to help me? Well, the audience couldn't help me, because they were falling about laughing. Finally, thank God, one bright spark gave the command to switch off all the headlights.

Why the attack?

Quite simple, I was a bloody foreigner whistling different sounds of songbirds into the dark of the African night which the native birds didn't recognise and so they started to attack me, diving out of the darkness from all angles, to drive me from their territory.

There was also a brighter side to this tour, we managed to fit in a mini safari and were able to see the fantastic variety of animal life. Having just met the famous couple Michaela and Armand Denis in the New Stanley Hotel and listened to their thrilling tales of adventure while filming the wild animals of Africa, I could appreciate why so many people find it so important to preserve all species God has given us.

My whistle held a strange fascination for the African children. First they hid themselves upon hearing me, no doubt believing I was a witch doctor, but after a while their curiosity would bring them out from behind the bushes and they would crowd around me, watching every move I made to produce those strange bird calls. When it was time for me to get back into the car, those who appeared to be in charge arrived with large sticks, hitting their own people with unmerciful vigour. I was quite sickened by this behaviour.

I even caused some havoc amongst the natives playing football. I just had to have my little bit of fun and imitated the referee's whistle when I saw what I thought was a foul. The game stopped at once, everybody looked at each other, then turned to the referee who just stood there looking at his whistle. Shrugging his shoulders he blew into it and the game continued. I gave it a few minutes and whistled again. That time the players didn't bother to find out why their play was stopped but immediately descended upon the referee and gave him such a hiding that I am sure he was not going to forget in a hurry.

We performed in Aden, Nairobi, Nanyuki, Nyeru, Naivasha, Gilgil and Nakobi and again I was pleased to bring a little bit of England into our soldiers lives and when I returned to England on Christmas Day, the Bernard brothers were presenting the last television variety show of 1955 with Alexis Rassine, Nadia Nerina, Arthur English, Eddie Gray, the TV Toppers, the Welwyn City Male Voice Choir – and Ronnie Ronalde. The choir sang 'Davy Crockett' with me, and to get into the spirit of the song, as well as the party, we all wore appropriate costumes.

Amidst fans

Troop concert

The overflow

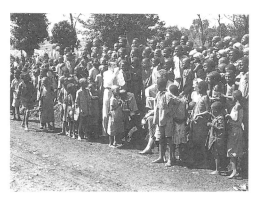

Birdie witch-doctor

The Silverbeck

Feeding time

That's when the birds came

Act Twenty-nine

DAVID AND GOLIATH

Recording new discs, a *Down Melody Lane* radio programme series, as guest star on the *Frankie Vaughan Show* on Radio Luxembourg with Geoff Love and the *Pied Piper Show*, numerous theatrical engagements also featuring Dickie Dawson a Canadian comedian and once married to Diana Dors, Bill Wareham, Rita Martell, Freddie Harrison, Dave Gray, Jimmy Wheeler, the Morton Frazer Gang and more, 1956 again proved to become very busy. I even received a request from Jack Jackson to take part on his TV show with Eve Boswell, Desmond Lane, Ronnie Carroll, Libby Morris and Glen Mason.

The time had come to make a decision, which house was I going to live in – Croylands in London, or Red Tiles in Beccles? It did not take long to opt for Beccles. There were many reasons, but the main one was my work. Soon my second Yarmouth season was starting. Both Steffani and I were also thinking that we could continue to present yearly shows in Yarmouth for many more summers. I did not think of putting myself into the staring position every year; I could easily book another 'top of the bill'. The added bonus I could offer of course was the storage space for the scenery.

I was sorry to leave Croylands but the wealthy Broadwalk area had become a prime target for burglars. Every door and window in my house was fitted with special locks and we tried never to be away all at the same time. Many of the transmissions at that time were of course live so one could read in the *Radio Times* when I was on air or TV but the 'Bing-boys' came any time. I remember sitting in the sun lounge late one night, eating my supper, when I heard glass smashing and a bump above me. 'Dear sister Vera,' I thought at first, 'she's smashed something – no, it's one of those aeroplanes going through the sound barrier!'

Next morning my father was asked by the neighbour: 'Did you have a visitor last night?'
'Visitor?' asked my father.
'Yes, I can see fresh footprints coming from your garden into my newly dug flowerbed'.
I went upstairs to investigate and found a window broken. Fortunately the thief didn't get into the house because of the special window locks. He must have lost his foothold, slid down the sun lounge roof, which I heard, and made his way over the wall back onto the street.

Watching the workmen packing up my Bechstein grand piano for its journey to Beccles made me realise that, over the years, I had managed to purchase a few nice things, making me quite proud of my achievement for somebody who had left school at 14. As the piano was mahogany and my Red Tiles rooms were all oak panelled, I went to the Piano Galleries Ltd. in Wigmore Street and asked them either to darken the colour of the piano or exchange it for another instrument. Before they committed themselves with an answer they wanted to know the number of the piano, which I had to phone them. A few days later I received a letter from one of the directors, explaining that according to their records my piano, made in 1914, was one of 'the best of the Bechstein make' and was bought first in 1916 by Mr. Stoner of Walton-on-Thames for 170 gns. He advised me to hold on to it. I have never parted with the piano and now it has pride of place in my music room at my home in New Zealand where it has often been played by Carl Doy of Candlelight fame, Quentin Gannaway, John Gibson, Reg Towers and Mike McCarthy.

I had become a firm favourite with the Swedes, who asked for a recording exclusive to their country, so in April 1956 I recorded 'Evening Chimes' and 'Beautiful Dreamer', which was flown to Sweden for immediate issue and later released by Capitol Discs of America and received a top 'sleeper' rating. The recording was made under the direction of Stan Stern, Head of EMI International, and my friend Norrie Paramour conducted the orchestra. 'Beautiful Dreamer', a most enchanting song – many would say the most beautiful song ever composed – was written by Stephen Foster who, with only 38 cents in his pocket was found lying dead in a New York gutter.

A new angle on listening to my records had come to light. Sidney Scarborough's record store in Hull had instituted, what surely must have been the most novel idea in disc publicity. You could dial a telephone number and immediately hear my latest recording. I was told that hundreds of fans had bought records by this means. All this had been made possible by the fact that Hull was the only city in Britain that ran and controlled its own telephone service, and Sidney had thus been able to enter into an arrangement with the telephone company to provide this wonderful public service to record buyers and recording artistes.

I had a good feeling about the Yarmouth Show. We were fully prepared with magazines printed by Feldman's Music Ltd containing my life story and pictures taken during my travels around the world. We had also written and recorded a catchy little number 'The Yarmouth Song'. Wherever one went in Yarmouth during the summer of 1956, one heard the song and Chappell's had printed its sheet music with my head on the cover. All the artistes for the Yarmouth *Ronnie Ronalde Show* had been booked and were ready to begin rehearsals. Billy Whittaker, Mimi Law, Eric Marsh, Helen Turner, Emerson & Jane, Hazel Ellis, The Cagney Bros, The Eight Eleanor Beam Girls, trumpet player Johnnie Lister and Terry Hall, television's newest sensation with his 'Lenny the Lion'.

One more week to go before the opening of the show and three times I had to drive back to London, first for a Radio Luxembourg programme, *Handful of Stars* and then for the Variety Club Tent 36 opening of the Festival Gardens at Battersea Park. To mention all the artistes I met there would take far too long, but here are just a few: Louis Armstrong, Avril Angers, Dora Bryan, Petula Clark, Ronnie Hilton, Jill Ireland, Dave King, Ben Lyon and Bebe Daniels, Elizabeth Larner, Jon Pertwee, Ann Shelton, Frankie Vaughan, Bernard Braden, Lonnie Donegan, Robert Desmond, Robert Earl, Bryan Forbes, Elizabeth Fraser, Kenneth More, David Whitfield, Billy Eckstine, Ian Carmichael, Dawn Addams, Vera Lynn and Shirley Ann Field. The third trip was to the recording studios, where Norrie Paramour was waiting for me to make another record. This recording produced the following in the *Sunday Pictorial* of 20 May: *Bang goes a whistle. Ronnie Ronalde can thank a golf club for the success of his latest disc. Customers were clamouring for a recording of the 'Happy Whistler' by the happy whistler himself. Columbia chief Norrie Paramour made haste to rectify this, but wanted it to sound different. This was eventually achieved by a rhythmical accompaniment, which featured hitting a drum with a number eight iron. This may appear stupid in print, but on wax it turns out to be a real 'birdie'.*

In those days, the sound engineer had to rely on impromptu ideas and, of course, on the talent of the artiste to make the sound different. These days everything can be altered, added, taken away – even the artiste's voice. No doubt this is one of the reasons so many pop-singers travel with train loads full of amplifiers to try and match the sound of their records over the loudspeakers. They have been known to mime to their own discs.

As well as heralding the beginning of our show in Yarmouth another long article was carried by *The Performer* May 17 with excerpts as reading:

…Let's face it, the BBC cut my business on this score in half… I don't expect people to come and hear me if they never manage to hear my records… does Mr. Cornell come here with no advance reputation… if he deems himself worthy of top billing in a Variety theatre, why does he need radio to bolster up his drawing powers?… Yes, why indeed?

Our show was an instant triumph, with everybody predicting that it would be an even bigger success than the year before. We always tried to show the lighter side of our individual scenes, and this year we had incorporated a 'Gardener's Dream' fantasy in which an enormous bee was whizzing around the stage on a wire; when she mistook the gardener for a flower, a huge sting protruded from the bee's behind, much to the hilarity of the audience. My recently recorded song 'Davy Crockett' was also included in a production called 'In the Land of Davy Crockett' with me playing Davy and for my own spot I had a 12-foot-high Columbia 'record' built with 'If I Were a Blackbird' written on it.

One of the main hits of the show was Lenny the Lion, the puppet Terry Hall used for his ventriloquist act. The lion was so endearing, that the audience, both young and old, absolutely fell in love with him. Every night at the finale I would let it slip that Lenny's feeding time was at 10 every morning at the end of the pier, earning a good laugh. But there were always the ones who couldn't see the joke and actually came, with their children, bringing bones and other food for Lenny. They paid the entrance fee and walked the whole length of the pier out to sea and waited for Lenny. When they realised that Lenny wasn't coming some holiday makers became very angry, especially if the weather had turned bad – so much so, that after a period the pier's manager pleaded, would I please refrain from mentioning Lenny's 'feeding time', he was fed up having to give the entrance money back.

Extract from the *Yarmouth Corporation's* statement to the Press, July 17:

'WELLINGTON PIER THEATRE. *While 1955 was an all time record we have already this season increased our turnover in advance bookings by 25 per cent'*

and nobody was happier about the show's success than Steffani and myself. It was only a matter of signing the following year's contract to confirming our verbal agreement with the City Corporation.

Halfway through the Yarmouth season, Cyril phoned; could I come to London, Bernard Delfont would like a meeting with me.

'Well,' I thought to myself, 'that sounds interesting!'

I have met and worked with many great theatre entrepreneurs, but he controlled such a great field of different aspects of show business that there was nothing in the British entertainment world he was not involved in. Through his agencies he presented many of Britain's great stars and some time earlier had made an offer to my agent Cyril to buy my services on a three-year contract. I had not accepted at the time.

The irony of this refusal, though, was brought home to me in later years, when London Management, my agency with Cyril Berlin, was already in 1955 incorporated into the Lew and Leslie Grade Organisation, both brothers of Delfont, and later when Lew Grade moved on to ATV Television, Bernard Delfont took over as head of the Grade Organisation, so he did end up in control of my agent.

Bernard Delfont had his headquarters in the *Prince of Wales* Theatre. He was not satisfied running solely London Theatres; he was after the provinces too. His first goal was Blackpool, which he soon dominated, beginning with the *North Pier*, then the *Central* and *South Pier* and then he made the takeover bid for the gigantic Blackpool Tower Company, which incorporated the *Opera House*, *Winter Gardens*, Zoo, Aquarium, Circus and the Grand Ballroom. With this scoop he had secured the working venues for his artistes. But this was not enough. He couldn't replay the same faces every year in the same town, so, where to next?

Yarmouth could pay stars to appear in their shows. I had, through Tom Arnold, been paid the highest salary ever in Yarmouth, plus a share of the takings at the *Britannia Pier's 'Ronnie Ronalde Meet the Stars Show'* during the 1951 summer season. Yes, Yarmouth had arrived and Delfont wanted it. He had read the newspapers that we had a good show – and that we were making money, 25% more money.

In Yarmouth Tom Arnold was in control of the *Britannia* and *Palace* Theatre, Jack Jay of the *Windmill* Theatre and later the Yarmouth Circus, and the *Regal* Theatre played weekly variety bills with tops like George Formby, Vera Lynn and Benny Hill. All other places of entertainment in Yarmouth were run by the Great Yarmouth Council's Tourist Committee, from which I held the contract for the *Wellington Pier*. Celebrity concerts had been booked for the pier on every Sunday during the summer season, Vic Oliver, Carol Carr, David Hughes, Henry Hall, Dick Emery, Petula Clark, Anne Shelton, Percy Edwards and Semprini amongst them.

After reading Bernard Delfont's autobiography in 1990, I wished he'd written his book before I mounted the steps to his office on that hot July day in 1956 because then I would have understood the deals he manipulated. And, more than that, I would have understood that I was about to take on Goliath, me, little David, and in my ignorance I had come totally unprepared – I had no stone, my sling was empty.

I was met with utmost courtesy and Bernard Delfont was Mr. Charm himself. He had a plan.

I would give him Yarmouth's *Wellington Pier* for 1957 and he would give me Blackpool's *Queens* Theatre, and then we could yearly alternate the shows between the towns. What a brilliant idea. There was only one stumbling block. Me! I am and always will be true to my word. I had given my word to the Great Yarmouth Corporation for the following year, and that was that.

It didn't take me long to realise that the meeting was only a farce, as arrangements between him and the Yarmouth Council were already well under way – he was going to put his show into the *Wellington Pier* the following year. I was sure that some of the council members had perhaps enjoyed a visit to London and being shown around various theatres finishing with a sumptuous meal and show at Delfont's *Talk of the Town*. It all seemed to add up. The Yarmouth Entertainments Council had not played fair and when their director, John Kinnersley, phoned me within days of my meeting with Bernard Delfont and asked if he could come and see me at my house in Beccles, Steffani and I knew what the visit was all about.

Within minutes of his arrival John Kinnersley informed us of the council's decision, they did not want us for a third year. I was disgusted with the Yarmouth Council for upsetting Steffani who was an East Anglian after all and felt badly let down by his own people. Strangely, I held no animosity towards Delfont, and I don't think he did towards me as he continued to book me into different summer shows and pantomimes over the following years. Perhaps little David did throw a small (honesty) stone at him and the great man respected it.

But life went on. A radio show had to be organised; beauty queens were waiting to be crowned; and there were boat regattas on the River Waveney to enjoy. That's when Benny Hill came one Sunday afternoon to take part in the Celebrity Regatta on my 'Blackbird'. He was not interested in the decorated crafts floating past our mooring, oh no, he was taken by a large box of chocolates. He didn't stop munching until the last one had vanished. I knew he'd enjoyed them because his smiling face displayed utter contentment as he, with a twinkle in his eye, gingerly replaced the lid, on the empty box.

When he told us the story about his experience as a ballet dancer during a TV scene, we laughed so much that the boat started to rock. Apparently he was dressed in close fitting ballet tights and, to make it look authentic, he used a rabbit's foot in his jock strap.

'But the thing kept on moving, Ronnie, and after my second 'entrechat' I didn't know what to do – it had slipped right down to my knee!'

As a co-writer of songs I belong to the Performing Right Society and as such had met Billy Reid, who was closely associated with Dorothy Squires, but when she came into my dressing room in Yarmouth she was escorted by actor Roger Moore. He had just returned from America filming 'Westerns', very unsure of himself, and certainly not ready for a James Bond.

Dorothy experienced many problems in her life, privately she had lost Roger Moore, financially because she had held great parties and theatrically because she had put her career on the backburner to bolster Roger. She found it difficult to get a London *Palladium* booking which she rightly deserved, so she put her two fingers up and under a false name booked a Sunday to stage her own 'Dorothy Squires Show' at the *Palladium* which was a complete triumph and sellout and simply astounded Val Parnell.

Her biggest 'Hit Song' for the night was: 'I did it My Way'.

The summer was drawing to its end and on 22 September the final curtain fell on my Yarmouth Wellington Pier season. It is very difficult to describe one's feelings when a show ends, but this ending happened to be more confusing as the large lorries arrived at my Beccles house with all the Yarmouth scenery, costumes, lights and machinery. Thousands of pounds worth – eventually it became a total loss although the chairman, F.H. Stone of the Entertainments Corporation admitted that we had played to 20,000 more people than the previous year.

During the first week in October I made another record, Norrie Paramour and his band supplied the accompaniment with Bert Weedon on the guitar and Harry Gold came into the studio as well to listen to the take as he had written one of the songs, 'Yodelling Rag'. When this record was released on the market the *New Musical Express* described it as sensational and Hubert David quoted:

...take a couple of high notes from Billy Daniels, a sprinkle of ha-cha-ma-cha-cha from Harry Roy, top it up with a drop of R'n'R from Elvis the Pelvis and add... A YODEL...

...anybody who can keep the till ringing to that extent must surely be in the nation's good books – but little good it does him if he is in the disc jockeys bad books...may carve him out of a hit record...

and... we shall never have another Ronnie, but we can always get more Liberaces... I would consider it an honour to shake the hand of Ronnie Ronalde... pop goes the whistler...

I was invited to appear in the Norman Evans TV show filmed from *King's* Theatre, Hammersmith. Taking part were Norman's daughter Norma, Jon Pertwee and myself. Then I was again packing my suitcase, first for a short family holiday in Majorca. We arranged to stay at the Villamil Hotel in Paguera, to have some peace and quiet, sun and sea. As we entered the hotel's dining room I could not believe my eyes. There they were, Frankie Vaughan, Peter West, Brian Reece, George Bolton and agent Jack Adams. Naturally we all gathered in the bar when Peter West's wife joined us. She couldn't help but remark about all the famous people staying at the hotel, 'and' she said, 'they tell me Ronnie Ronalde is here too!' Poor Peter didn't know where to put himself, so after a little whistle we all had a good laugh.

And on to Denmark where a remarkable amount of my records sold. It had been decided that a concert coupled with a TV and radio broadcast for 7 December would be very appropriate. Steffani and I were really looking forward to this trip as it brought back quite a few memories I had spent in Denmark with the Silver Songsters, way back in 1939. This time it was different – I was known. As I walked into one restaurant with Norrie Paramour and Michael Holliday, the orchestra struck up 'In a Monastery Garden', making me feel quite humble.

Edna Savage who had also flown to Copenhagen to feature in the concert had disappeared the moment we arrived in the hotel. Seeing my perplexed face, Michael, without batting an eyelid said: 'you are looking for Edna? she's gone and left me high and dry when this dashing cunt, sorry Ron, count came in.'

During the concert when Edna was singing the microphone suddenly went off. Without thinking, I immediately walked down into the audience and told them that my whistling must have upset their sound system, so 'I'll whistle a little more until the mike's back on again'.

Afterwards Michael remarked that he couldn't have done that, he would have frozen and I always thought he was so relaxed when he performed. I found out that he had fears sometimes beyond belief and, in the end, these sadly drove him to take his own life.

I had to dash back to Britain for a live Jack Payne's *Off the Record* TV show, Peter Sellers, Spike Milligan, Eve Boswell, Julie Dawn, Terry Burton and Desmond Lane were the other artistes taking part and a Christmas Party get-together organised by EMI was a befitting finale for an eventful year, some of the revellers were Alma Cogan, Kathy Kay, Ambrose, Geoff Love, Ray Martin and Bert Weedon. I must have done something right. Two days after my TV appearance, Cyril phoned. He had closed a deal for my very own live Thames Television series, *Meet Ronnie Ronalde*, 'The Voice of Variety', beginning on 4 January 1957.

Robert Tronson as the director/producer and the Jackie Brown Quartet was to accompany me, so for every song I anticipated performing, Steffani, with Jackie, had to rewrite all my music parts. I also tried to give the show a more relaxed feeling and decided to wear different pullovers. Wow, the reaction came in hundreds of letters, asking where I'd bought them? I didn't tell them the secret of why they fitted so well – elastic bands, safety pins and Elastoplasts held everything in place. The so-called tricks of the trade.

Busy with my own TV shows, I was also invited to appear on the *Jack Jackson Show* with Don Peters, Bert Weedon and Shirley Bassey, who was just about to leave England for a three-week engagement in America. A further TV show with Eamon Andrews featuring Ruby Murray, Max Robertson, Brian Johnstone, Freddie Mills, Bob Monkhouse and myself was televised over the BBC and on *Midday Music Hall* I was heard over the radio. But that was not all. Benny Lee, Eddie Calvert, Jimmy Parkinson, Arthur Muxlow, Mel Thompson, Norrie Paramour and myself were special guests at Capitol's first year birthday party; a recording was made for later inclusion in a Radio Luxembourg programme;

A guest at the recording session, was Ramsden Greig of the *Middlesborough Evening Gazette*. He described the set-up very accurately:

On the way out I noticed that many of the walls in the recording studios were padded in the manner of lunatic asylums...

Kenneth Allsop, from the *London Daily Mail* wrote a very nice long article about my life and included a picture of me, dedicated 'To the Budgies!'. He had made a seven-hour return journey from London to Beccles especially to interview me for this article. Why did he show all that interest in me? He was an ornithologist and had to find out for himself how I lived among all these songbirds in East Anglia.

Charlie Chester, who was standing in for Alan Melville on the *A-Z programme* made a joke over the air, which was immediately picked up by the press all over England and Scotland:

They were going to have Ronnie Ronalde, but somebody put a ring on his leg and he has flown south.

Music publishers party

'Meet Ronnie Ronalde' TV show

Girls...

... and more girls

It's a dirty job...

Michael Holliday

Ronnie & Steff

Winifred Attwell

Film actor Lawrence Harvey

Rosalina Neary & admirers

Donald Campbell

We lived to tell the tale

Act Thirty

BACK ON BROADWAY

A cable had arrived, from *Radio City*. Would I be available to star in the stage show that was to accompany Marilyn Monroe's much vaunted movie *The Prince and the Showgirl* and to boost its premiere in America at *Radio City's Music Hall*? The show and film, were to open on 13 June. Again Cyril had the job of cancelling and rescheduling my pre-booked theatre shows, as this was one offer I wasn't going to let slip past me, especially as the *Record Mirror* wanted me to send weekly articles about American show business back to London. I was delighted by this request; my 'Dear Pop' letters would now be printed and provide me with an accurate record.

Before boarding the plane to New York I signed a contract presented to me by Geoffrey Everitt of Radio Luxembourg. He had offered me a long-term engagement as a DJ, starting immediately after my return from America and the programme was to be called *The Happy Spin The Platter Boy*.

The papers, after they'd picked up the news printed:

Seems all in all the birds in that Monastery Garden will be warbling extra loud from now on.

The opening night really was an event. At seven in the evening Broadway was a fantastic kaleidoscope of colour. Giant signs flashed across the New York skyline and from my dressing room window at *Radio City* I watched the swelling crowd of fans. Some were waiting to go in, others were just hoping to see their particular idol arrive. Mounted police had been called out to control the situation, though they did their job with patience and good humour, and when Marilyn Monroe arrived she looked the complete star; she not only created a sensation, she was one. The theatre was full of

America's dignitaries – the Mayor of New York, the Rockefellers, Hursts and Rothschilds – as well as half of Hollywood. Despite having done it so often before, I felt all keyed up waiting in the wings until I stepped onto the vast stage and into the spotlights.

I was delighted when I heard Marilyn Monroe comment that my whistle made her all shivery and that whistling was the one thing she couldn't do. With her percentage of the takings I failed to see how she could do anything else *but* whistle!

Thereafter a midnight supper-dance was held at the *Waldorf*. This venue reminded me of the time, in 1947, when I was asked to perform there in the Grand Ballroom in front of the Mayor of New York and a Congress of United Nation Members. Standing in the wings also waiting to go on was a very nice gentleman who offered to swap places with me after hearing I was pushed for time. When he was called to make his speech he simply walked onto the stage to a tremendous ovation and announced me instead. He was none other than General George Marshall, 'Mr. Lease Lend' himself, in whose honour that event was staged. A great man and a good friend to Britain.

My weekly columns in the *Record Mirror* gave British readers an indication of the hectic life in New York, with five shows a day, seven days a week to get through in temperatures of 94 in the shade, engagements to be kept, visitors welcomed and friends to look up. Furthermore, America already had nine television channels.

Ray Martin, who resigned his post as A & R Manager of Columbia EMI and emigrated to America, took me, in his terrific new multicoloured Chrysler, to Johnny Johnson's restaurant where the celebrities gathered for steak dinners, cooked barbecue fashion. If you were bold enough to cook your own steak you received a cook's hat as a diploma. I saw hundreds of these hats hanging all around the walls bearing the names of famous people; unfortunately they did not have one to fit me.

One thing that puzzled me was seeing so many people with hearing aids, literally hundreds of them. My curiosity was roused and when I gathered courage and asked one of the Glee Singers from *Radio City* why there was such an outbreak of deafness in New York, he laughed and took the aid out of his ear and as he was holding it to mine at the same time produced a little radio out from his breast pocket. It was connected with a wire to the 'hearing aid' and transmitted music. They called it 'personalised radio listening'. Whatever next!

I managed to see the final performance of a show at the *Roxy Theatre* featuring Tommy Sands, one-time son-in-law of Frank Sinatra, the latest teenage craze in America. His fame had arrived quite unexpectedly. Tommy was asked to appear in a TV show that Elvis Presley had turned down, and, wham, he hit the jackpot overnight. Joe Mathews of Capitol had arranged for us to meet for a photo-call as Tommy's record and my 'Yodelling Rag' were both promoted by Capitol.

One of the first showbiz friends to come and say hello was Lester Ferguson, appearing as Petruchio in *Kiss Me Kate* I hardly recognised him as he had lost five stone. (Comedian Joe E. Lewis, on a diet too, said: 'In fourteen days I almost lost two weeks!') Lester introduced me to Abe Saperstein, owner of the famous *Harlem Globe Trotters* and his personal manager, Olga James.

And then I had a very special visitor. Lovely Jane Russell visited me in my dressing room at *Radio City*. She was so friendly, nothing like the characters she portrayed in Howard Hughes films such as *The Outlaw*. To make her look more provocative he had designed a specially wired bra, but Jane preferred to wear her own, stuffing the cups with tissue paper and pulling down the straps. Jane was very interested in my whistle and I tried to teach her, but we didn't get very far.

My forthcoming assignment as a disc jockey on *Radio Luxembourg* made me curious to meet as many American DJ's as possible, to see and hear their style. The first thing that struck me was their unbelievably high earning power – around $100,000 a year – but in spite of that I found them very easy to talk to. Dean Hunter, Peter Tripp, Joe Sacconi, Lonnie Starr as well as William B. Williams, Bob Howard, Bob White, Allan Lober and Jack Lacey all appeared very relaxed, a style I liked.

Then I heard from Dave Dexter in Hollywood, vice-president of Capitol, that they were releasing my Christmas record in America so I was pleased to see, that Joe Mathews (Capitol), Charlie Hall (RCA Victor), Marty Selken (DECCA) and Dick Linke (Columbia) were boosting the British records and it was a pleasant change to hear more British recording stars mentioned and played over the American radio stations. Jack Mills and Mack Stark, after hearing my rendering of 'The Alpine Polka' at *Radio City*, renamed it 'New York Polka' with special lyrics by Al Stillman, who had also written the words to 'I Believe', and decided to publish this song in America. They gave me a grand tour all over the vast publishing organisation of *Mills Music* where I met Eddie Kassner as well as Jacques Kluger who owned a publishing house in Belgium and was told that he was the publisher of 'The Yodelling Whistler'. The world indeed was becoming smaller and smaller in more ways than one.

A very enjoyable show came to the end, and, once again, I had made many acquaintances such as Clark Terry, Duke Ellington's first trumpeter and Billy Graham to whom I spoke at *Madison Square Garden*. And I ate in many restaurants such as Tappens, Lindy's, Jack Dempsey's, Count Basie's as well as Sugar Ray Robinson's 'niteries' and even watched American TV with their version of *What's My Line?* and guess who came on as one of the guest celebrities – Eamonn Andrews!

In London again a welcome-back party had been arranged for me by many of my friends and took place at the *Renomme* Restaurant, the large table bore many famous names, Jack Fox, Mildred Mayne, Roy Burden, Pam Butler, Elizabeth Larner, Peter Page, June Smith, Sheila Bradley, Johnny Roberts, Chris Barnett, Peter Grant, Betta St. John, Wally Peterson, Noelle Adam, Dick Tatham, Isidore Green, Dickie Henderson and Shirley Bassey who arrived last and gave me a welcoming kiss making me realise she was all woman.

It was a must to put the 'Alpine Polka' onto wax. This melody was coupled with a composition, which had been sent to me by publisher Max Diamond. He first heard it hummed by pianist-comic Peter Maxwell in Eddie Calvert's office and because it had a 'birdie feel', he immediately thought that I might like to record it. So on my return from America 'A Bird Sings' and the polka number were born.

I was determined to make my engagement on *Radio Luxembourg* a success because I had turned down an offer from the top Australian impresario David Martin who phoned me at *Radio City* all the way from Sydney, to secure a date in the autumn for me to make a lengthy tour down under, in a show called '*Sugar and Spice*' at the *Tivoli Sydney* and Mick Edgely's *His Majesty's* in Perth. Australia was a country I dearly wanted to see. My decision not to go wasn't taken lightly and I knew that I must find time to go there soon.

Radio Luxembourg had made a big drive to sign up seven well-known names for their new nightly series, *Record Request*, which included ITV's MacDonald Hobley and Libby Morris as well as George Elrick, Beryl Reid, Richard Murdoch, Teddy Johnson and myself. My broadcasting day was Thursday. Other stars to be heard over the *208* wavelength were Hughie Green, Winifred Atwell, Eddie Calvert, Tommy Trinder, Anne Shelton, Michael Holiday, the Deep River Boys and Dennis Lotis.

The *Radio Show* was on at *Earls Court* and one of the most impressive stands was EMI's. It made you realise what an important part records were playing in home entertainment. The spotlight was on a new 7-inch record, but the piece de resistance was a so-called 'Selectogram' record cabinet. It held a hundred 10- or 12-inch discs and any one could be picked out in a second with a sliding selector – in short, it was a *juke box*.

Because the first four Ronnie Ronalde DJ programmes, which I shared with Beryl Reid, proved immensely popular I was given a further weekly show *Sing and Be Happy* but with a live audience and to be broadcast from different halls all over Britain. Also featured were Geoff Love with his orchestra, organist Jackie Brown and tenor sax Betty Smith. There was a feeling of tremendous power, holding all those different records by different artistes in your hand and having to choose which ones should have some airtime. I tried to stay patriotic in my choice of records and received many letters of thanks, from, among many others, David Hughes, Ronnie Carroll, Mantovani, David Whitfield, Frank Chacksfield, Johnny Duncan, Malcolm Vaughan, Michael Holliday and Max Bygraves.

One of the greatest ever all-star shows was presented at the *Victoria Palace* in London on 9 December, a midnight matineę in the presence of Prince Philip. The names of those involved read like an encyclopedia of British artistes – everyone from Arthur Askey and Max Bygraves, Charlie Chester, Alma Cogan, Tommy Cooper and Bud Flanagan to Vera Lynn, Wilfred Pickles, Sandy Powell, Ted Ray, Harry Secombe, Frankie Vaughan and more. Christmas week itself was busy, with a *Jack Jackson TV* show on the 22nd, Glen Mason played Father Christmas and included the Beverley Sisters and Johnny Dankworth, which was followed by *Radio Luxembourg Shows* on the 23rd, 24th, 26th and 28th,

I decided to stay at the Mayfair Club to cut out the daily travel to and from Beccles. During dinner one night raffle tickets were sold. Steffani bought two and we carried on eating and discussing the next day's programme and didn't realise that all ticket holders not drawing a prize had to perform a forfeit. I had to dress up in furs to look like a caveman, and Steffani was forced to don cross-country running gear. Then I had to ride around Berkeley Square on a horse while Steffani had to run, to see which one of us would be first. What a sight! A wild man on a horse racing a puffing cross-country runner through London's traffic at midnight. Steffani gave up halfway, mounted my horse and together we rode back to the club.

We had broken the rules and as punishment I had to ride around the square once more, but this time a most beautiful 'Lady Godiva' debutante had been placed in front of me. With a slap on the horse's behind we took off and won the race.

We halted outside the Berkeley Square Gambling Club where we were trying to collect some money for our Variety Club Charity when a guy dressed in a light raincoat and trilby started to pat our horse:

'I like your horse fella!'

The moment he spoke I recognised him, it was George Raft. Riding back around

Berkeley Square with my Lady Godiva's hair blowing in my face and with my arms aside her the caveman in me urged the thought that we would have made even more money if my beautiful debutante had played her true part of Lady Godiva and taken her cloths off.

Finally I had some time to look through the mountain of mail on my desk. I reached for the first letter. 'Oh God! Not again! What's wrong now?' I should have guessed. A brown envelope with HMS Services, Income Tax Dept. embossed on it. 'Dear Mr. Ronalde, With reference to your accounts forwarded to us by your accountants we notice a difference of figures submitted by you and the one showing in the accounts of the record company. Please clarify.'

I hit the roof, immediately shouting for Steffani.

'What have you done?' throwing the letter in front of him.

'Son,' he said quietly (that's what he always called me when I needed calming down),

'if the record company sent you a cheque for X amount, I paid X amount into the bank account. I'll check.'

And check he did. Apparently the amount I had been sent was only the interim amount, as the record company themselves had not received the full amount from their foreign branches. After so many years in the business I should have been used to receiving these brown envelopes, but every time another one arrived I felt my whole integrity was being questioned. Nobody could have been more honest than me. Every penny I earned went into the account. Mind you, every possible allowance was charged; the Tax Office could have always turned round and said no.

London City accountants, Arthur Heyward, had to deal already from the start of my theatrical career with questions like a sum of £8-14-4 with an avalanche of Tax letters and argue the percentage of living space I was using to rehearse, Steffani's, my secretary's office space, and mine along with all the cupboards, files and Roneo cabinets used for my theatrical business and fan-club, in my house.

Another time, because I had been in America and my car-travel expenses were much lower than the previous year they asked:

'Did I really need a private car? Couldn't I use public transport?'

I really could not see myself, after a show, TV or radio broadcast, coming off stage sweating and getting onto a local, drafty bus to travel home with all my theatrical luggage, I could have also been mobbed by fans.

I really do believe that all those rather thoughtless, niggling questions, and to pay tax to the amount of 19/6 in every Pound caused many a public figure to leave Britain and more so when Aneurin Bevin started to call some of us big money earners in the Houses of Parliament

These vermin

END OF FIRST HALF

Interval

Ice Cream – Chocolates – Teas – Coffee – Drinks

The Sparrow:

A Chinese Emperor declared war on the sparrows. He believed them to be pests because they were picking all the rice and grain, so reducing the harvest of his farmers and therefore reducing his income as they could not pay his taxes.

So the farmers were ordered to go out into their fields and start banging their woks, thus terrifying the poor little sparrows and forcing them to stay aloft in the sky until they were so exhausted that they couldn't fly anymore when they fell to the ground, dead.

Good, thought the Emperor, next year I will get my full taxes paid by the farmers.

Next year came and again his coffers stayed empty.

What had happened?

Insects had started to eat the crops, the fields were barren.

The Emperor soon realised that his greedy order had unbalanced nature and it was him who had to pay the price for it, so wisely he lifted the ban and soon the crops started to bloom and grow again and the sparrows returned, to keep the peace in nature.

One can truthfully say that birds save our lives. We could not live on this planet without them because the insects would become so great that man could not survive.

SECOND HALF

BEGINNERS PLEASE

A business card

Loni Saton, Arthur Maxlow of EMI

Pianist Dorothy MacCartland

Ray Martin

Tommy Sands

Father 'Knickerbocker' on stage

203

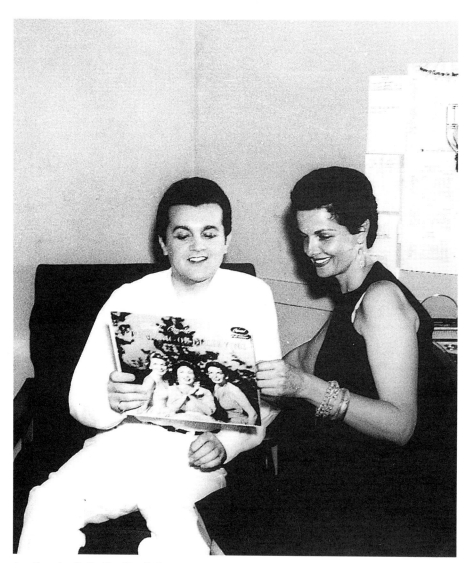

Jane Russel at Radio City, New York

Act Thirty-one

AUSTRALIA CALLS

'Steff, I'm going to leave England!'

'Now hold on, son! Let's talk about this in a sensible manner!'

We talked, and as so often in my life, certain events happen which seem to guide me exactly into the right direction.

A theatrical engagement of 20 weeks minimum in Perth, Sydney and Melbourne, Australia, starting in April, had landed on Cyril's desk. Would I sign on the dotted line?

Sometimes I wondered if all the problems with the tax authorities were brought about because Steffani was handling my affairs. We Silver Songsters sold thousands of our photographs and because we were always on the move, the monies taken were never correctly shown in Steff's accounts. So the Income Tax Office charged him on all the sales on the figures received from the printers, not accepting that some cash went towards special treats and the many giveaways for publicity. So he sold everything he owned to pay off the tax demand. He never recovered from this financial setback.

The *Record Mirror*, reporting that I was off to Australia, headed their announcement with: 'RONNIE RONALDE WILL BE GOING'.

Little did they realise there was a deeper meaning to those words.

While I was still busy with my weekly *Radio Luxembourg* programmes the Rank Organisation asked me to whistle the soundtrack for their latest film, 'Innocent Sinners', starring Flora Robson and David Kossoff. The tune, written by Philip Green, was then recorded.

Different papers wrote: *...greatest novelty record of the week... I was struck by the haunting theme tune... R.R. is back on the hit parade...* and Paul Dehn wrote: *'I leave*

my heart in little Miss Archer's garden'… and the *London's South Western Star…*
*Ronalde at his very best when whistling a tricky number, excels in every direction and
scores a splendid success…*

That's when Hughie Green had a novel idea – one of his Jack Hylton *Monday Shows*
on ITV was going to be different. How different? 30 000 feet high different and it was
all summed up with the headline and photo of a plane featured in the *Financial Times*:

'B.O.A.C. BRITANNIA MAKES AVIATION & T.V. HISTORY'.

*A BOAC Britannia jet-prop airliner is today the scene of the most ambitious airborne
TV project ever undertaken…*

The idea was to film Jack Hylton's show aboard this magnificent new British airliner
as it flew high over the Atlantic between London and New York!

*Variety Show from the Stratosphere, Mr. Hylton tries a High-Flier and The Highest
Flying Blackbird.*

Celebrities taking part were Hughie Green, the curvaceous Rosalina Neri, Winifred
Atwell with her piano, Donald Campbell, Laurence Harvey, impresario Jack Hylton
and myself. Hughie Green, who held a commercial pilot's licence, had been flying for
years and when he was asked why he chose the Britannia for this stunt, his answer was:

*'Because it's quieter and smoother than any piston-engine plane, which makes filming
possible. The Britannia is more like a sky yacht than an aircraft, spacious, free from
vibration and excessive noise.'*

A BOAC spokesman confirmed that this flight was going to make TV and aviation
history as it involved the solution of a number of technical problems, as for instance the
supply of power for the lighting. Apparently the plane could also fly above the weather
as its radar equipment enabled the pilot to 'see' bad weather 150 miles ahead and so
plot a course around it.

We all met at 8.30am on 6 February at Hylton House, 3 Savile Row in London and
from there cars took the whole company to London Airport North. Preliminary publicity,
customs check and filming prior to takeoff, scheduled for 10.30am, were all organised
by Jack Hylton's Television Production Ltd, as were the arrangements for our arrival in
New York after the 12-hour flight.

We took off and with champagne cocktails in our hands waved goodbye to London,
waiting for lunch to be served. Good God, a second champagne cocktail had arrived!
I hoped I wouldn't become too tipsy; I wasn't really used to drinking.

Winifred Atwell's husband, Lou sat next to me and looking out the window exclaimed:

'Look Ronnie, they're pushing all the petrol out!'

'That's not funny, Lou,' I answered and then I realised that something was wrong.
We were right over the Irish Sea, dumping 3000 gallons of fuel, and the reason for this
manoeuvre?

The undercarriage was stuck – it would not go up, it would not go down; in short, the
hydraulic system of the plane had collapsed so the captain decided to return to London.
Fire engines and ambulances stood by as the Britannia, with its cargo of 52 entertainers,
crew and TV people attempted to touch down at the airport. Just before the expected
crash landing a steward came up the gangway, checking that every passenger was securely
strapped in the seat. As he reached my row he took one look at me and then asked
confidentially:

'Are you Ronnie Ronalde?'

'Yes?'

'Can you whistle like a bird?'

'Yes?'

'A pity you can't bloody well fly like one!'

The ordeal was over and safely back in the airport lounge, we were informed that there would be a 24-hour delay. None of us was very happy.

After an overnight stay at a nearby hotel we took off once more and this time everything went like clockwork. Again four rows of seats had been removed in the plane to secure Winifred Atwell's famous honky-tonk piano and after we had settled down with our champagne cocktails and the daily newspapers we took one look at the headlines and disbelieving what stared into our faces, silently folded them again. The Manchester United Football Team had been virtually wiped out as their plane crashed in Munich during bad weather conditions a few hours ago.

At last we were ready to start filming. Everything was going extremely well and the plane was flying exceptionally steady. As the cameras rolled, Hughie Green interviewed Donald Campbell, who talked of his plans for an attack on the world's land speed record in Utah and showed a drawing of his car, which used a Bristol Proteus engine, similar to those in the Britannia. Lawrence Harvey was giving his latest film on *Commander Crabbe* the *highest* plug. Four-year-old Helena played on her trumpet Mike Todd's theme song *'Around the World in 80 Days'*. Rosalina Neri's neckline was nearly as low as the 70 degrees of frost outside the plane whilst her highest C nearly shattered us at 30,000 feet. I produced my highest bird whistle – at least higher than any real bird – and when it was Winifred Atwell's turn to tickle the ivories, we all stood round the piano, singing along with her melodies.

Did somebody write in a newspaper that this plane's new radar system could spot bad weather from miles away? While Winifred was playing, the plane started to shake. We looked at each other –

'I don't like this!'

As the shaking grew stronger, one or two hands were seen to open shirt buttons and then it started. The plane did absolutely everything. Poor Winifred couldn't get off her stool quick enough and she was white as sheet. We had hit what they called cobblestones, so Hughie, the expert, tried to explain to us while we were all holding on for dear life, when suddenly he shouted:

'Christ, hold the piano fellows!'

'I hope that's not our last flight Ronnie!'

said Lawrence Harvey and with that we all took one dive at the piano, which had loosened its ropes and could have slid towards the tail-end of the plane and disappear through it, no doubt taking us all with it. Then the captain informed us he was diverting the plane to Labrador's Goose Bay and would wait there for the weather to clear before making his final approach into New York. Finally, late in the evening, we arrived in New York and all I could think of was food. I was starving; I had left everything behind, in one of those brown paper bags.

The reason we got caught in the bad weather was because we had been flying low so that the film crew could establish a link with the weather ships cruising below us via radio telephone, another novelty to add to their show.

I had admired Donald Campbell who had sat through the whole drama in complete calmness, not one hair out of place, he must have nerves of steel, what a man! Next morning I was sitting in the hotel dining room with James Green of the *London Star*, enjoying my ham and eggs, when Donald Campbell joined us. He looked deathly.

'What's up, Donald?'

'My dear boy!' was his answer. 'I felt sick all night – and what with the honeymoon couple next door! Waiter, just coffee, black!'

Within a couple of days of our return to Britain, which was safely accomplished, I had to travel to Hull to appear at the *Palace* Theatre. The theatre could not have asked for a better advertisement than the screening that week of Jack Hylton's Britannia Show. Both the theatre and the TV shows received very good write-ups; in fact the TV crew and engineers had done such an expert job that the viewers wondered to why there had been so much fuss about the high-altitude filming.

At the *Opera House* Cheltenham, my next theatre engagement, I found the Amazing Fogel, Eddie Fox and Harry Shields on the bill too. That week it rained and rained so I looked forward to the 26 March 1958 when the SS Orsova lifted her anchor and slowly started her journey towards Australia.

Many passengers were families emigrating to Australia or New Zealand and it was interesting to learn their different reasons for doing so. We shared a diningroom table with the ship's surgeon commander, also a very sweet lady, returning home to Australia, a relation to the Tate & Lyle Sugar Company who asked me to call on her and have a round of golf at the Royal Sydney Golf Club and a young married couple destined for New Zealand, where he held a position in Shellmex.

Two of the Orsova's passengers, who also stand out vividly in my memory, because I had the privilege of holding some very interesting conversations with them about their home country, were Sir Clifton Webb, New Zealand's High Commissioner in the UK, and former Minister of Justice in New Zealand, and his wife, Lady Webb.

At the port of Navarino, in Greece, another 100 immigrants were taken on board, all destined for Australia. It was so sad to see them with their bags and bundles saying their good byes. As the weather became hotter, I became lazier and my trousers grew tighter – how many more days to Australia?

'Steff, how long is it to Ceylon?'

'Another week or so, son! Why?'

'That's where we'll be getting off this ship. We're going to fly to Perth!'

While we were making our way south, through the Red Sea, towards Aden, a horrific tragedy had occurred in the Indian Ocean. The Norwegian emigrant ship Skaubryn caught fire and our ship was asked to pick up 250 survivors out of the 1200 original passenger complement of the ill-fated ship, which sank while being towed, still aflame, into Aden. These poor survivors had lost everything – all their money and belongings apart from what they stood up in. They were on their way to Australia, to start a new life. Some of them looked so very young.

Eventually we docked in Colombo. The news of my arrival must have preceded us because within minutes of booking into the hotel, newspaper and the local radio station wanted me for interviews. This proved to be very profitable, as the bosses of the radio station arranged to have a chauffeur-driven car at my disposal and, to make my brief stay in Ceylon more interesting, organised a two-day trip into the mountains. We had a wonderful expedition which was quite breathtaking in its magnitude and beauty;

we even saw the film bridge replica of the *Bridge over the River Kwai.*

Enduring a seven hour flight from Colombo to Singapore Steffani and I were pleased to get out of the plane as we felt uneasy. All during the flight crew members had walked up and down the aisle looking at the floor, never saying a word. During the last hour of the journey the captain appeared and giving the order to pull up one section of the floor, looked inside the plane's belly with a torch.

Still nothing was said.

'Will all passengers on flight 536 to Perth please board the plane!' Another nine hours of flying and then, at last, Australia, here we come.

'Come on Steff, let's go!'

Shortly after takeoff I was asleep only to be woken up by a torch shining right into my eyes.

'What's up?'

'Could you please move your feet? The captain wants to look under the floor!'

I sat up with a jolt and looked. The whole of the bloody gangway was up! 'Didn't the previous captain tell the new crew that there was something wrong with the bloody plane, and why didn't they change it anyway?'

'There's nothing to worry about, Sir, it's only a minor fault in an electrical circuit.'

On Wednesday 16 April, we landed in Perth and for the first time I set foot on Australian soil.

The sun was shining and everything looked so beautifully white and bright. Jack Neary waited for us with the press at the airport and soon we were on the way to the hotel and on to the theatre, where we met Mick Edgley, the management and artistes. They really made us feel at home and soon we were Ronnie and Steff to everyone. The theatre… well, we might just as well have walked into the Finsbury Park *Empire* or the Manchester *Hippodrome*, I really liked Perth.

What is a Connie? You may well ask. I found the answer in the *Perth Daily News* under the headline 'PEOPLE YOU MEET ON A CONNIE'.

There was my picture.

'No he's not biting his nails. Whistler Ronnie Ronalde shows his stage technique at Perth Airport.'

Apparently the Australians called their Qantas Super-Constellation aircraft, the plane I had arrived in, a Connie.

Edgley & Dawe, by arrangement with Jack Neary, presented the show at the *His Majesty's Theatre* in Perth. Eric Edgley, himself an artiste, took part in the show as well as Margo the Z-Bomb, (what a lady!), Buster Fiddess, Alwyn Leckie (a New Zealander), Johnny O'Connor, The Two Earls, Michael and Shirley Davies, Margot Glancy, Marlene, Patti Munro, Edna Luscombe, Brenda Rowe, Rickie Herder, Aquina and Bobby Limb, an excellent comedian-raconteur, singer and sax player – in short very accomplished. He would be just perfect for a Yarmouth Summer Season, so much so, that we wrote to John Kinnersley to that effect, after we'd made a tentative approach to Bobby. John Kinnersley's reply, unfortunately, was in the negative, although, in the same letter, he conceded that, for the first time in his life, he had the 'second best show' in town (Yarmouth) and not the best.

Sadly, only weeks before my arrival in Perth, David Martin, who initially booked me for this Australian tour had died an untimely death. For the past eleven years he had been represented in London by Lew and Leslie Grade, so Eddie Jarrett's visit to Australia was to meet the new management headed by Neil S. Maver who himself had been connected with the *Tivoli* circuit for the past thirty years and Gordon Cooper, the new General Manager. Upon Eddie Jarrett's return to London he featured an article in *The Stage*:

...the show I saw in Perth featured Ronnie Ronalde... House Full notices before curtains go up...

We were invited for Lunch at Parliament House with Sir Charles Latham, the Prime Minister and members of the Cabinet. Sir Charles had been to see the show three times. This was the very first time that civic recognition had been given to a visiting theatre star. His Excellency the Governor Sir Charles Gairdner and his wife also attended a performance at *His Majesty's Theatre*. Then I achieved another first: for a theatrical artiste to be featured on the front page of the *West Australian* newspaper with a picture of me whistling to a little blind boy who was smiling while his fingers felt over mine whilst I was chirping some bird notes and was headed *'Feeling the Notes'*. I had met the boy, Keith Hayes, at a concert I'd given for blind children.

Perth was busy, the Lord Mayor of Perth invited me for tea at the *City Hall*; I had drinks with the Edgleys at their home; Tony Martin, a policeman at Yanchep, some 35 miles outside Perth, who patrolled 500 square miles around that area, invited us for a barbecue in the bush with prawns the size of a crayfish and beer served by the jug and David Howard, the Variety Chief of the Australian Broadcasting Commission in Perth invited me on his *Memory Time* radio show.

Interestingly, Perth had no Television in 1958 although Sydney was served by a TV station. To buy a radiogram was around the £200 mark.

Many of the people who came to the theatre to hear me had emigrated from Britain and wanted to listen to the British birds sing again, my different chirps and whistles made them feel quite homesick, so much so that many of the women were crying after the shows. During one of the record signing session at 'Wyper Howards' where the fans had bought up every single record available, one Aussie come up to me. Angrily he threw my record on the table and in a brusque manner demanded for me to sign

'this bleed'n record. All bleed'n night the bleed'n wife was bleed'n crying. All because of the bleed'n birds!'

I didn't know whether to bleed'n well laugh or cry!

One day, while we were eating our lunch at the hotel, the waiter brought a note which read:

'Dear Mr. Ronalde, I was the lime boy at South Shields for your show. I have emigrated and live here, I would love to say hello!'

I asked the waiter to show the fellow in but the answer was:

'Sorry, he can't come in, he hasn't got a jacket on!'

A similar problem arose on the train journey from Perth to Sydney, an experience I would not have missed for the world, 2694 miles across the great Nullabor Plain in a virtual straight line.

Dressed in a sort of shantung silk trousers and shirt suit I'd walked all the way along the train to the dining car, when the waiter politely informed me that he could not let me in dressed as I was.

'What's wrong with my suit?' I asked, looking to make sure I'd done up all the buttons.

'You can't come in here without a jacket!'

'A jacket for breakfast?'

'Yes, Sir.'

I had to walk the whole length of the train back to my compartment, put on a jacket, and repeat the long walk to the front of the train again to have my breakfast.

One of my 'Dear Pop' letters, written on 8 May 1958, tells what it was like on our last night in Western Australia: 'The theatre was packed to suffocation. They sold every chair from the offices. People stood, sat and knelt in every gangway and all around. They were literally hanging from the rafters. Hundreds were turned away and if the police had walked in I'm sure they would have closed the theatre for dangerous overcrowding. After the most terrific reception I had received anywhere, all the balloons came down from the roof and everyone was throwing hundreds of coloured streamers. It was an unforgettable sight on an unforgettable night.'

In Sydney we took a flat right in the middle of Kings Cross with a lovely view across Sydney Harbour for the duration of our season at the *Tivoli Theatre*. Every day I was taken out somewhere different by Vic Leeson the representatives and Head of EMI, John Burnett; John Harper of 2KY; Georges Dwyer; Ron Wills and so many more, who had all taken it upon themselves to really look after me. Over lunch one day I was offered a complete radio series by the head of the ABC to follow the *Tivoli* show. Jack Neary, and his wife June, were also fervent hosts. Jack ran a show on one of the large Sydney Harbour cruise-boats to which he invited me. Jack also offered me a season in his show after I finished playing the *Tivoli* circuit. Everything looked very promising for perhaps a future in Australia.

The *Sydney Telegraph* showed a picture of me cooking spaghetti in the flat and printed recipes of some of my favourite dishes. In another newspaper I was pictured as a wolf with his fingers in his mouth, whistling after some girls. The *Sydney Daily Mirror* reported:

'THIS'LL MAKE YOU WHISTLE: World famous whistler Ronnie Ronalde (pictured) got a shock in West Australia when he heard a lyre bird imitating his imitation of a blackbird.'

The *Tivoli* show opened, called 'Sugar and Spice' and also featured Vic Hyde, George Holmes, Clifford Guest, with whom I had worked with before *at Radio City Music Hall* in New York, Joe Martin, The Curibas, Eleanor Gunter, Michael and Shirley Davis, Joe Jenkins, Buster Fiddes, Bill French, Alwyn Leckie and the Tivoli Ballet.

In the following morning press was criticism that the comedians were *too 'blue'*, but I received high praise – *'Outstanding. It goes down big here as in Blighty or the Bronx.'*

There was absolutely nothing I could do about the context of the show. Although I was doing well Steffani was concerned. When we signed contracts at Fosters Agency in London we were told the theatre's weekly take was in excess of £5000. Steffani was flabbergasted when backstage staff told him that it was nearer £4000, which of course showed on the pay cheque.

One of the visitors to my dressing room was the famous footballer, Sir Stanley Mathews. He and his team had just beaten the Australians by 8 – 2. I really idolised him, and when he knocked on my dressing room door and meekly asked: 'May I come in, Ronnie?' I was lost for words.

In one of the Sydney stores, looking to buy a boomerang I had to pass the pet department where all the birds were singing away, so I thought I'd give them a bit of my whistling and, as I did so, all the birds shut up. I suppose they thought: 'Another bloody foreigner!' A man who was sweeping the floor stopped and slowly inching nearer me he asked:

'Was that really you doing the whistling? It's not bad!'

'Thank you,' I answered.

'In fact,' he continued, 'it's as good as him over there at the Tivoli.'

In July the show finished its run at Sydney's *Tivoli Theatre* but before then I'd received a cable from Cyril informing me that he had accepted on my behalf Howard & Wyndham's *Cinderella* pantomime in Liverpool for the forthcoming winter season. Steffani was able to negotiate my release from the *Tivoli Circuit* contract and, instead of appearing in Melbourne we boarded a plane back to London.

Cyril asked me to come to his London office and discuss some bookings before the pantomime.

So between signing for another 13 weeks with *Radio Luxembourg*, a further year's (my thirteenth consecutive) recording contract, another tour to Ireland under Philip Solomon, concerts ad Blackpool's *Opera House* and the *Town Hall* Yarmouth, a *Wish You Were Here* TV engagement in Lowestoft, a Lew & Leslie Grade contract for the *Empire* Newcastle where the clause had been added:

Ronnie Ronalde to receive full top billing, with no other artiste billed in equal or larger type, Cyril said:

'Now here's one, Ronnie, which I'd like you to take.'

Apparently over the last two or three years, an impresario by the name of Sydney James had wanted me for a Sunday concert on the island of Guernsey. He could not afford to pay much, although the figure had gone up with time and he would also provide two return flight tickets, accommodation and meals while I was on the island.

'Why don't you go, Ronnie? I'm sure it won't be there next year!' Cyril urged.

I signed to appear at the *St. George's Hall* in Guernsey on Sunday 17 August 1958. Little did I know at the time that with this signature I was to enter another life.

SS Orsova

Lady Godiva

Racing the New Year in

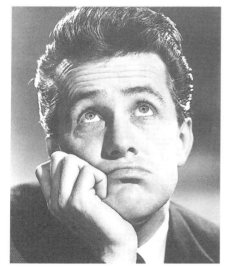

Bobby Limb

MARGO THE Z BOMB

Father George & Father Ennio

Blind boy, Perth school –
seeing with your hands

Act Thirty-two

CINDERELLA

After an hour's flight in quite a small plane we landed in Guernsey, on grass. Thank God it hadn't rained!

We were met by Sydney James who drove us to the *Channel Hotel* near the evening's venue, *St George's Hall.*

Rehearsal was to be in the hotel's bar and when I eventually found and opened the doors I was greeted by a crowd of people drinking and laughing. Every time I asked Sydney when the rehearsal would start he just laughed and put another drink into my hand. How could I resist this happy, carefree atmosphere? I had to join in.

Somehow the evening arrived and with it my first performance in Guernsey. After my last number unsuspectingly Sydney came up on stage and urged me to whistle 'The Monastery Garden' with him. It brought the house down. Later I learned that it had been one of his dearest wishes to stand on stage with me and whistle.

After the show a most welcome supper was waiting in the hotel, not only for us, it seemed the whole of Guernsey was present judging by the number of people. I had never realised how French champagne can accompany lashings of bacon and eggs in such a pleasant way.

Next morning, on the way to the airfield, I asked the taxi driver,

'Which hotel would you buy if you had some money?'

'I'll show you!'

Sure enough, halfway between St Peter Port (the capital) and the airport he turned into a drive.

'That's the one, Ron! That's the one I'd buy!'

He drove once round the hotel's carpark and carried on to the airport. As the plane gained speed, lifting its wings skyward, I felt as though I was leaving another world. It was a strange feeling.

I felt unsettled, I needed something more than theatre, although I did not know what I was looking for. There I was, a 35-year-old bachelor with a large entourage, huge fan club, money in the bank, friends worldwide, known worldwide, travelled worldwide, but still so very much alone, that of course is the price of fame.

'Let's pack our bags Steff, we'll go to Guernsey for a few days!'

Steffani booked a house in St Peter Port, only to be told later that it was in the red light district. Mind you, considering the mood I was in at the time, this location might have suited me had I been alone.

One evening we went to the hotel shown to me by the taxi driver for a drink. The place was in poor shape but had potential. We left Guernsey again and I began my tour of Ireland appearing in Castlebar, Dungarven, Clonea, Lobinstown, Youghal, Galway, Waterford, Dublin and Glenfarne.

As always, touring in Ireland was an experience very hard to describe – you really have to go to the lovely Emerald Isle yourself and feel the warmth of the people. I always remember one place where the piano simply did not have the note I needed to start me off on the right key for the 'Monastery Garden'.

'Don't you worry,' I was told, 'it'll be all right on the night'.

And all right it was. The organiser of the venue located another upright and with the help of a local priest and a handcart had it delivered to the hall.

Driving to another evening's show it became more and more difficult for our car to move forward. On either side of the road one car after another was parked and a human line, all holding up their black umbrellas as it was pouring with rain, shuffled slowly forward. Surely I was not at the tail end of a funeral procession? When I questioned our driver he laughed and told me that they were all coming to see me. When, at last, we arrived at the stage door not just a puddle but a lake with all that rain had formed in front of the door. No way could I have jumped this distance when suddenly, out of the waiting crowd a man came forward and virtually carried me over the water to reach the front steps. Then, with a 'God bless you, Ron', he took up his place in the queue again. That's the Irish.

Driving back to the hotel after the night's show our car was suddenly flagged down by Military officials wearing armbands and carrying firearms. They demanded to see our driver's papers to prove his and our identity. One of the officials, after beaming his torch into my face, turned to the driver and said:

'You can whistle off now'.

It was already becoming quite evident that this beautiful land had a few problems.

The reviews in the Irish papers were very kind.

...his greatest success... 'In a Monastery Garden'. It was worth the money to hear this alone... There was not a murmur in the hall, one could hear a pin drop... it was an experience that few of those who had the pleasure of enjoying will forget in a lifetime.

The *Stage* wrote:

Will the Variety Theatre Survive Into 1959?

Well, I surely hoped so as I did look forward to playing 'Buttons' and a meeting that had been arranged by Freddie Carpenter with my leading lady for the forthcoming

Cinderella pantomime, Barnsley girl Diane Taylor. I had some time in hand, so had a look at the Rolls Royce showroom in Conduit Street. Maybe I was engrossed in what I saw through the window, or in thoughts of the panto meeting, but when a young woman called out to me 'Hello, Ronnie', without thinking I turned round and acknowledged her greetings.

'I've seen you perform recently and you made me very happy!'

'Thank you' I answered, 'I'm pleased.'

'Now,' she said, 'I'd like to make you happy!'

That's when I realised which way the wind was coming from and quickly made my polite excuses. The words 'Perhaps another time' echoed in my ears as I made my way to the offices of Howard & Wyndham's where I sat in my chair, not hearing a word that was spoken – I was mesmerised by the attractive *Leading Lady* and her vivacious smile. All sorts of thoughts were running through my head. How was I going to get through this pantomime without making a fool of myself? My Aunty Blanche had often told me that one day Miss Right would come along and I would know. Was this her? Was this Miss Right? I couldn't wait for the rehearsals to begin. I knew I wanted to be with Diane and find out.

On 8 December the rehearsals in Liverpool started. Diane played Cinderella, Joy Turpin Prince Charming, father and son Albert and Bryan Burdon represented the Ugly Sisters, George Neil portrayed Baron Overdrawn, Stella Lowe Dandini and Ronald Scott the Lord Chamberlain. Also taking part were Judith Harte as the Fairy Godmother, Brenda Last, Ronald Emblen, The George Mitchell Singers and the illuminated coach was drawn by Ruby Vinning's famous ponies. And then there was me, Buttons, who had to be Cinderella's friend in adversity on stage; little did anyone realise that I was one off stage too. Life had become suddenly so very complicated.

The *Royal Court* pantomime opened to rave notices:

The star was Ronnie Ronalde; Ronnie Ronalde picks up the biggest hand of the night after he has persuaded the children of the audience to join in with him; Ronnie Ronalde fits into the Button's role in the manner born; his cheerful personality and powerful singing was most enjoyable; He is not an assiduous trouper like Tommy Steele rather an individual and well-liked artist who can happily co-operate in what's going on; He makes a Buttons utterly different from the versions of the late whimsical Jack Buchanan, the genial Al Reid or zany Ken Dodd...almost genteel.

I nearly forgot to mention another star of the pantomime. He was my bird, a hand-puppet named Joey who was with me on stage during various scenes of the pantomime, especially in the kitchen setting where I had to try to make a crying Cinders laugh which I succeeded with Joey's amorous actions towards her. Because Diane played her role as Cinders not in the usual singing but a dancing version, I had to dance certain routines with her. This closeness on stage made me fall even more in love with her and the passion grew to such an extent that I had to ask Steffani if he could get me something from the doctor to cool me down.

The most demanding scene of the pantomime was, when I had to pacify Cinders because she could not go to the ball. That's when I was happy that my costume sported a large green baize apron that also acted as a cover-up to my manly virility. To be together on stage twice a day, for two and a half-hours each time, proved to be a distraction that I could not cope with. You might well ask to why I did not declare myself to her?

I couldn't, she was engaged to be married. The man in question was a member of the Howard & Wyndham family who had contracted me to play Buttons; there was no way I was going to behave badly. The situation was hopeless.

Diane did tell me that it was only an infatuation on my side, but I can honestly say that after the show finished this passion took quite some time to fade away. I never saw Diane again. For a while I carried her photo everywhere with me, and to this day, I keep the little charm she gave me on the last day of the show, reading 'I Love You', among some other trinkets on a gold chain in my waistcoat pocket.

Liverpool's University Guild of Undergraduates had invited me to judge the annual 'Miss World University Service' contest. Little had I bargained with the determination of the students to make money out of this occasion to bolster the kitty for their week's liquid entertainment. They kidnapped me and only after Steffani paid a handsome ransom was I allowed to rush back to the theatre, nearly missing my first house.

The year of 1959 had crept into the land and brought with it worrying uncertainty in many of the British theatres. At the Pantomime Ball, with all proceeds going to the VABF, one heard many entertainers present voice their concern with regard to empty date books. Many of them were playing to half empty houses, some theatres had shortened their running seasons and even cancelled future engagements, however, according to the *Liverpool Daily Post* on 3 February, our pantomime at the *Royal Court* was *still going strong*.

Gone were the days when Liverpool theatres were packed with pantos, revues and Variety with many magicians on their bills. The Songsters days working with the Great Lyle, the Amazing Chan and Horace Goldin were fun times for us boys. We often worried the magicians, I think they thought we'd pinch their magical tricks so they would ban us from standing on side stage. So we would then go up into the flies and watch from up there and on last nights if one of the magicians had been too stroppy with us we would drop a few stinkbombs during his act down onto the stage and sometimes put itching powder in his cloak.

Jasper Maskelyne we liked though one Songster did try to replace the strung together mock razor blades Maskelyne brought out of his mouth with real razor blades.

Cingalee's flower spectacle of coloured flowers with dart points falling from everywhere massed over the stage caused one boy to borrow the stage carpenter pliers and bend a quite few points, that night the carpet of flowers looked somewhat flat.

Devenne and his New York Blondes always intrigued us how he had his cigarettes coming out from thin air and we laughed at Benson Dulay cutting off the head of the black boy stooge with his rolling eyes of fear.

Cinderella scene

Diane Taylor – 'Cinderella'

'Buttons' in Cinderella

ROYAL COURT THEATRE LIVERPOOL
PROPRIETORS HOWARD AND WYNDHAM LTD.
MANAGING DIRECTOR   STEWART CRUIKSHANK
MANAGER C. H. MASON   ASST. MANAGER F. DENOVAN

Commencing

FRIDAY, 19th DECEMBER, 1958
EVENINGS AT   MATINEES AT
7   STEWART CRUIKSHANK   **2**
Presents

RONNIE RONALDE

ALBERT BURDON

JOY TURPIN

in
AN ORIGINAL AND DAZZLING PRODUCTION
of

CINDERELLA
THE IDEAL FAMILY PANTOMIME

With Fabulous Supporting Star Cast

A HOWARD AND WYNDHAM PANTOMIME
THE HALLMARK OF GOOD ENTERTAINMENT
Directed by FREDDIE CARPENTER

Mary Marshall & Sydney James

Act Thirty-three

MINE HOST

It is impossible for me to put down on paper the emotions I went through at that time in my life. The pantomime had finished, the first person I had really been in love with had disappeared on the stroke of twelve – only she hadn't left her glass slipper behind. I had come to a crossroads. Which route was I going to take? Was I going to carry on solely with my theatrical profession or should I try my hand in the hospitality trade, which is very closely related to entertaining people?

'Steff, let's phone Guernsey and see if that hotel is still for sale?'

On 22 February Steffani and I flew across, and yes, the hotel was still for sale. Now the bargaining began. Have you ever tried to bargain with a Guernseyman? I always thought I was good at that game, but wow, I had met my match but all through the proceedings the hotel owner's wife used to whisper to me:

'It's yours, Ronnie!'

During the ironing out of the sales contract between Monsieur Le Caer and my advocate, Steffani and I were staying at the Royal Hotel in St Peter Port. What a way to live! Even the water supply in the tap took its time. Before the maid came in with the morning tea you quickly turned on the bath taps, then back into bed to drink the tea at a leisurely pace, hoping when the teapot was empty the bath was full.

Then, on 19 March 1959, the *Guernsey Evening Press* announced:

STAGE STAR TAKES OVER AT HOTEL. Les Merriennes Hotel, St Martin's has recently changed hands. Its new owner... is that well-known artiste Ronnie Ronalde...

The hotel was mine, lock, stock and barrel, including seven acres of land (a lot in Guernsey). It was a very proud *mine host* who flew back to London.

My first stop was to Cyril announcing the purchase of my hotel. He looked at me, aghast – didn't I know that I'd be cutting myself off from the theatre? The media quickly picked up the news that I was the owner of a hotel in Guernsey.

The family was another matter. The same objections were tabled: the shops didn't carry everything they were used to, the beer wasn't as good as it was in Beccles, now where had I heard that argument before?

During March, the filming of a special TV series took place at the Wood Green *Empire*. This was a new concept by Associated-Rediffusion titled *Circus-Variety Hippodrome Show* and featured Danish clowns Les Freres Steckel, from Italy The Fredanies, the Three Merky's and D'Angolys Junior from Germany, Noberti the Swiss clown and the Thedar Sisters as well as Britain's Sheila Buxton, the Michael Sammes Singers and myself. But that was not all. This hour-long show also included animals. Among them were Holland's Jean Farmer with his football dogs and Joan Rosaire with her horse named Goldy.

Norrie Paramour's Orchestra accompanied us artistes, human and animal. The musicians were positioned very near to and facing the circus ring which was completely caged in. During one of the breaks, Norrie, a gentle gentleman through and through, was telling me, with much distress and displeasure, what had happened during the filming of the previous circus TV show. He was conducting some African music with his back to the cage where seven large lions, one of them a huge male with a massive mane, were performing. As the trainer cracked his whip this lion gave an almighty roar. But it was not the lion's roar that wiped the smiles off the musicians' faces, but a smell. One musician laid down his instrument and left his place, trying to escape from the foul smell that was drifting from where Norrie was standing.

'What happened, Norrie?' I asked, hardly able to keep a straight face.

'Ronnie,' he answered, in his very quiet voice, but sounding greatly indignant, 'this bloody lion behind me had let an almighty fart and my musicians thought it was me!'

Everybody got to hear of this story, as poor Norrie so desperately wanted to clear himself, much to the amusement of his musicians who kept mocking him with:

'Oh yes?' and 'It wasn't me!'

It was April of 1959 and there I was, in sunny Guernsey. My railtrucks from Beccles had arrived and so had the new staff for our opening in May for the hotel's summer season. The bar was in good hands with resident head barman and licensee Tom Robson, a wonderful character. My stepmother, Win, took over the running of the kitchen, my sister Vera looked after the housekeeping side and reception and my father was to oversee the tradesmen. This left Steff and me free to return to London for a *Jack Jackson TV Show* which also featured Lonnie Donegan, Chris Barber's Jazz Band, Cliff Richard, and Marion Ryan, a *Midday Music Hall* presentation *and Alan Melvill's A-Z* show with James Robertson Justice, Beryl Reid, Rita Reys and Ginger Rogers (all the R'r).

For the first time in my life I had found that I could no longer hide from the public. My home had become open to anybody at any time. I used to eat my meals in the hotel dining room and every time I tried to put the spoon into my mouth someone would stop at my table and start a long conversation about where and when he or she had seen me last. Rehearsing for my new records too had become a nightmare. The visitors used to watch Steffani like hawks and the moment he made a move towards the piano, out of nowhere they came, armed with chairs and there they sat ready to be entertained.

Their attitude was that they were entitled to it – they had booked to stay in Ronnie's hotel. Did they expect the Queen to be behind the reception desk if they stayed at the *Royal Hotel* in St Peter Port?

Forever the 'improver', I was already drawing up plans to alter the hotel – adding bedrooms, a larger dining room and a new visitors' lounge. There was already a very large lounge bar with a dance floor. Everybody on the island seemed to make a beeline for this bar, especially if a ship was in the harbour. Spirits were often drunk in trebles, champagne flowed, the band played and different 'singers' were coaxed with free drinks to perform; in short, a good time was had by all.

But it didn't end there. On opening-night my sister came running to me, quite horrified.

'Ronnie, they're upstairs, in the rooms!'

What could I do?

So upstairs I went, gingerly knocked on some doors and asked the culprits to leave.

'Don't spoil our fun, Ron,' they begged.

Not wanting to have too many problems on that very first night of being mine host, I replied,

'All right, I'll give you 10 minutes, but then it's curtains!'

'Thanks Ron, okay Ron'

came from behind the bedroom doors. And okay it was; it never happened again. No wonder when I bought the hotel my accountant asked me if I realised what sort of a hotel I was buying – it wasn't one that he'd take his wife to!

Yarmouth was calling again for a Sunday concert at the *Wellington Pier*. How does the proverb go? Absence makes the heart grow fonder?

There was a reason why I did not mind accepting, I had to organise one more railway truck full of scenery from my Beccles store to the *Garrick* Theatre Southport, where Steffani and I were putting on a summer show beginning in July. In that production we presented the little bear *Sooty* with his partner *Sweep* and their father, Harry Corbett. Supporting these two top stars were Smoothey and Layton as well as the Two Rexanos, Helen Turner, the Two Exelsiors, Raymond Newell and Perry McCann and, of course, the indispensable girls – in this case Betty Lunn's Cavalcade Girls. Jack Upson was the musical director. Once again our show had catered for the family audience:

…the Ronnie Ronalde Show at Southport's Essoldo is a happy and unified production, which caters for everyone…

and named all the different scenes as in 'Neptunes Domaine' with all its luminous fish; the 'Temptation of the Orient', the 'Jackdaw of Rheims'…*the red-robed Cardinal… what a welcome change from Osborne's horrible skit on the clergy in 'The World of Paul Slieckey'…*

As a bachelor I had no wish to complicate my life again but, on the other hand, I must admit, it hadn't taken me long to cast my eye on one of the show girls. She was fun to be with. Years later Joan Turner told me that her sister, Helen Turner, would not have said NO either to an invitation by me.

Theatricals often had difficulty in finding food after they finished their last performance, this of course has changed now drastically but through backstage talk one soon learned to know where the best places were. One late night, I was sitting in the back of my parked Bentley with no lights on, eating fish and chips with this particular young lady when suddenly a policeman knocked on the half-open car window.

'Are you all right, Sir?'

'Oh yes, Officer, I'm quite all right!' I assured him quickly.

I wonder if I would have answered him in the same easy manner if I had realised that the young lady with me was just 17?

After driving her back to her digs I returned to the Royal Hotel where I was staying. As I walked up to the front door, I found it locked. So I rang the bell, nothing happened. I knocked. Still no reply. Where was that night porter? Either he was on his rounds or he was having a quiet kip. What was I going to do? I couldn't afford to stand much longer in front of the hotel's entrance door in case another passing policeman questioned me, by this time it was well past two in the morning.

Next to the door was a large, slightly open, sash-window. But there was a snag – to reach it I would have to jump approximately a yard from the elevated hotel steps, across a 15-foot drop.

I had no alternative I risked the leap and safely landed on the window sill holding on for dear life. I tried to open the window further to climb through when glancing through the glass, what did I see? Lying on a settee right in front of the window was the night porter, looking up at me curiously as I squatted precariously on the sill. Slowly he sat up and asked:

'What do you want?'

Naturally I answered very quietly, 'I want to come in!'

'You can't!' he whispered, 'we're closed!'

Well, I did have to laugh and nearly falling off the sill still managed to open the window far enough to climb through and then the penny dropped, he realised who I was. He ran to the reception desk to give me my room key and offered to make

'a nice cup of tea, Sir?'

That was most welcome, especially when he brought some biscuits as well.

Many funny gags grow out of an impromptu episode on stage which, because it gets a laugh, often will be incorporated into an artiste's act. One night, at the end of my spot I whispered to the audience in a very confidential manner:

'Have you been to the Channel Islands for a holiday?'

I looked off stage, mock-checking if the stage manager could hear me, then continued:

'It's marvellous, there's plenty of sunshine, good food and wines'.

This time I looked to the other side of the stage and making out I saw nothing, turned again to the audience with the words:

'I often go there but I can't tell you the name of the hotel I stay in because that would be advertising, but I can give you a clue – the fellow who owns it, whistles.'

That caused an uproar of laughter.

Next morning the receptionist of the Royal Hotel phoned me in my room.

'The mayor's office is on the line for you, Sir. Will you take the call?'

'Good morning, Sir, this is the mayor's office, we'd like to make a booking for a double room, please.'

'I'm sorry, the receptionist must have put you through to me in error, I'll try to get you transferred back to the desk.'

'I am through to Ronnie Ronalde?' she asked quickly before I could hang up.

'Yes, that's me.'

'I wish to make a booking on behalf of the mayor and mayoress. After seeing your show last night they would like to spend their next holiday at your hotel.'

I kept the gag in all season.

Little did I realise that Southport's *'Ronnie Ronalde Show'* was to be my last production I would personally finance and present in Great Britain, so with the Betty Lunn's Girls giving the grand finale of my show a patriotic note being dressed in glittering Union Jack costumes with bells draped around their shoulders and dancing and singing to the tunes of *'There'll Always Be An England'* and *'Land Of Hope And Glory'*, in retrospect, made this scene even more moving.

Before returning to Guernsey I appeared at *Drill Hall* for the 9th Derby RTRA Radio Show *'Fair of the Airs'* with Noele Gordon, Patricia Cox, Pat Astley, Barbara Clegg and Charles Tingwell. Victor Buckland, their publicity officer had been responsible for a demonstration of 'television' at a radio exhibition in Derby as early as 1933 when together with Ethel Noton, a six foot screen was set up in the exhibition hall and they transmitted half hour long programmes with some of the revenue coming from advertisements before each performance. (Was this the start of Commercial TV?)

Back in 1922 Mr. Buckland had pioneered the first loudspeaker system at an exhibition in Eltham near Woolwich, opened by Sir Kingsley Wood, using the 2LO radio station. He also owned the recording studios London Road, Derby where many programmes had been recorded like Richard Dimbleby's *Down your Way*.

My hotel's summer season had finished but Tom Robson, our barman thought it would be better to keep the Ballroom Bar open during the winter so patrons could dance to the music of the resident band, the Martinis. Quite often I used to join the locals in the bar where, warmed by a crackling fire and a soothing liqueur, they would tell me many a folktale and of course, about their period of occupation by the Germans during the wartime.

It was on 19 June 1940 that the British Government announced the demilitarisation of the Channel Islands and on 28 June low-flying German aircraft carried out a vicious bombing raid on St Peter Port. An ambulance was machine-gunned, as was the Guernsey lifeboat – the son of the coxswain was killed, along with 29 civilians on the town waterfront. On 30 June four Junkers 52 troop-carrying aircraft arrived at Guernsey's year-old La Villiaze Airport and the German occupation of Guernsey began, to last for five dreary years.

Tom proved to have been quite a character himself at that time. Apparently, during 1942, some 2000 people from the Channel Islands were sent to concentration camps in Germany. At one camp, called Laufen, Tom was put in charge of the islanders, because he had been a military policeman in England before his hotel work in Guernsey.

'Mr. Ronnie,' Tom reminisced, 'the Germans relied on me to march our people to and from work. They preferred to do other things!'

'Yes,' said another local in the bar, 'and he wouldn't even let us pick an apple from the trees we passed on the way!' pointing at Tom.

Tom's strictness was not because the apples were German, but because he had been given an order and his own honour and loyalty to his superior at that time would not allow him to waver, whatever the circumstance. I was to experience the same loyalty from him right to the end of his life.

To turn Guernsey into an island fortress by the Germans, vast quantities of concrete and steel were poured into it and thousands of slave workers were brought from all over

Europe. Since my hotel was on one of the highest points in Guernsey, the German officers had taken over the place and White Russian prisoners of war had been housed in the cellars.

Now I understood why I had found all those iron beds, huge cooking pots, war helmets as well as outsize cartwheels originally belonging to an iron mobile German kitchen. Lots of this German regalia I buried, not thinking that later it would be regarded as valuable; eventually I gave permission to have them all dug up and many of the articles are now in the 'German Museum' in Guernsey.

Frank Stroobant wrote a very informative book called *One Man's War*, retelling many of the stories and a Television series was made, '*Enemy at the Door*' showing Guernsey Occupation life during the war years between 1940 and 1945.

For so small an island, 24.5 square miles, Guernsey is rich in evidence of its colourful past, not only of these concrete fortifications and tunnels from the German Occupation years, but also in form of ancient dolmes and their witchery, castles, forts and finds dating back as far as 4700 BC.

In the December issue of the *New Musical Express* Keith Goodwin wrote an article in which he said:

The last remaining days fade into the twilight; December 31 closes the most exciting and flourishing chapter in the history of popular music. The 1950-1959 decade can truly be described as 'The fabulous Fifties'.

I had been blessed to be part of that era.

Act Thirty-four

GYPSY ORACLE

I became quite a busy commuter between London and Guernsey and thoroughly enjoyed the island's tranquillity at the end of each journey.

One of the first things I tried to change was the name of my hotel, Les Merriennes. Guernsey-French Patois underlines the Norman origin of the island and to this day all states meetings and court sessions are carried out in French. After my Aunty Blanche heard the name of my hotel she could not pronounce it correctly, calling it everything, from 'Mary Ann' to 'Merry N'. So we thought we'd call it St Martin's Hotel. Later, though, it became simply known as 'Ronnie's Hotel' with the taxi drivers calling it 'RonRons' for short.

I also changed the front and ground floor area of the hotel completely.

As an *Evening Press* article said:

St. Martins Hotel is gaining in popularity among visitors and residents and that is likely to increase still more as time goes on.

I must have hit the right note.

These alterations to the Hotel were soon put to the test, when a charity football match was arranged for the British *'Showbiz XI'* All-Stars team to play against the Guernsey *Island XI,* to aid the Bailiwick of Guernsey World Refugee Year Fund. Some of the players came a few days earlier and stayed with me.

Quite a crowd welcomed the others at the airport and followed them to my hotel, from where they officially left for the football pitch. Nat Gonella kicked off for the showbiz side which also included Tommy Steele, Ronnie Carroll, Billy Cotton JR., Dave King and my 'ref's whistle' was heard all through the game. I think the Guernsey people were surprised that the stars played so well: the result was a 3-3 draw.

Cyril had booked me to appear at the *Empire* Cleethorpes.

...The Empire Management can congratulate itself... Mike and Bernie Winters proved popular... Hylda Baker a winner... Jimmy James ideal choice... Peter Brough, Archie Andrews and Reg Dixon go down well... the biggest hit was undoubtedly Ronnie Ronalde...

After each show the manager came backstage and asked if I would see a palmist who had repeatedly been in to see my performance. She wanted so much to read my hand. At first I declined the offer, but after some persistence she got her way. She took hold of my hand and began telling me things I was sure she could have easily read in any newspapers. Then she said that I was soon going to go on a trip abroad. Well, that I didn't believe – I had just returned from Australia and I'd been everywhere else, round the world and back. But to be told that I was going to meet a tall, blonde girl, and I would have three children, topped the lot. I laughed, but she insisted that what she saw would come true.

Soon I had forgotten about the whole episode. I had been in love and as the outcome had only been hurt, I had closed the door to any thoughts.

I could not wait to get back to Guernsey and once there, didn't take much notice of anybody around me but retreated immediately to my private lounge.

What was up with my father? He was stalking in and out of the room, not at all his usual self. And he kept on chatting and chatting, asking how I was and how I felt. What was he getting at?

'We had a few new staff arrive, son.'

'Yes?' I looked at him. 'I knew that, Dad.'

'That new receptionist...' he said. 'If I were younger, son, she'd be the one for me. Her luggage, ooh, and the moment she arrived she asked where the nearest bank was! She's from Austria.'

That night, on my way to the dining room, I passed through the reception when suddenly a young lady hurried forward to open the door for me and greeted me with 'Good evening, Sir, welcome home' in a lovely foreign accent. Looking at her, I realised that this must be the girl my father had been talking about.

Days later I was invited to open a film show – would I bring the wife or a lady friend?

'You'll just have to say, Steff, that I have neither.'

He looked at me and thoughtfully said:

'What about the one at the reception desk? She looks decent enough, why don't you take her?'

Yes, indeed, why not?

I had been quietly watching her performing her duties, how she moved, heard her talk in German to her friends and in her broken English to the hotel guests and very often getting the wrong end of the stick. How do you explain to a foreigner, that when somebody asks for horseradish it does not mean going to the stables to find a horse that eats radishes? There was also the occasion when a French couple tried to book into the hotel and were told that the office had not received their 'French letter' confirming the reservation. I enjoyed listening to this girl's laughter when she realised the real meaning of these misunderstandings – it was like a breath of fresh air. Not that I was running after the Austrian Fraulein, oh no, but I'll take her out.

The evening of the function arrived and she was a treat to look at. Steffani had my Bentley brought round to the front of the hotel and in full view of everybody dining that night, helped her to get into the car, leaving me to fend for myself to get into the driver's seat. After closing the car door on her side, with a little bow, he beckoned to me:

'Drive on, son.'

What was up with Steffani? What was he trying to accomplish?

The evening was a success. During our drive home I asked her if she would go out with me again?

'I will look forward to it,' was her reply

Hold your horses Ron, I said to myself, don't run before you can walk, but try as I may to have an unnoticed courtship was not on. It became so bad that I had to ask her to meet me in the nearby church graveyard. One evening she had to wait there for quite some time as I was on the phone to Norrie Paramour arranging my new recordings due in September. To make up for it I took some chocolates and a bottle of wine and drove to the meeting place. She was still there but, oh boy, not in a very good mood. She had never waited for anybody, I was told in no uncertain terms.

I asked her to get into the car and we drove towards Cobo Bay. I parked the car among the sand dunes, turned on the radio and, by then sitting in the back of the car, opened the bottle of wine, gave her a silver thimble full while I filled my goblet. That's how it carried on until the bottle was empty. I didn't want anybody to tell me that I made a girl drunk!

I had to find out so many things. I already knew that she was a good cook, because after some of our evening walks she would prepare tit-bits for me in the hotel kitchen. I enjoyed the taste – it was different, continental. I was happy that night on the beach and reluctantly drove back to the hotel.

What was up with the car, coughing and spurting? and I couldn't see the road properly, everything seemed so dark! Eventually we arrived back at the hotel and that's where the car stopped, in the middle of the long entrance drive. The battery was flat. The following day rumours started to fly around the island.

For a small island Guernsey was very well catered for entertainment wise. My hotel, with my cabaret act thrown in, Sydney James' Old Tyme Music Hall at the *New Theatre Ballroom* and *Candie Gardens* starring Ronnie Corbett.

I will always remember meeting Ronnie in the High Street of St Peter Port, and we stood there, chatting, in the middle of the road for a good hour. But that's theatricals, oblivious to everything going on around them. I met him again in 1990 at *the Logan Campbell* Theatre in Auckland where, backstage, we chatted, again oblivious of others, about handmade shoes we both adore.

The summer of 1960 during which my courtship had blossomed, with little glamour but a lot of intrigue, was coming to its end. I did not relish the impending departure of my summer romance, but there was nothing I could do. Work permits for foreigners in Guernsey were only stamped until the end of September, after which date they all had to leave the island; it was as if the final curtain of a show had come down again. Norrie Paramour had already arrived to work through the music and songs I was to record the following week in London. Perhaps it was for the best that we should part when one evening, during our by now customary walk through the moonlit lanes, she invited me to come to Austria and stay with her family and she could drive me to her Hotel Training School in Bad Hofgastein, which could send staff to my hotel every summer.

I discussed this proposal with Steffani.

'Well son,' he said, 'next week we'll have to record in London. Let's take her with us, then you go to Austria with her.'

For the first time in my theatrical life I had a girl accompanying me to my work at the recording studios.

Steffani had booked a suite of rooms in a London Hotel. No problem, until the following morning, Steffani suddenly stormed into my bedroom and quite indignantly pointed to his head. All his hair was coated in a white paste.

'What's happened, Steff?' I had to hide my laugh.

'Somebody has put their toothpaste next to my Brylcream!' he moaned. He had left his glasses off and confused the two tubes, both red and white.

How did pressman Tony Austin know how I felt, did it really show through in my new records when he wrote in the *Music Man*:

...Ronalde yodels his way around the groove with enough power to bring avalanches tumbling from all the mountains in Switzerland, and a few in Austria, too... there is a swing in the Ronalde voice...

As we waited at the airport I looked at my companion and suddenly it hit me like a sledgehammer. The gypsy woman in Cleethorpes, what had she said? I would meet a tall blonde girl? Well, there she stood. And I was going to go abroad – to Austria. My God, am I heading for trouble! What else had she said?

At that moment we were called to board the plane.

'Your passport and tickets, Sir?'

'Here are the tickets!' I said.

'Passports?' The official held out his hand.

'I haven't got my passport, it's packed, in the suitcase!'

Where the hell was Steff? I'd never had to do these things before – he always looked after me.

To cut a long story short, the airlines had to bring my suitcase back from the plane, I had to find my passport and then at last I was allowed to board. All that for a woman? Within a few seconds I had made up my mind – the slightest thing I could find wrong in or with Austria and I would be on the very next flight back to Guernsey; suddenly I had cold feet.

In Austria I was welcomed with open arms.

'So far, so good. I think I can survive the fortnight. I don't think there'll be any need to book into a hotel.'

During the next few days I was passed around like a piece of china. From Rosemarie's friends who, fortunately all spoke English, to her father's friends and colleagues, the mayor, government officials, police inspectors, surgeons, dentists, opticians... We drove round the lake and up the mountain, ate in cellars and danced in village halls. It really was *The Sound of Music* country and I expected Julie Andrews any moment to appear and sing The *Lonely Goatherd* which I had just recorded. I had to extend my return ticket for a further week – well, I had to go to Hofgastein, which was, after all, the whole purpose of my journey. We arrived in the *Grand Hotel*. After talking with Director Reith of the college I realised that he knew Harold Fielding, the English impresario I had worked for many times and who, at that time, owned the *Chalet Hotel* in Jersey.

Another extension to my ticket was needed. Rosemarie wanted to show me Venice, which was beautiful and so very romantic. We had booked into one of those aged palazzos near the Rialto Bridge alongside the Grand Canal. The hall, adorned with its Venetian glass and chandeliers, was magnificent and the bedroom had to be seen to be believed. It was huge and so was the canopied bed. I sat on it to take off my shoes. Well, the croak and the groan that greeted me made me jump a mile; both the springs and the bed were antique too! Immediately it went through my mind that this would be no good for a honeymoon couple.

Rosemarie's father had another journey arranged for us. Vienna. After visiting the Big Wheel in the Prater, the Lipizaner horses, the Heurigen Taverns and eating the famous chocolate torte at Sacher's, I had to loosen my belt again. The time had come for me to say goodbye and return to Guernsey. I had not bargained on Rosemarie's reaction. She feared that, once I was back in Guernsey, our romance would end.

Suddenly I found myself taking a 21-year-old Austrian girl back with me to Guernsey. As what? To do what? She could not officially work, she had no permit. I was caught.

It was mid-November and Bernard Delfont wanted me to take the star part of Idle Jack in the Dick Whittington pantomime at the new *Pavilion Theatre* in Weymouth with Diane Noble, Claire Ruane, O'Duffy Bros., Susan Irvine, Susan Caddy, Ruth Calvert, Tony Menray, Marie Lynn, Ernest Bale, Charles French, the Keefe Bros. & Annette, Tobie Darrell and the girls and boys.

When the script arrived, I experienced another first. Rosemarie was helping me to learn the lines by reading all the other character parts. I must admit it did sound humorous when I heard her speak the words of the fairy with a German accent. Steffani concentrated on the music and at the same time tried to organise the smooth running of the hotel during our absence over the Christmas and New Year period.

'We've got a problem, Ron. Immigration has been on to me again – what is Fraulein Burschberger doing in the hotel?

'What did you tell them, Steff?'

'What can I tell them? That she's your lady friend? I can't keep on stalling them. You'll have to do something soon!'

Rehearsals and the fitting of costumes were scheduled for the second week of December in London. I returned to Guernsey for Christmas Eve as we had previously advertised that I would perform in my ballroom, an event that was already sold out. During the early hours of Boxing Day morning Steffani and I had to board the Guernsey to Weymouth four hour long sea ferry as the pantomime was due to open that very night. A few hours before my departure my father suddenly informed me that he did not want the responsibility of looking after the hotel. This shocked me tremendously and I had to ask Rosemarie to take charge. I could see that she was not very happy, especially as this was the first Christmas that she had been away from her family in Austria. I promised that the moment the show was running I would have her come to Weymouth. I had to look after her; the time had come where I realised that she meant more to me than just a passing affair.

Again my ability to make a hit with the children from the audience was specially remarked upon and the London *Record Mirror* under the heading of *Panto Parade* informed its readers where their favourite stars will be entertaining, showing photos of Norman Wisdom, Bruce Forsyth, Ruby Murray, Yana, Roy Castle, Harry Secombe, Gary Miller, Lonnie Donegan and me.

I was not unhappy when the show finished its season, I wanted to get back to Guernsey and I am sure the Showgirls felt the same. The *Pavillion Theatre* had been built without any thought given to the width of crinolines to get through firedoors onto the stage. After many of the scenes the girls had to quickly get undressed on stage as their costumes had to be hoisted up in the flies for storage until they needed them again. The timing had to be impeccable for a smooth running show.

Everything seemed to be moving ahead. I was adding a wing, my personal flat, to the hotel when a bombshell in the form of a letter came. It was from the Guernsey Immigration Authorities advising me that Rosemarie had to leave Guernsey. That night I went down on my knee and asked her to become my wife.

Her reply was an excited yes, but she had one favour to ask. Could I please change my name by deed poll from Ronald C. Waldron to my stage name of Ronnie Ronalde! She did not want to marry me and become Mrs. Waldron and share a bedroom with Mr. Ronnie Ronalde. And anyway, she said, looking at me.

'There will be the children to think about.'

That was it! The palmist's words were ringing in my ears. How many did she say? Three?

I changed my name by deed poll to Ronnie Ronalde on 28 February 1961 at the Guernsey Greffe.

Football fever

Act Thirty-five

MR AND MRS RONALDE

The news of my engagement went round the newspaper world like a whirlwind. Cecil Wilson of the *Daily Mail* flew to Guernsey specially to get an exclusive for his paper. According to him, he had to meet the girl who was to end Ronnie Ronalde's diehard bachelorhood.

The wedding date was set for 15 April 1961. A special licence to marry in my hotel was soon obtained. Rosemarie's parents and her sister came from Austria, loaded with presents and, of course, the contents of the 'bottom drawer'. That was a surprise. Everything had been beautifully embroidered by nuns, from bedlinen and towels to tablecloths and napkins with our initials: her name first, then mine. Burschberger and Ronalde, BR.

Oh no! the BR's looked just like the ones on the back-head covers of British Rail seats!

I knew I was in for it when my friends from London arrived – Mr. and Mrs. Leslie Reynolds (HMV Records), Mr. and Mrs. Norrie Paramour (EMI), Mr. and Mrs. Leonard Smith (EMI), Norman Newell (Columbia), Mr. and Mrs. Geoffrey Everitt (Radio Luxembourg), Teddy Holmes (Chappells), Hyman Zahl (Foster's Agency), David Jacobs and Eric Spear (composer of the Coronation Street theme music). Sure enough, the minute they walked into the hotel and saw the display with the BR's, the jokes started flying; after all, they were all theatricals.

The ceremony was conducted by the Greffier of Guernsey, Mr. R.H. Videlo, Master of Ceremonies was Sydney James who took great delight all evening in announcing the names of Rosemarie's father and sister with their German pronunciation, Vater (Faaater) and Puppi (Poupeeee).

Still somewhat new to the island way of life I had advertised my wedding dance in the local newspaper first and then applied to the Royal Court for an extension to my hotel's licensing hours.

It turned out to be a chicken and egg situation and this once in a lifetime celebration was declined.

But the Guernsey newspaper was very helpful and printed the alteration in their Saturday 15 April edition:

RONNIE RONALDE'S HOTEL TONIGHT GALA WEDDING NIGHT
fully licensed until 11pm (not 11.45pm).

The day was exactly as a wedding day should be, perfect in every way – especially my bride, Mrs. Ronnie Ronalde. Honeymoon? We did go on honeymoon, yes, I had to make another record for Columbia in Abbey Road and yes, I did point out Buckingham Palace to Rosemarie on the way to the studio.

The photo of our wedding and write-ups – *'Radio Star's Holiday Isle Gala Wedding'*, *'Whistling Wonder Weds'*, *'Singing Star Married at his Hotel'* – were carried in most national newspapers and still the reporters could not get enough: they were at Gatwick to meet our flight from Guernsey, by this time Rosemarie was starting to complain:

'I believe you married me under false pretences,' she cried. 'Will there ever be peace?'

Steffani had always pushed me through doors or into taxis first. Now there was suddenly someone else who should precede me. Well, that took some time for me to get used to especially as I preferred not to touch anything foreign, my fingers had to go into my mouth to whistle so it surely was understandable that occasionally I forgot to be chivalrous and walked through the door first and only realised what I had done when Rosemarie yelled after the closing door had hit her once again. I had developed the habit of opening doors with my elbow or shoulder if nobody else was there to do it for me. I have also been known to get into a cab and drive off, leaving Rosemarie behind only having to shamefacedly ask the driver to please turn back and pick my wife up.

But I did learn, especially after I knew that Rosemarie was expecting our first baby. One evening, we had already gone to bed when quietly she asked me to drive her to the maternity hospital. I wasn't worried about my wife having the baby, oh no, *'I'* had to get dressed again. It was all right for Rosemarie to sit in her dressing gown, waiting, but me? I was going to make an appearance at the hospital. People were going to be there, doctors, nurses, and I had to look my best.

Oh! I could hear her all right! These theatricals are the end, everything has to be a performance.

At last we drove off. Steffani had already alerted the doctor and the hospital; unfortunately he could not come as well, although, given the chance, he would have been there too, organising things.

After giving my wife over to the care of the nurses I was ready to settle down and await the arrival of my first child.

'You can go home now, Mr. Ronalde,' the matron informed me, 'the doctor will call you when the baby is born.'

There I stood, all dressed up and ready for the big moment and I wasn't needed.

Back at the hotel Steffani kept me company until after agonising eight hours the much awaited phone call came. Carolyn had made her entrance and the doctor called her a 'smasher'.

The rest of the day passed in a haze.

Leonidoff had been in London and wanted to know if I would be interested in another Christmas or Easter Season at the *Radio City* in New York. What a dilemma. My first Christmas with my wife and my beautiful baby daughter – I couldn't leave them. Geoffrey Everitt was also eager for me to do another series on his *Radio Luxembourg* – to begin in January 1963. It would have been nice too, after listening for many years to the weekly BBC radio programme *Desert Island Discs* to be featured as their guest, especially as I was living on a real island. I wrote a letter to Monica Chapman at the BBC to that effect and received a reply stating that, although Miss Chapman was at present on leave, she would be in touch when she returned in a fortnight's time. I am still waiting!

The *Weekend* magazine carried an article written by Norman Newell:

The top names in the Hit Parade are my best friends. They deserve the fame and happiness they can get, but... I wish they wouldn't get married... it is sad to stop recording with artists you like. Like Ronnie Ronalde. He was in small type on the bill at Chelsea Palace when I first saw him. And there was a small audience. But at the end of his act they went wild. Ronnie was one of the sensations of the last few years, but now he and his wife live in a beautiful hotel he has bought in Guernsey...

February 1963 arrived and with it my son Ronnie. This time Rosemarie did not put me through the agony of having to get dressed in the middle of the night; she timed it so I could have my cup of morning tea first. And to celebrate his arrival I went to London and recorded an album.

Trumpeter Humphrey Lyttleton, did not seem to like my new disc in his write-up but had to admit in the end that ...*you can be sure that he (me) is an institution as permanent as the Tower of London...*

The date of this article coincided with his appearance with Chris Barber and Johnny Dankworth heading the panel of judges in a *Jazz Festival* contest. Well he always liked playing his own trumpet.

The *New Record Mirror* wrote: ...*evergreen Ronnie Ronalde comes up with an album which must be a best seller...*

It was not easy to leave a wife and two young children behind, but I did answer Leonidoff's call to America for my tenth *Radio City* show called *The Glory of Easter* which opened on 4 April 1963 with Louise Armstrong, Francoise Szony, Nancy Claire and the British puppeteers Pinky and Perky.

The famous *Radio City* Rockettes had recently opened a new hotel, the *Americana*, situated only a couple of blocks away from the theatre, so Leonidoff suggested that I should stay there. The room was very well equipped and even had a second telephone in the bathroom, mounted on the wall by the throne and as nature will have it always rang when privacy was most needed, resulting in a very strained:

'Helloooo!'

Once the show was up and running Steffani returned to Guernsey and I was left alone, appearing in five shows a day, seven days a week. Every evening I phoned Guernsey and speaking to my wife was agony, so I decided that she should come to New York. My dear friends Sam and Mary Eisner were absolutely delighted.

'We'll show her New York, just give her to us.'

The moment I returned to Guernsey I received a phone call from Holland. Could I come to Hilversum to take part in AVRO's 40th anniversary *Cavalcade* Television programme, scheduled to be shown live on June 30? As always, I enjoyed Holland and stayed at the Hilversum *Gooiland Hotel* where I met some of the other special guest artists, one of them Catarina Valente.

The summer season at the hotel was in full swing when:

'It is imperative for Ronnie to open new production at *Radio City Music Hall* first week in August.'

A cable from Leonidoff arrived, he had produced a show called *Europe* and just had to have me in it. Rosemarie was getting thoroughly sick of me flipping off halfway round the world at the drop of a hat but did realise it was my work after all.

This time, alas, I was in for another first. A fire shut *Radio City* down, for the first time in 32 years, although it opened again the following morning; a large electric transformer had exploded in the theatre vaults.

The eight-week season dragged, with the same routine every day, so when I finally returned to Guernsey, Rosemarie and I flew to Majorca for a holiday on our own. But poor Rosemarie went down with the bug. For two solid days and nights she was absolutely delirious, and all I could do was to sit on the balcony and watch the people at the swimming pool below and decided that when my hotel pool was built I would have enough deck-chair space for everyone. I didn't like the way some guests claimed their chairs with towels well before breakfast time.

The hotel manager presented us with two seats for the bull ring but when Rosemarie, still feeling very shaky, saw the first beast arrive in the arena, she had enough.

'I want to go, I want to go,' she moaned and, with that, buried her head in my lap and would not look up until I got hold of her and guided her through the crowds, back to the carpark. We returned to Guernsey the following day.

Our hotel was going from strength to strength. We needed more bedrooms, a larger kitchen, dining room, lounge bar and ballroom and, of course, a swimming pool and tennis court. One could not build one area without the other. Oh well, in for a penny in for a pound. Let's do the lot! The incidents that happened during that time were maddening, frustrating, discourteous and downgrading, while others were hilarious, bordering to the point of stupidity. To write about every detail of the rebuilding process would fill another book.

And then the last prediction of the palmist in Cleethorpes was fulfilled our third child, Christina, was born.

How would I like to try an altogether new concept of entertaining? at the Greasborough *Social Club* near Rotherham. It sure was different: the concept of entertaining in a working man's club, where gambling took place and drink and food was served during a performance, was new to me but did give me the idea of doing the same in my hotel. I had entertained visitors in my lounge bar on previous occasions, but my sister Vera did not like it:

'Everybody hushes when you're on, Ron, and my tills aren't ringing. You're no good for business!'

Nobody tells me twice that I'm stopping business. So after I got back from Greasborough Steffani and I put together an *'Evening with Ronnie Ronalde'* act and from then on, all during the summer, we held a dinner cabaret. Every week the room was fully booked out. Who wants to go away for work when it's all on your own doorstep?

'Ronnie, come to England and be our guest on the *Black and White Minstrel Show*.'

George Innes, producer of the popular TV show had been in touch.

Yes, why not. A few days in Britain wouldn't do any harm so I accepted the booking, which was a great success, and I'm pleased to say that the TV film was afterwards sold to other countries, among them Australia, Gibraltar and Sierra Leone and revamped episodes will again be seen on TV during 1998. It was a very impressive bill with the Mitchell Minstrels, John Boulter, Dai Francis, Tony Mercer, Herb Alpert and his Tijuana Band, Margaret Savage, The Television Toppers, Delia Wicks, Penny Jewkes, The Jolas Puppets and as special guest: Ronnie Ronalde.

My dear wife had taken it into her head that she did not feel she was married in the eyes of God. What on earth had brought that on? Suddenly I realised the reason. Our eldest daughter Carolyn had started to go to a Catholic school run by nuns. My wife, a Catholic, and being in daily contact with the nuns had made her vulnerable so to please her I agreed to marry her again, this time in a church. We asked Reverend Reeve from St Joseph's Church in St Peter Port to come to our private flat in the hotel and over dinner he was supposed to instruct me in the catholic faith and what I was going to take on, as if I didn't know already.

After that first night of instruction, and having wined and dined, the Reverend drove back to his church quite happy, so much so that for the next meeting he asked if he could bring his assistant too, after which they both drove back to the church quite happy. Rosemarie and I married again on 15 April 1966, five years to the day after our 'first' marriage, with our children present. Carolyn was very proud too and told everybody at her school: my parents are getting married today!

And Dick Tatham wrote a beautiful article about me, my life, my family and my hotel in the British *My Weekly* magazine. I felt very proud and honoured that a journalist of his standing went out of his way to write so nicely.

Then the childrens' convent school was celebrating its centenary, with very special guests from England, His Eminence Cardinal Heenan and the Bishop of Portsmouth, the Right Reverend Derek Worlock and our hotel provided, cooked and transported all the food to the convent. But that wasn't all. Reverend Mother again approached my wife:

'We have a concert tonight at *Candie Gardens*, Mrs. Ronalde, all the nuns are singing to honour our special guests, it wouldn't be possible…? Would it?'

How do you say no to a Reverend Mother?

Next morning the *Guernsey Press* gave the Sisters front-page with a huge picture showing them on stage:

…Concert was quite out of the ordinary! There was a gasp of delight when, unannounced, Ronnie Ronalde and Steffani walked onto the stage. This great artist was excellent in his rendering of 'Lo, hear the gentle lark'…

Well, I reckon I was giving something back to the Sisters for putting up with my children. The evening was a success according to His Eminence, who sent a letter graciously thanking us.

On 1 July 1967 the European Common Market had been signed. Through Britain, Guernsey was in the EEC – but, at the same time, not in it. Guernsey did exactly as it saw fit for its own people. That's very clever, you might think, but unfortunately not so for my wife, an Austrian who, on the advice of the Guernsey lawyers, had been sworn in as a British citizen in Guernsey and not London, before our marriage. Suddenly she found herself an outsider and hit the roof when she applied for an extension on her passport only to find that a special clause had been added:

Holder has the right of abode in the United Kingdom. But has no right to employment or establishment in the remainder of the EEC.

When she asked the Guernsey Immigration Officer, Rodney Le Lacheur, about this ominous-sounding statement she was told exactly what it meant. If I died, Rosemarie could carry on living and working in whatever I leave her, the hotel, but should she decide to sell, she would have to move to Britain which she did not know never having lived there and bring up our three Guernsey-born children.

It was time to build a house for Rosemarie in our hotel grounds, so she could carry on living in a home with our children if circumstances would necessitate a sale of the hotel. It would also assist me with my rehearsals and not use the hotel dining room stage where the waiters were thoroughly fed up having to reset the tables and chairs every time they came back on duty. It was and still is vitally important that I rehearse every day to keep my lips in a supple condition, they are as important to me as they are for a trumpeter; if I don't use them they become soft and split.

On 14 August 1968 I met with the architect to start drawing up plans for a bungalow within the hotel grounds and we sent a letter and a copy of the site plan to the Secretary of the Island Development Committee. We waited and we waited for permission to build until, on 31 January 1969 we found that our request had been turned down; the committee didn't have to give the reasons for their decision.

We were back to square one. Let's write a new letter asking permission to build a bungalow on the other side of the hotel grounds, where there was already a large wall with an entrance to my private lane leading onto the main road. Again, after a somewhat shorter waiting period, the answer arrived: NO.

They did, however, upset my wife with a compromise they suggested.

The committee would allow us to add some more rooms to an already existing staff block and I would be permitted with my wife and three young children to occupy some rooms in it and at the same time share the staff facilities!

These constantly frustrating setbacks planted the seed of thinking about an eventual move from Guernsey.

I still needed a room to rehearse. If the States of Guernsey would not allow me to build my house in my own grounds, there was only one way, to go up. I was going to build one on top of my hotel with a lounge 40 feet long by 30 feet wide with a large Guernsey granite fireplace and sliding doors leading onto my private patio. Eventually those plans were passed.

Channel Television in Jersey asked me to take part in one of their programmes called *Mainly Live*. The programme director, John Rothwell, had also invited Susan Hampshire onto the show. One remark Susan made I found very unusual for a woman to say to a man:

'I love your shoes Ronnie!'

I was very interested to see how the new TV setup in Jersey was working. When the original CT Company was about to be formed, tenders were invited from both islands, Guernsey and Jersey, to see where the new channel could best operated from, it was inevitable that the larger island, Jersey, would pick up the contract.

Jimmy Henney and BBC producer Steve Allen came to the hotel. This one-hour interview, *Be My Guest*, was aired over the BBC Radio 1 and 2 during October 1969 and repeated January 1970 and Jeffery Barnard wrote in the January *Radio Times:*

If the blackbirds on the island of Guernsey feel insecure, then it's not surprising. They are competing against the master: Ronnie Ronalde, the island's leading hotelier.

The producers Brenda Luce and Adam Clapham of the BBC TV programme *Braden's Week* came with the request that Bernard Braden wanted to see me on his show.

The very next day Cyril called. He had an urgent request from David Frost, he also wanted me on his ITV programme. Brilliant. The unfortunate part was that both programmes were to be screened on the same night, at the same time, but on different channels. Cyril reminded me that I had not as yet signed the Braden contract and therefore could do the Frost show instead, but I had promised Bernard.

'I can't break my word, Cyril. Please tell David I'd be happy to come on his show another time.'

The *Braden Show* was screened in December; I never heard from David Frost again but this was understandable. Both shows were rivals and screened at the same time but on different channels, one obviously tried to outdo the other.

The pressure from England to produce another record could not be ignored any longer. Norman Newell was adamant and had already pre-booked the recording studios for January 1970. I had to deliver 12 new songs, one of which had to be 'Wanderin' Star' as the film of *Paint Your Wagon* was about to be released, with Lee Marvin singing this number. So I could get the feel of this song, Norman arranged for me to see a special preview of the film. I was most intrigued by the melodious call of one of the birds which had been taped for a special scene.

Before the recording I took my family to Tenerife for a Christmas holiday where I had arranged to visit Jack Jackson, who had retired to the island. It was strange seeing him at his house, halfway up a volcano, so far away from London where once he had ruled the lives of so many entertainers by playing – or not playing – their discs.

The *'Sweetest Sound of Ronnie Ronalde'* was solely a whistling album. Steffani took it upon himself to send a copy to many radio and TV producers with varying results including the BBC Head of Variety Light Entertainment and TV, Bill Cotton JR. whose reply was encouraging whereupon the letter from the BBC's Barry Knight quite clearly wrote, that my record, after showing it to Eric Robinson for a possible inclusion in the aptly named programme *Melodies for You* is really not quite the sort of ingredient he is looking for.

One can't win them all, therefore it was especially gratifying when a letter arrived from Yorkshire Television's Jess Yates. His programme, *Stars on Sunday*, was a Sunday night institution on ITV – would I be available for two Shows?

I had no time in answering his letter, Jess Yates, quite impatiently phoned from Leeds: 'I'd really like you to do these shows, Ronnie, they are you!'

The dates were 28 June, with Dame Anna Neagle, Harry Secombe, Eartha Kitt, Los Picaflores and Miss Violet Carson, and 1 August, featuring The Bachelors, Cliff Richard, Patricia Cahill, the Archbishop of York, Dr F.D. Coggan, and The Seven Poole Children.

These two programmes were such a success, that Jess Yates sent a further letter, this time from Capri where he was interviewing Gracie Fields, asking if I would be available for a further six programmes. In his letter he also wrote that 'he was so glad that I liked the way he had been able to present my wonderful talent and that he was looking forward to fixing the new dates'.

Over the next four years I appeared in many more *Stars on Sunday* shows and met many entertainers and dignitaries, such as James Mason, Roy Orbison, Nina, Bobby Bennett, James Peglar, His Eminence Cardinal Heenan, Stephanie Powers, and a very young New Zealander, Kiri Te Kanawa.

Kiri was to be filmed during the morning and I had gone for lunch as my filming schedule was in the afternoon. Back in the dressingroom suddenly Jess Yates came running in:

'Please Ronnie can you help me?'

He begged me to be filmed straight away otherwise all his crew would be standing idle.

'What's the problem Jess? You know, I can't blow on a full stomach, I've just eaten!'

'These bloody amateurs' he shouted, 'why can't this Kiri-cow come tuned up? She's holding up the whole bloody show.'

I was none to pleased, but *The Show goes on* and I whistled 'Sanctuary of the Heart' on a full stomach of Roast Beef and Yorkshire Pudding. Kiri Te Kanawa was already playing 'Dame'.

1971 started on a good note with an article in the *Guernsey Evening Press* reporting that St Martin's had joined the Old Government House Hotel and the Royal Hotel as one of Guernsey's four top grade hotels:

For international singing and whistling star Ronnie Ronalde... the achievement of having raised it to 'top billing' has been as exciting as his own climb to stardom... the largest in the island.

A hotel owned by an entertainer attracted not only holiday makers but also other celebrities. The list of names was endless and if I included each and every one, this book would resemble an encyclopedia of show and sports celebrities: Peter Aliss, Dickie Henderson, Ken Dodd, Bill Waddington, Cyril Fletcher, Meatloaf, Avril Angers, Kenny Baker, Ralph Bates, Charlie Chester, Harry Corbett, Matthew Corbett, Fanny Cradock, Tommy Docherty, Fred Gee, Geoffrey, Harry Gold, Nat Gonella, Terry Hall, Jimmy Henney, Donald Hughes, Gareth Hunt, David Jacobs, Dave King, Richard Loaring, Phillip Madoc, Malcolm McDonald, Middle of the Road, Ken Morris and Joan Savage, Nick Owen, Jack Parnell, Morris Parsons, Mike Reid, Willie Rushton, Brian Sinclair, Joan and Helen Turner, Ken Dodd and many more.

Once Victor Seaforth came for a visit and as we were sitting around the dinner table he started to tell us every detail of his recent operation. Being an artiste, he made it into a performance, giving a colourful account of the surgeon's every move and cut. Suddenly I realised that my wife was no longer sitting next to me. Where had she gone? 'Oh my God, Ron,' cried Steffani, 'she's under the table!' Rosemarie, with her vivid imagination, had visualised every detail of Victor's explicit account of every cut and stitch, so much so that she had fainted and quietly slipped under the dining table.

It was nice for *The Times* to include four pages, all about the Channel Islands, in one of their editions. Writer Robin Mead had interviewed, what he thought were, the five most prominent people of the Channel Islands: Gerald Durrell, author, naturalist and conservationist, Len Matchan, Chairman and Chief Executive of Cope Allman Int., William Davies from Jersey, Raymond Falla and me. Press coverage of this magnitude definitely helped to put a lot of bums into beds.

America was calling again. Leonidoff wanted me for another Easter show, would I be interested? Alas, there was one problem. The ongoing British postal strike. Leonidoff's contract, dated 11 February, did not get through to Guernsey and I needed it to obtain my working permit from the American Embassy. I ended up having to write and sign a letter of acceptance myself and then fly to France to post this self-made contract to New York. Leonidoff in turn managed to inform the American Embassy in London of my dilemma and they permitted me to bring my passport to their offices on my way through London to New York and receive their working visa stamp. This was the most expensive letter I had ever posted. Leonidoff's contract eventually arrived in Guernsey, on 16 March, two weeks after my 'First Night' in New York.

Walking back from *Radio City* to the *Americana* hotel I saw in big letters the words: 'London Fish and Chips'. Wow, that's for me tonight.

'One fish and chips, please.'

'Okay, honey. With ketchup, Thousand Island….?' and she carried on running down a list of different sauces.

'Any vinegar?' I asked. Again she started to recite all varying kinds so I interrupted: 'Malt vinegar?'

'That's one fish and chips with malt vinegar.'

Looking up I noticed an advertisement for Guinness – 'and one Guinness' I added.

The fish and chips arrived fairly quickly but no vinegar. After sitting there with my mouth watering, I asked if she had forgotten about my vinegar?

No, she hadn't forgotten, but the boss had had to go to the storeroom and broach the barrel because I had been the first customer to ask for vinegar.

Halfway through my meal I had to call her again:

'My Guinness?'

'Its in the icebox but if you want it now I'll put some ice cubes in it for you!'

She obviously was not an Irish immigrant.

Rosemarie decided from one day to the next that she would join me in New York and came armed with a shopping list as long as her arm. Walking back from Macy's to *Radio City* we saw in the distance a figure approaching who looked rather familiar. It was a very dear colleague of mine, Frankie Howerd. He had come to New York to see if the British comedian could gain a foothold in America. This proved to be an impossible task as the American sense of humour is very different from the British.

We were chatting away when Rosemarie kept on nudging me. I grew somewhat impatient with her until I realised what she tried to tell me. Frankie Howerd had forgotten to close his flies and was running round the New York streets exhibiting more than British humour.

'Well now, now, er, I wondered where all that draught was coming from! Anyway, hm, old birds never fall out of the nest.'

Meeting Tommy Cooper in New York also had its funny side. Apparently when he saw me from the distance, dressed in my dark blue overcoat, he thought that I must be either his solicitor or his bloody bank manager, ha, ha, ha.

After another record 10-week season at *Radio City Music Hall* I flew back to Guernsey and found that my new penthouse was ready to move into; the only problem we experienced was moving the Bechstein three storeys up into my new lounge. At last everything was in place, I was happy I had somewhere completely private where I could rehearse.

In the middle of July Steffani, for no apparent reason at all, suddenly succumbed to a heart attack. After a few very worrying days and nights, the doctor permitted him to stay at the hotel where we could look after him ourselves on the proviso that he was strictly confined to bed. Thank God, the imminent danger was over.

'Jess Yates here, Ronnie. Would you be available for some more TV concerts on Stars on Sunday? The first one is in two weeks!'

Sure, I would have loved to do it, but I had to think of Steff. Yet perhaps this phone call was just the trigger to bring him back to health? With this in mind I collected Steffani's afternoon tea tray from the waiter and took it to him myself. Talking away about one thing and another I casually mentioned the phone call and that I was going to turn the offer down.

Well, you've never seen anybody get out of bed so fast! In his dressing gown he went straight up to my lounge to the piano and immediately started work on his beloved music and when it came to record the new programmes for Jess Yates in Leeds, Steffani was on top form again.

Mr & Mrs Ronnie Ronalde

Hyman Zahl – my first agent

The Wedding Cake

Len Smith & Norman Newell

David Jacobs

*The boys from Radio Luxembourg,
Chappell & EMI*

Act Thirty-six

THE GOOD OLD DAYS

Dick Hurran, Producer of the Bernard Delfont Organisation wanted to know if I would be interested in a summer season in Blackpool as their Guest Star in a BBC TV show called *The Good Old Days*, produced by Barney Colehan. Sir Bernard Delfont wanted to present the show from *City Variety's*, Leeds at the *Winter Gardens* Blackpool for its first public stage presentation during the 1972 summer season and then onto a season at London's *Victoria Palace* Theatre.

The *City Variety's Music Hall* had been entertaining audiences for well over 200 years and had staged the *Good Old Days* over the past 19 years for its Television presentation.

I remember when our Songsters' act had completed their Monday morning band call and the conductor, because he had a new drummer, decided to have a run through of the *National Anthem*. What he didn't know was, that the music of *God Save the King*, normally played at the end of the show, was the cue to the rats to appear for a feed, eating up all the food strewn over the floor by the audience during the performance. The rats came out in their hundreds, well, the musicians couldn't move fast enough, falling over each other to get out of the pit, I don't think they rehearsed *God Save the King* again.

Now I had to tell my wife that she wouldn't be seeing much of me during the coming summer. So what better way to tell her than to say:

'Darling, you've worked very hard this year, let's all have a holiday!'

So over Christmas we went to Torremolinos with the family and had a bloody awful time.

In Blackpool Steffani booked a house for the summer which would give us more privacy, especially as the season would be 15 weeks long and the children were coming to stay with me during the school holidays. The property also had a garage where I could park my new car, a red 300 SEL Mercedes, which I had recently bought to replace my black Bentley. I was told that, with only 54,000 miles on the clock, the Bentley was a danger on the road. I was so disgusted that I gave the car back to Rolls Royce for a nominal fee of £100. I certainly was not going to sell it to an unwary driver. I'm sure that this change of car and colour came as a relief to the Guernsey police, as my black Bentley had often been mistaken for the Governor's official car, especially when we were both attending the same function. Everybody would be standing to attention, awaiting the arrival of the Island Governor's black Austin and I would arrive in my black Bentley, the tic tac would start: *the Governor's here*! and then the frustrated look on their faces: *Christ it's not him, its Ronnie Ronalde*!

The cast in Blackpool included Tessie O'Shea, Joe Church, Rod Hull and Emu, Bernie Clifton, Rob Murray, Tony Cawley and Wendy Bowman – each one of these artistes a star. Rod Hull, originally from Australia and his Emu, a large puppet bird had everybody in fits with their antics. After the finale of the show Rod used to go forward and have his Emu pick and peck at anybody who was passing him. One day, though, he had a mishap. He pecked on a gentleman's head and as he turned away the hair became entangled in the Emu's beak. He tried to pull away but unfortunately took the gentleman's hairpiece with him. The bald victim, I can assure you, did not join in with the hilarity.

Ben Warris was the chairman. He'd been for 30 years in partnership with Jimmy Jewell as a comedy double act. Wee Georgie Wood wrote in his article in the *Stage* a sentence overheard by him from a man sitting next to him during the show: ...*well he's (Ben Warris) better off, t'other chap's (Jimmy Jewell) running a pickle factory with Hylda Baker...*

Blackpool had always been the Mecca of Showbusiness and in this year of 1972 it provided entertainment for the holidaymakers second to none. Cilla Black was at the *Opera House*, Lovelace Watkins at the *ABC* Theatre with Ted Rogers, Arthur Wolsley, the Clarke Brothers and the Rockin' Berries. Jack Douglas was at the *Grand* Theatre together with Lucille Gaye and John Inman and of course one must not forget the *Tower Circus* with Charlie Carioli, surely one of the most famous resident clowns of Blackpool. Joe Loss and his Band played nightly at the *Stardust Garden*. Frank Carson, George Roper, Duggie Brown, Colin Crompton, Mike Burton and Steve Faye could be seen at the *North Pier* and the Grumbleweeds, Syd Francis, Barbara Law, Alan Fox and Lambert and Ross at the *South Pier*. The show on the *Central Pier* starred Clinton Ford, Ryan and Ronnie and Alec Pleon.

Cilla Black, too, had rented a private house for the summer season where she invited a few of us artistes for a get together. I always remember following her Corniche Rolls Royce along the colourfully lit Blackpool Front.

After having been invited to the Water Rats *'Big Night'* charity gala at the *Jack of Diamonds* Theatre, no summer season would have been the same without the inevitable football match between the stars of the various theatres with the proceeds going to a theatrical charity, this was staged at Blackpool's famous Stanley Park Oval. The stars were lined up, the Blackpool Dolly Birds acted as cheerleaders, the ball was kicked off by Tessie O'Shea ably assisted by Jack Douglas, the game was refereed by Ted Rogers and ref-whistled by Ronnie Ronalde, the commentary was by Ben Warris and the whole event was managed by Joe Loss. We had a ball.

Rosemarie wanted her aunt (her mother had died 10 years earlier) to come from Austria to Blackpool and see me on stage, even though she couldn't understand a word of English. At the end of my performance I really did get a rousing reception, with shouts of 'More' and much whistling from the audience. That really upset Auntie Lilly, because in Austria shouting and whistling at an artiste shows one's disapproval, so she thought that I was getting the bird. Indignantly she stood up and started to shout out in German, waving her arms frantically and nearly giving herself a heart attack. After the show a very subdued aunt came to my dressing room and gave me a wonderful hug. 'Oh Ronnie!' she kept repeating all night 'Oh Ronnie!'

I remembered some years ago at the *Vienna Ice Revue* in Klagenfurt when I started to whistle because I'd recognised two of my British artiste friends performing on ice. How could I ever forget? The people in front of us and even the police turned round to show their disapproval. Different countries, different customs; and the stamping feet in Scandinavia?

Every weekend Rosemarie flew from Guernsey to Blackpool. The children, staying with me, decided to wait up for Mummy one Saturday.

'Well, have you all been good, children?' she greeted our dear little ones.

'Yes Mummy,' they chorused. Only Carolyn had something more to say. 'Mummy?'

'Yes darling?'

'You know Daddy?'

'Yes? What about Daddy?'

'Mummy, he's taking out another girl!'

When I returned from the stage to my dressing room, instead of being met with the usual hug and kiss I was suddenly confronted by a stony-faced woman.

'If you have to take another girl out it would have been kinder not to do it in front of the children!' she hissed.

'But, but, I haven't taken anybody out!'

Right at that moment the dressing room door opened and one of the dancers whose duty it was after each performance to return my straw hat from the stage, entered and, as every night, wore a see-through negligee, barely covering her panties and bra. I hasten to say that this was the norm backstage.

I took one look at my daughter and immediately realised the little game she was playing. Unfortunately my wife did not take it as such.

Then the stagedoor-keeper came with an arm full of autograph books for me to sign so I said:

'Now tell me Jock, how often have I taken a chorus girl out?'

'Hm,' he paused. 'Now let me see', making a very thoughtful face, 'well, no more than five times last week!'

I could have throttled him. How on earth was I going to get out of this one?

I didn't, for a long, long time.

The *Sunday Express* on 13 August 1972 carried the following:

'I'll go to jail rather than pay Yana's tax says Alan... of his former wife, blonde singer Yana... Their two-year marriage was dissolved in 1966... The Inspector of Taxes says he sent the assessments to her agents but got no results. Says Yana, 39, who lives in

Jersey and has been working in cabaret since she and her third husband, hotelier Ronnie Ronalde, separated three months ago: 'As God is my judge I know nothing about this at all.'

This news item was read by my wife and of course all hotel guests in Guernsey as well as me and the rest of Britain. The telephone lines between Blackpool, Guernsey, London and the *Sunday Express* were running hot. We'd had problems before with a fellow who called himself Ronnie Ronald. He owned a hotel in Jersey and people who dined in his restaurant were not discouraged from believing that he was me, with Yana, a singer, I had worked on my *Radio Luxembourg* series. So people asked my wife if she had given it all up (singing) and that they enjoyed her performance at such and such a theatre. Also the way the article was written made my fans and friends and relations believe that my marriage had broken down.

With not much response from the paper's editor I had no alternative but to put the matter into the hands of my London lawyers who, after a year's persistence, received compensation on my behalf and a retraction in the newspaper. Ronnie Ronald had died in 1972 and I worked with Yana again in 1974 on the TV show *This is Your Life* featuring Jimmy Jewell. In 1988 Channel TV had me die this time in one of their news programmes, in 1990 the editor of *Call Boy* magazine, Barry Balmain, wrote an article about Yana as she had passed away and mentioned Ronnie Ronalde as her deceased husband. My children received phone calls of condolences and again the telephone wires were running hot, this time between Auckland and Britain. Mr. Balmain tried his best to put the matter right in the following edition, especially as his magazine was read in New Zealand and Australia as well and in 1995 I died again in the USA *Whistler's News*. I must have the seven lives of a cat.

September and the Blackpool season was drawing to its end when I had a visitor in my dressing room. Jock Jacobsen, Max Bygrave's agent, brought impresario Lionel Abrahams from Australia in to see me. Would I be interested in appearing at the *South Sydney Junior Rugby League Club* in Sydney during October and November? 'You'll enjoy it,' said Jock. 'Max has been there and liked it.'

Within a day of our arrival in Australia, Steffani and Rosemarie had come with me, Lionel Abrahams sent his car and from then on we were taken everywhere. One of the first ports of call of course was the club where I was to appear for the next four weeks. I could only say: 'Wow, what a place!'

Not only were we met at 10 in the morning by doormen all dressed in evening suits but the club had everything; theatre, dancing, gambling and restaurants, bars, swimming pool, squash courts and of course the inevitable poker machines.

Then on to the *Bob Rogers'* TV show where I appeared with Rex Harrison's son, a musician, the Australian tennis champion Yvonne Goolagong, the new Miss South Wales and David Whitfield, whom I knew very well. David had brought a 'friend' to the studio who had a funny habit of tangling her keys on her key-ring. How strange? A few days later I took Rosemarie to Kings Cross where I'd stayed before and what did we see? Quite a number of young ladies walking around and they were all tangling their keys. I should have known.

All during my four weeks in Sydney we were kept busy with the shows at the club but also with TV shows on *Channel 7* where I met Bert Newton, radio and newspaper interviews and record signing sessions at the *Roselande Shopping Centre* where some of the people would not let go of my hands. EMI sold out every one of my records much to the pleasure of the head of the EMI in Sydney, Mr. Burnett, especially as he had invited me for dinner at his home. Rosemarie liked the house very much; the only thing she didn't appreciate was the Burnett pet, a huge, hairy, black tarantula, towering in a corner of the ceiling in the kitchen. We didn't have to worry about spiders when Lionel took us on his *Captain Cook's Floating Restaurant* in Sydney Harbour. Oh no, we only thought about all the sharks in the harbour.

During my engagement with the *SSJRL* Club various supporting artistes had been booked: Jean Michelle, Sylvia Raye, Barry Krause, Carl Barateau, Wendy Wayne, Joan Laurie, Dorothy Neale and Paul Newton. It was very gratifying when somebody in the audience, in the middle of my act, shouted: 'Ronnie, you're the best in the world!'

And another stood up and yelled 'and I second that!'

I was pleased that the president and directors of the club thought so too. Not only did they have the champagne flowing freely after my first night's performance but they also picked up the bill when I tried to give them something back by eating in their restaurant.

Lionel Abrahams had arranged the homeward flight via Hong Kong. Rosemarie wanted to do some shopping and I must admit I wanted to see the place too. There was only one snag: we had to have cholera injections. Just go to a chemist, we were told, buy the stuff, take it to a doctor and, hey presto, he'll shoot it up your arm. That was easier said than done, I had to work with my arm, I had to whistle. Hong Kong won the argument and I worked with a painful arm.

Hong Kong was fantastic and we did find some time amongst the shopping for some sight seeing too. I'll never forget the trip up in the cable car to the Peak. The moment the cabin pulled away from the station and started to climb up this very steep mountainside, Rosemarie realised with horror that she had to come down the same way.

'I can't do it, I can't do it, Ronnie,' she started before we were even halfway up the mountain.

'Hang on,' I said, 'we'll see what's up there – we can't just jump off!'

At last we arrived on the top of the Peak and were overwhelmed with the vista over Hong Kong. We sat in one of the cafes surrounded by greenery, with hundreds of multicoloured birds all flying in and out of the bushes. I felt quite at home and enjoyed my chat with the birds, although I saw them sometimes shaking their heads as if to say:

'I can't quite understand you. What are you saying?'

We came down the Peak by Taxi.

We had one more stop before arriving in London, Istanbul where Steff had to purchase 3 kilos of Turkish Delight. His sweet tooth could not miss out on this opportunity.

Before I knew it, the New Year had arrived and with it another *Black and White Minstrel* TV show, and a summer season at *Radio City* in New York. So once again it was time to pack my suitcase, but not before I had played host to a *National Enquirer* team who came from Florida to Guernsey to write a lengthy article about me for their magazine. They were fascinated by the formation of my teeth and took a large photo of them, which they printed beside the article.

It was gratifying to hear from visitors who came all the way from Canada to see my performance at *Radio City* that my records were often played on the Canadian Radio *Calling Britain* programme and of course many questions were asked how to whistle and what about the pea-less one?

In 1976 Canadian Ron Foxcroft was refereeing the Olympic Basketball Finale when his whistle failed because the pea jammed.

Eight years later, in front of some basket ball players in South America it happened again, forcing Foxcroft and his partner Joe Forte to make a hasty exit.

They spend the next three years trying to perfect the pea-less whistle and in doing so re-invented that tiny instrument that sports fans take for granted.

So why did a whistle need a pea?

The reason was to give it the trill that makes the sound more piercing. The trouble with the pea – actually a small cork sphere – is that it wears out and in cold weather gets wet and freezes up. Foxcroft lived in Canada, so his search for the perfect whistle started in 1984 when he enlisted the help of an engineer/inventor by the name of Chuck Shepherd.

They made 14 prototypes costing US$50,000 and finally made the perfect referee's whistle as used today.

Terry Thomas told me he experienced a similar problem on a tram in Spain when the pea blew out of the tram-conductor's whistle.

The conductor stopped the tram at the corner chandlery shop but could only get split peas, so he put one in and after blowing his whistle only half the tram moved off.

Blackpool residents, 1972

That's the way to travel... Tessie O'Shea, Ben Warris, Rod Hull & Emu

That's the modern way

Act Thirty-seven

THE ISLE OF MAN

As a Silver Songster in 1939 I had written in my diary that 'I could live here', so after my return from America Rosemarie and I flew to the Isle of Man. She was not very happy with Guernsey – having to watch a huge house being built within 10 metres from where our plans had been turned down.

We had a wonderful week at the 'Castle Mona Hotel' and left the island loaded with brochures of different houses for sale. We also found a lot out about King Williams College and Lady Buchan School if we were to make a move.

Before Michael Aspel, the 1990s host of *This Is Your Life*, Eamon Andrews, presented the 'red book' for many years on the British TV screens, but before him Wilfred Pickles sprang the surprise of a live interview on his unsuspecting victims. I was one of the few who declined Wilfred Pickles' challenge, as at that time I would have found it very embarrassing to have my private life paraded in so many homes. On stage I had always tried to portray myself as a happy fellow, when privately the scene was quite the opposite. My mother had died, my brother Alf had been killed, my father's second wife was robbing us left, right and centre, Father himself could become quite argumentative when he'd had one too many, my uncle knew all about life in prison, one of my cousins was quite familiar with the famous education Borstal provided and one of my aunts (whom I later discovered was not in fact my aunt) had tasted life behind bars for a period. I would have shrunk on stage with embarrassment if that information had been made common knowledge during the 1940s. In the 1990s, however, the more sordid or notorious your life has been or is, the more accolades you seem to acquire, irrespective of your talent as an artiste.

Naturally the television producers were not happy with anyone who upset their schedule, as they quickly had to find another programme to slot into the live network system and say sorry to the huge disappointed audience. Later, this sometimes very costly dilemma was solved by filming the shows some time before the actual date of transmission. Interviews started to be arranged and accepting them became quite an honour, more like receiving a television knighthood. In hindsight, I realise that I'd possibly made the wrong decision in upsetting the producers and studios, as I was never asked again to play the surprised, unsuspecting, innocent victim of *This is Your Life* although Thames Television did ask Steffani and myself to come to London on 9 January 1974 and be surprise guests on *This is Your Life* featuring Jimmy Jewel and was hosted by Eamon Andrews. Both of us agreed to go and honour a fine comedian I had often had the pleasure of working with and, of course, Jimmy's lifelong partner Ben Warris. I must say a good time was had by all. The programme was scheduled to be screened towards the end of the month of April.

Over Easter of 1974 our three children departed on a holiday to the Eisners in New York and Rosemarie and I were in the Isle of Man to buy a house and finalise the arrangements for the children's education. All day long my mind and thoughts were going back to Guernsey. In the evening Vera phoned to tell us that Steff had been rushed to hospital with a heart attack and had gone into a deep coma. He never recovered.

How is one supposed to feel when the man who has been your Boss, partner, friend, tutor, manager, a brilliant musician and pianist, your second self for nearly all your life has suddenly left you? I wasn't ashamed of my tears.

Steffani had died on 22 April 1974, aged 70.

National newspapers wrote lengthy tributes, as did the theatre world's *Who's Who, The Stage, The New Musical Express* and many local newspapers, including the *Beccles and Bungay Journal*, his hometown paper.

Thames Television were very worried in case I would stop the screening of the prerecorded Jimmy Jewell *This is Your Life* programme which was due to be aired a couple of days after Steffani's funeral. I had no objection but, sitting in my lounge in Guernsey, watching him on screen, gave me a strange and eerie feeling. It appeared that he was looking straight at me and was saying:

'I'll never leave you Ron, I'll always watch over you'.

Then Jess Yates wanted me to appear on a further series of his Sunday TV programmes, to be filmed in Leeds during June and August. Suddenly I realised there was nobody to rehearse with me. I had a band playing nightly in my hotel - maybe I could start rehearsing with them? It's amazing what one can do if one has to, although the feel and expertise of music which Steffani had towards every note he played in relation to my work I was never to meet again.

There was a little ray of sunshine when a phone call came from the owners of the house I had made a bid for in the Isle of Man, they accepted my offer. I was pleased with this turn of events as all three children were ready to start boarding in their new Colleges in the Isle of Man during September. In October I began rehearsals in Coventry for the *The Good Old Days* show at the *Coventry Theatre* with Max Wall, Jean Bayless, Audrey Jeans, Joe Church, Gil Dova, Regina Baranton, Ken Wilson and Leonard Sachs as chairman and opened on Friday, 4 October. The next morning the first review, in the *Coventry Evening Telegraph*, praised the show as *fun and lavish* and said that

...The unbelievable whistling of Ronnie Ronalde makes you wonder whether the birds go to him for lessons...

An hour before the opening of the show, Rosemarie received a phone call. My father had been rushed to hospital and operated on. She didn't tell me, the show had to go on. Why worry me? I couldn't do anything, she thought.

On 12 October at 10pm, while I was on stage, my father, aged 81, died; Rosemarie told me the next morning.

Over the war years Coventry had its share of bombings which unfortunately was brought to the fore again one evening when the IRA exploded a bomb in the middle of the city, causing tremendous havoc. We all heard and felt the destructive explosion, the theatre had to be vacated and after an hour's interval the cast and the audience were permitted to re-enter the theatre and continue with the show.

The *Coventry Theatre* had a busy schedule. Not only did they host our show during the week, but on Sundays different one night performers, groups or bands had been booked to appear. On Sunday 20th Slim Whitman and his group were the entertainers and unbeknown to us artistes all our dressing rooms were opened and used by them. When I arrived on Monday afternoon to prepare for my evening show I realised that someone in my dressing room had taken a very treasured gift presented to me by Rosemarie's father. The police were called and took a description of the item. It was an Austrian Maria Theresa silver taler (coin), sliced through in half with a magnifying glass emerging between the two halves. The taler, on a silver chain, never surfaced again.

The novelist Heller Toren, estranged wife of Jess Yates and mother of Paula had written from Majorca, asking if I could give her some tips, as she was interested in moving to Guernsey. I knew that Jess and his wife were living apart as I had met Jess and daughter Paula at Manchester Airport where he was seeing her off for a holiday with her mother in Majorca. As we stood talking, an announcement came over the airport tannoy:

would Mr. Jess Yates please come to the information desk to take a phone call?

He didn't seem to take any notice so when the announcement was repeated I urged him to answer – it could be something important.

'Oh no,' he said and with a sideways look explained that he always had the information desk call him at regular intervals to let the waiting travellers know that he was in the airport and it also allowed him to cut a conversation short if he found himself caught up with someone he didn't want to talk to. Presumably I didn't fall into this category!

Jess was in a spot of bother at that time. In *Stars on Sunday* he always portrayed himself as a 'holier-than-thou' producer, earning himself the nickname of 'The Bishop'. He would scrutinise every performer on the show - they had to be clean living and free of scandal. Alas, it turned out that 'The Bishop' himself had been found guilty of the sin of being human. He was ousted from Yorkshire Television after his affair with busty actress Anita Kay, 33 years his junior. To put it bluntly, he was out of a job and had returned to his native Wales, outside Llandudno.

Consequently I found it very endearing to read the last paragraph of Heller Toren's reply.

'I too have great regard for Jess,' she wrote. *'It's my belief we'll always be friends even though living together wasn't anyone's idea of happiness we just weren't temperamentally suited. I've never met such a talented producer or such a dedicated*

man to his work. I'm hoping his friend will keep her mouth shut these next few months and allow him to get back to work in peace if YTV (Yorkshire Television) will open the gates again!'

Sadly, for Jess Yates, they never did, dear old Jess, he had taken an almighty drop.

But it didn't take him long to re-establish himself as an impresario and organist at the 2000-seat *Astra Theatre* in Llandudno: *Jess Yates and his Friends* played every Sunday to full houses during the summer season. Jess was able to attract notable guest acts: Dai Francis, Don Estelle, Millican and Nesbitt, Cerys Hughes Taylor, Glynn Poole and his Sisters and the 70 strong full-throated Welsh male voice choir under the baton of Glynn Hughes.

After appearing for Jess at the *Southport Floral Hall* during the hot and sticky summer of 1976 Jess booked me for three different Sundays at the *Astra Theatre* in Llandudno. On the first occasion Rosemarie and I flew to Southampton and drove with a hired car to Llandudno which Rosemarie swore she'll never do again. During the drive I managed to undress myself more and more and ended up wearing only my underpants. Rosemarie could not quite do that, and when she eventually got out of the car the back of her skirt was drenched. The show went splendidly and that evening I was introduced to Anita Kay. She was everything they said she was - a blonde Jane Russell.

My Guernsey lawyer wrote a letter on my behalf to the Guernsey Housing Authority, seeking permission to buy a local market house where I could live with my wife and three Guernsey-born children. I was seriously starting to think of selling my hotel. I waited a long time to receive an answer. The first three lines of their reply were an apology for the delay in answering my letter and the next three lines, which constituted the rest of the letter, went as follows:

'If your hotel is inscribed on the Housing Control Register, i.e. is open market, then you will not be permitted to occupy a local market dwelling on ceasing to occupy the hotel.'

And that was that. Lump it or leave it. It really was like a chicken and egg situation. I just could not believe it.

In the midst of all this upheaval I received a letter from Cyril Berlin, thanking me for some comments I had put in a note to him after reading an article in the newspaper.

'There is nobody,' Cyril wrote, *'with whom I have been associated in this business who I regard more highly than your good self... You say that you were lucky in having me as your agent and this I find a coincidence as I have always told others that I was lucky as an agent, so soon after my return from the Army, to have found a potential star like Ronnie Ronalde, and it was my good fortune to recognise at the time the sheer talent and ability was there to be encouraged. The fact that you were always a credit to the profession in the way you carried the success, and the fact that we became such sincere friends, made the exercise so worthwhile.'*

Working in the garden of the hotel I was suddenly doubled up with an excruciating stomach pain. I opened my trousers and, with one hand holding them, pulled myself up the fire-escape stairs leading to my penthouse. There I collapsed into a chair. After a while the severe cutting sensation had subsided but a burning soreness all over my stomach remained. About half an hour after this dramatic and painful event the phone rang:

'This is King William's College in the Isle of Man. We're sorry to have to advise you, but your son Ronnie has just undergone an emergency operation on his appendix. He is out of the operating theatre at Nobles Hospital and doing fine.' I was absolutely astounded. I must have felt the surgeon's knife at the very minute it was cutting into my son's body so many miles away.

On a lighter note, the *Sunday Express* of 26 October 1979 told how *A silent canary finds its voice after phone call.* Apparently, a Mr. Gerard Kingston had bought a yellow canary which he called Sweety-pie and he waited expectantly for the bird's first song. *And he waited and waited. Days, weeks and months slipped silently by. Both he, his wife and friends whistled notes of encouragement, but the songbird that could not sing did not even tilt its head to listen. Obviously it needed singing lessons. But from whom? Mr. Kingston said: 'I was getting desperate. I have had canaries before – I have bred them too – but I have never come across one that could not sing.' Then he suddenly thought of the man who filled a monastery garden with bird song – entertainer turned hotelier Ronnie Ronalde. Mr. Kingston traced him to his hotel in Guernsey in the Channel Islands. 'Please give my canary a singing lesson,' he pleaded.*

Mr. Ronalde told me: 'I was taken aback but agreed to try to help. Put the canary on the phone I said. As I whistled Mr. Kingston told me the canary, in its cage beside the telephone, was tilting its head.

The lesson lasted about 5 minutes. Then to continue the lesson I sent Mr. Kingston my record of 'In a Monastery Garden' on which I do bird impersonations. It was a weird experience whistling down a phone to a canary. I was so intrigued I was prepared to fly over to give Sweetypie some tuition.'

Back to Mr. Kingston at his home in Fulbeck Road, Scunthorpe, South Humberside. 'I played and re-played the record which I am keeping as a souvenir, to my canary. To my delight Sweetypie listened with obvious interest. Then came the day he gave out his first whistle. Now I can't stop him. He has turned into a lovely little songbird. I think I will call him Tweetypie from now on. Without Mr. Ronalde I am certain I would still have a canary without a whistle.

A 10-foot satellite dish had been put into position outside the Ebenezer Methodist Church on Guernsey. A special *Sunday Worship* programme, followed by *Spotlight Southwest* and *Swapshop*, were going to be filmed and beamed, via a satellite which was positioned above the equator, to Goonhilly in Cornwall, the GPO tower, the BBC in Plymouth and, within microseconds, onto television sets in homes throughout Great Britain. Further to these live transmissions, the BBC team expressed the wish to record and interview my hotel and me for their *Pebble Mill at One* programme presented by Don McLeod. It was fantastic how an army of technicians with lights, cables, microphones and everything one could possibly think of moved into the hotel to tape half an hour's interview for TV. It was not at all like that when the crew from *Channel Television*, based in Jersey, came to my hotel to film interviews; there were usually only two of them – one carrying the video camera, which included the microphone and the other was the interviewer.

I had been invited by Tyne Tees Television to take part in two *Friday Live* programmes, both of them were filmed in Newcastle. Talk about adulation!

...Ronnie unable to walk through Newcastle... police thought he was a street hawker and asked him to move on...

One of the programmes, was all about spiritualism, the sixth sense, seeing and feeling beyond you and rebirth of souls. Rula Lenska was in the show with Denis Waterman keeping an eye on her. As well as taking part in the discussions, I was also asked to perform 'In a Monastery Garden'.

After the show we were all invited to a supper that had been laid on in one of the private rooms at the Royal Station Hotel. While I was talking to Rula Lenska a gentleman came up to me. He had been one of the invited guests in the audience as he had claimed to have some supernatural powers.

'I hope you don't mind me telling you,' he started, 'but as you stood on the stage, whistling, I saw a very strong aura above your head.'

We carried on talking and when he took my hands – many people over the years had shown interest in my hands as they are so prominent when I perform – he remarked:

'You have healing hands! You should use them!'

Boarding the train from Newcastle to London I recalled 'Hutch' travelling with me after he said his goodbyes to some beautiful blondes who showered him with goodies including a bottle of some special alcoholic mixture which we drunk until empty.

On arrival at Kings Cross, Hutch opened the carriage window and shouted:

Porter! Taxi! as he was waving a Pound note.

Hutch was the first away in a Taxi, he did not have to queue.

Once we worked together at *Shepherds Bush Empire* and as he was doing his 'Begin the Begin' someone in the audience shouted what sounded like a derogative remark. Hutch stopped playing the piano and said:

'I beg your pardon? and leaving his piano walked forward to the stage footlights calling to the person to:

'Speak up, I can't hear you?'

The silence was deathly. I gave Hutch top marks for that bit of stagecraft.

Steffani

Hutch

We'll give 'em Hylton...

Victor Seaforth & Billy Moore

THAT'S NOTHING – YOU SHOULD
HEAR HIM IMITATE RONNIE RONALDE!

Act Thirty-eight

INTO A NEW FUTURE

The hotel was working well, open all the year round which I had reluctantly agreed to after the Guernsey Tourism Authorities had asked me time and time again, with many different functions taking place; at some, theatrical artistes from Britain were invited to be guests of honour, other dinners were presided over by dignitaries from our local community. Gareth Hunt (who not only advertised coffee on television, but also drank gallons of it), David Jacobs came in support of a fund-raising ball to aid Oxfam and Phillip Madoc and I enjoyed ourselves among the many   Ladies of Variety at a special Guernsey Variety Club Tent 55 Charity celebration luncheon because the right for Ladies of Variety to become Barkers had been passed during the Variety Club Convention in New York on 24 May 1982.

It was also the year that my daughter Carolyn announced her engagement. She had met her husband-to-be, Lloyd, at the Blackpool Catering College and on 5 January they were married. She looked so beautiful, my little girl, walking on my arm up the aisle, and I was going to give her away.

After the couple was pronounced man and wife and walked to the vestry to sign the register I stayed behind in front of the altar and with a prearranged signal to the organist turned to the wedding congregation and started to whistle Gounod's 'Ave Maria'. I was told there was not a dry eye in the church.

Radio Guernsey, in conjunction with the BBC started to transmit their own programmes on 16 March from their very own St. Peter Port studios and we were all asked to re-tune our sets. Guernsey and Jersey were to be the first stations to be opened outside the UK by the British corporation in a self-governing community and was officially opened by the Bailiff, Sir John Loveridge as well as George Howard, chairman of the board of governors of the BBC.

Then I heard from Mary Charles from Newport in South Wales that her cousin, Raymond Chilcot, brother of Bernard – both were at one time Silver Songsters – had fallen ill with multiple sclerosis, could I write him a letter.

Certainly, and at the same time invited Raymond to come to Guernsey for a little break and I was so pleased when my offer was accepted. When he arrived it was a shock to see him handicapped but he was as bright as ever, just as he was as a boy, getting up to all sorts of tricks, and we managed to have quite a few laughs. Although I felt very sad when he left I was glad that I had helped to bring a little sunshine into his days.

Des Yarr, a former Silver Songster, had also stayed in contact and was organising a reunion of as many Songsters as he possibly could find for an evening at the *Sports Club* in Barry, Wales and of course he would have liked me to come as well.

Life can sometimes be so cruel. One could have hit me with a sledgehammer when, one evening over dinner, my wife broke the news to me that she had to go into hospital the next day for an operation.

'What on earth for?' I asked, somewhat perplexed.

The doctor had confirmed her fears that she had a lump in her breast, a rather large one, she confessed quietly. Apparently she had known for some time that something was not right but foolishly hadn't gone to the doctor, partly because she was afraid as her Mother had died of breast cancer, but also not to upset our daughter's wedding arrangements. So when she did pluck up courage to see him, he booked the operation for the very next day.

I sat there, dumbfounded. The woman of my life, who had worked so hard in the hotel and had been at my side for 22 years, was in trouble. What on earth was I going to do about it? After the initial devastating shock my brain started slowly to work again. The name of John Pollock leapt into my mind. He was the gentleman I had met at the Tyne Tees TV studios, who told me that I had healing hands.

'I know what I'll do, we'll go to bed and I'll put my hand on her breast!' My whole body started to burn as I tried to concentrate and gradually I felt a stream of fire going through my hand and into her body. I managed to keep this intense pressure up well into the night, until, exhausted, I fell asleep. The next day I took Rosemarie to the hospital and after the surgeon removed the tumour, thank God, it proved to be nonmalignant.

Those hours, minutes, seconds of waiting to hear the result, with every nerve in my body stretched to breaking point, were the most horrifying I have ever lived through.

The surgeon's scalpel had performed a work of art – you can't see the scar. Two years later Rosemarie again seemed to detect a small lump in her other breast. This time she owned up very quickly and once more I tried to put my prayer into my hands and when she went to the doctor he could not find anything. Since then she has been very conscious of self-examination and keeps up regularly with the screening test.

'*I wonder where Ronnie Ronalde is now?*' remarked disc jockey Stuart Hall playing my 'Monastery Garden' over the BBC Radio 2, a few weeks later he called out again:

'*Ronnie, where are you?*' So somebody in the BBC was starting to miss me?

Alex Lindsay followed suit by writing an article in the *Express* titled:

Whatever happened to…? and went on to say that *In the Fifties Ronnie Ronalde whistled his way into millions of homes, bringing the sound of summer to the mills of*

Halifax and the backstreets of Bermondsey. No edition of 'Housewife's Choice' seemed complete without his rendering of 'In a Monastery Garden'.

It had also come to my notice that *Reader's Digest* was offering their subscribers a set of 128 songs on LPs or cassettes and my 'Birdsong at Eventide' was included, my first record with Decca who told me it would never get anywhere.

My mind was turning again to Australia and New Zealand. There wasn't much more I could do around the hotel. We had led the way over the years beginning with the introduction of contracts for staff, building the swimming pool, tennis court, rooms with bath (when we were told that if all the guests bath and pull the chain at the same time we would flood St Peter Port) and ended with an award given to us by the AA.:

The AA have chosen Ronnie Ronalde's St Martin's as the first Guernsey Hotel to receive the 'H' Award for Hospitality.

As usual, if I think long enough about something, it happens. Impresario Roy Watterson JP from Sydney, was in Wales, trying to book some star attractions to appear in his shows back in Australia and he wanted to engage me. He concluded his letter by saying:

'I had the privilege of working with you years ago when I was one of Billy West's Harmony Boys'.

I invited him to come over to Guernsey so that we could talk more about the subject with the result that Roy would travel back to Australia and start booking different venues for a tour.

In the meantime the hotel went on in the normal busy way and it was always good to see familiar faces booked in as hotel guests. One of them was Harold Snoad, the BBC TV producer with his family (*Keeping up Appearances* with Patricia Routledge) but when he stayed with us he had another series in mind called *Barber*. For this he contracted me to whistle the famous melody from the *Barber of Seville* as the theme song for the series.

Another visitor to our hotel was Nick Owen – presenter of the *Morning Breakfast TV* show with Anne Diamond – with his young family which resulted in my being invited a few times onto his programme, waking Britain to another new day with my dawn chorus of birdsong.

On one of those early morning programmes I met Christopher Timothy, the actor who portrayed Dr. James Herriot in the long-running TV series *All Creatures Great and Small*. Some weeks previously the German Sheepdog Breeders Association at a dinner in my hotel had a guest speaker, Brian Sinclair, the real Tristan Farnon, brother of the vet and author Donald Sinclair who had written the original books under the pen-name of James Herriot. One of these books had been given to me as a present by one of Lloyd's relations as I was an ardent watcher of the TV series. Naturally I asked Brian Sinclair to sign this book for me. When he realised that I was Ronnie Ronalde, he asked me for *my* autograph –

'It's an honour to meet you, Sir,' he said.

I felt very humble to be held in such high esteem.

Our first

Act Thirty-nine

JOURNEY TO AOTEAROA

Cyril had arranged for me to take part in a *Thames Television* programme called *Looks Familiar,* prior to my tour to New Zealand, chaired by Denis Norden and also featuring Ivy Benson, George Meaton and Dickie Henderson. The programme was fun to do but sadly the last time I saw Dickie Henderson.

Rosemarie and I both loved New Zealand and on our return to Guernsey started quietly the emigration procedure with New Zealand House and of course indirectly put the Hotel up for sale. It was therefore somewhat ironic when the Guernsey tourist offices compiled a hotels brochure and to add credibility asked me to write an article to why I came to Guernsey and together with my photo must have appeared in countless Travel Agencies all over Britain and Europe for that year.

Easter 1985 I had departed again for my tour with Roy Watterson to Australia.

This trip proved to be very hectic. In Sydney Roy had already arranged for many TV, radio and press interviews to advertise his shows, not giving me much time to acclimatise nor, indeed, to rehearse. Our first show was at *City Hall* Brisbane with James Pegler, The Barrinos and Roy Watterson himself took part with Jack Thorpe. After the next show at Sydney's *Town Hall* with Horrie Dargie and The Rhythmaires and organist David Parsons we immediately boarded the plane for Melbourne where we played at the *Dallas Brooks Hall* the following day. In Melbourne I had the chance of meeting up again with a dear friend and fellow-whistler, Jim Campion. My last concert was at the *Town Hall* in Adelaide.

On the Spot writer Malcolm Andrews summed up a very successful tour with:

...Ronnie's on a Whistle Stop Tour... Whistling is an interesting art form. Most of us

can whistle the odd tune... Greensleeves... Colonel Bogey... We are the World...
We may not be as tuneful... or as piercing... We don't take the Seven Dwarfs to heart
and whistle while we work... Ronnie Ronalde... whistling so well that critics have dubbed
him the world's greatest whistler... and when you realise that his concert this week at
the Sydney Town Hall and similar performances interstate sold out before his arrival
yesterday who would argue?...

The article was accompanied by a picture of me under an umbrella, titled: – *whistling*
in the rain –

Yes, it does rain sometimes in Australia and in New Zealand too, buckets of it.

When I arrived back in Guernsey two letters were lying on my desk awaiting an
immediate reply. Both were from the States of Guernsey Housing Authority. The first
informed me that the States of Guernsey had agreed to the Housing Authority's
recommendation that my hotel could be added to Part B of the Open Market Housing
Register, Signed Elizabeth Lincoln MBE President and the second letter said that if the
form wasn't completed and returned by 24 July, the authority wouldn't be able to add
my hotel to the register. Signed E. Barbe Administrator.

What a welcome home!

If these two letters meant what I thought they meant, I was in deep trouble. My hotel,
unbeknown to me, had been *Local Market*. I had been incorrectly advised and could
have bought a local market house all along but at the same time if I wanted to sell my
hotel it would have had to be at local market value as well. This was indeed quite
a worrying situation financially.

On 16 July I filled in the registration form to have the hotel included on the Open
Market Housing Register; the inscription was confirmed on 6 August 1985 and in the
accompanying letter it stated:

I am directed to draw your attention to the provisions of Section 38 of the Housing
Law 1982 concerning your occupation of any other dwelling on the island. Under this
section of the law you lose the benefit of any residential qualification which you hold.
The effect is that you are not entitled to occupy any other dwelling in Guernsey save one
inscribed in the Housing Register, unless the Authority is prepared under Section 38(7)
to grant you permission in writing to do so.

The situation most certainly had been clarified – it was time for me to go, after 27
years, a marriage and three Guernsey born children, I was not going to test the last
sentence of the letter.

I was soon proven right to be cautious when son-in-law Lloyd was offered a position
with a Computer company. Within hours of his decision having become public knowledge
a phone call came from the States of Guernsey Housing Authority, advising us that
Lloyd, daughter Carolyn and Samuel, our first grandson, no longer had the right to live
with me in their apartment in the hotel, the only home my daughter had ever known.
They were given a month to get out, this naturally left them bitter especially as Lloyd
had given so much service to so many islanders in the hotel.

I'll always remember when he became a little flustered. He happened to answer
a telephone call from one of the hotel rooms.

'Could we have a pot of tea for two, please?'

'Certainly, Sir,' Lloyd replied, standing motionless. When he eventually managed to
put down the receiver, he shouted:

'I know this voice, I know this voice! Who's in that room?'

He was quite right, the voice he'd heard over the phone was known to millions of cricket fans in Britain and, no doubt, all over the world – it belonged to Sir John Arlott.

The hotel once again was fully booked with salespeople from all over Britain and the continent to exhibit their food lines for the local buyers and referred to by the staff with names according to their sales line; Mr. Icecream or Mrs. O/J (Orange Juice).

So when my wife received a phone call if we could accommodate meatloaf? she replied: 'Well, the exhibition is in full swing, but I'm sure we can find a corner'.

She wrote a memo to the reception staff that a 'meatloaf' wants to come and stay at the hotel.

My daughter Christina, after reading the note, asked her mother: 'What do you mean, Mum? m.e.a.t.l.o.a.f?'

Christina had heard that singer Meatloaf with his group was coming to Guernsey for a concert and had immediately realised that her mother had got hold of the wrong end of the stick. My dear wife had thought it was a salesman for meatloaf, as in food!

One could not have wished for a nicer group of people. One of our teenage hotel guests, who went to the concert (incidentally a false bomb alert interrupted their performance), came back thrilled, saying that she had managed to get very close to him, only to be informed by one of our receptionists that Mr. Ronalde personally pressed Meatloaf's trousers and surely nobody can get closer to a man than through his trousers! Christina still has a framed photograph, showing her together with Meatloaf.

Ralph Bates too had spent a few days with us during his filming of a car commercial and Deputy Show Business Editor of the *Daily Mirror* Clifford Davies, onetime 'TV's Mr. Nasty' honoured us with his '*Magic of the Mind*' routine in our ballroom. I also played host to the leader of the band 'Middle of the Road' and Harry Corbett's son with his puppet 'Sooty'.

Cyril Fletcher, the famous odd-ode comedian, who with his wife Betty Astell had come to live in Guernsey, asked me if he could use a corner of my land to construct a garden from scratch and have every step filmed by *Channel Television*. Michael Lucas, Head of Programmes CTV25 confirmed the arrangements and Director Alastair Layzell had me introduce the TV series and my interpretation of birdcalls was used to enhance the background music.

I never saw the finished project but hope that the *Guernsey Lily*, nerine sarniensis, Guernsey's national flower was incorporated into the garden as I had always been very fond of the flower and the rather romantic legend of its first appearance on the island that lay behind it:

When the fairy king won the heart of the beautiful Michele DeGaris and persuaded her to go away with him to his faraway kingdom she thought of her family and how they would be grieving for her. She asked her elfin lover if she could leave a small token by which she would be remembered by. The fairy king gave Michele a bulb which she planted in the sands of Vazon Bay before she embarked on the journey to her new home. Later, when her distraught mother came looking for her she did not find her daughter but this bulb which had by now burst into a tall, beautiful flower with scarlet blossoms sprinkled with fairy gold.

The first listing of the Narcissus Japonica appeared as far as I know in 1664 in John Evelyn's Gardeners' Chronicle.

Very often through the years pieces of my music, whistling or indeed yodelling, were used for different projects. I received a letter from Caryl Wright, production researcher for Thames Television, asking my permission to use a piece of film of me shot way back in 1975 during an interview with James Hogg for the *Nationwide* TV programme. The letter stated that I gave *'a wonderful example of yodelling which is what I would like to use. Our programme is for schools and aimed at 5-7 year olds, and shows the different ways the voice can be used musically . . .'*

A well-known Guernsey personality had left for ever. Sydney James, the man who had brought Variety Theatre to Guernsey, founder member of the Guernsey Variety Club, the man who had originally brought me to Guernsey for a concert in 1958, had died on 23 April. He had been ill for quite some time but nevertheless it was sad to see a friend depart. His widow, Mary, phoned me with a special request made by Sydney before he passed away: would I whistle 'Monastery Garden' at his funeral service?, a song he and I had often whistled together over the years in his shows. What could I say but yes. As I stood there in St Peter's Church in front of the casket, and reached the Kyrie eleison which I translate with a cacophony of many birdcalls, suddenly from nowhere a bird flew into the church. A robin sat on the coffin and tilting its little head, appeared to be listening and when I had finished it sort of nodded, chirped and flew away again, through the open church window, towards the sky.

Agent Ken Earle had a surprise 80th birthday gathering arranged for Cyril Berlin at the *Wellington Club* London. Ken had invited only a handful of guests as he wanted every person to have a special meaning for Cyril on this auspicious occasion. They were the Head of London's *Palladium* Louis Benjamin, New Musical Express Maurice Kaufman, Agents Billy Marsh, Nat Berlin, Sydney Grace, Producers Robert Luff (Black and White Minstrel Show) and Dickie Hurran, George Graham, Mike Wall, Des O'Connor, Roy Castle, Alan Sinclair, Cyril's sons Marc and Simon and me as Cyril's first star. We all had a wonderful time recalling anecdotes of different artists we had worked with. Roy Castle told a story about Jimmy James.

One night Jimmy's stooge had not turned up for the show so he asked his nephew, who happened to be visiting him backstage, to help him out. He wouldn't have to say anything, just lie there, kind of dead. After some persuasion the terrified nephew took up his position, the tabs opened and Jimmy soon had the audience in uproar when Jimmy's nephew playing the 'dead man' couldn't hold himself any longer and started to shake with laughter. Of course Jimmy encouraged it and so had the audience laugh even more until the 'undertakers' arrived on the scene to carry the 'dead man' off. As they lifted him all his loose change fell with a clatter out of his trouser pockets onto the stage. A mighty roar went up in the audience finishing up with Jimmy James on his knees, picking up all the cash. BLACKOUT PLEASE!

Once more I was asked to help the Guernsey Tourism Committee with their 1986 brochure *Guernsey Holiday* News promotion: *'Tune in to the Charm. Ronnie Ronalde's home is an Aladdin's Cave. It is an artist's dream, a collector's paradise, and the champion of anyone who thrives on the joys of memorabilia...* ' It was that little word *'home'* they called my abode that had taken on such a hollow meaning.

Life had to go on as normal so I was doubly pleased when my good friend Charlie Chester responded to a long-standing invitation of mine and came for a week's visit.

And after an ardent fan's visit, Terence Cheese, who has many of my original records all in mint condition, another surprise, Mike Craig, producer of *BBC North West Light Entertainment*, also spent a few days with us and during that time taped an interview with me for his radio series *It's a Funny Business*, which was transmitted on *BBC Radio 2* and proved such a success that it was repeated again in *Pick of the Week*.

All these activities and friends' visits proved to be very therapeutic at this anxious time.

Yes, yes, yes, going, going gone!

The Hotel was sold. Rosemarie and I had come through it together, still loving each other. Unfortunately the New Zealand Emigration Office was not ready with our entry visas, so during August all the family and our furniture trucks moved to the Isle of Man house.

The Sunday *Highway TV* series, which was to be filmed with Sir Harry Secombe during October in Guernsey wanted me in it. The recording of 'Plaisier d'Amour' was done during September at the *Wembley CTS Studios* in London so Rosemarie and I returned to Guernsey for a couple of days for the filming at the *Pierre Park Hotel*. I made a mistake. We should not have stayed in 'our' hotel.

There was another programme on TV which used my whistling, Dennis Potter's *The Singing Detective* showed an actor miming to my 'Birdsong at Eventide', which was included on the cassette and CD of the programme's music.

During our wait in the Isle of Man to receive our entry visas to New Zealand Roy Watterson had been in contact with me again and asked if I would tour Australia and New Zealand during February and March 1988 so Rosemarie and I set off together. The tour started at the Sydney *Town Hall* where I was to meet a very long-standing fan of mine, Virginia de Cruz. During the show Television were whizzing around, filming my dressing room and part of my act on stage. I also met Mary Schneider, Australia's Queen of Yodelling, an encounter that was arranged by Paul Hazell, who had interviewed me for one of his radio country music programmes earlier that week.

Walking along Circular Quay towards the ferry boats I heard one of my discs being played. I stopped and looked around trying to find the source. It was a newspaper stand where, on the table among all the papers and magazines a cassette player was belting out my whistling and birdcalls. Rosemarie went up to the paper man, waited until the song finished and then asked the chap why he played this music.

'I like it,' he said, 'I'm always playing it.'

'Well,' answered Rosemarie, 'the fellow who whistles on your tape is standing just over there' and she pointed to me.

'Yes,' answered the man, 'really?' and carried on serving the other customers, not taking any notice of what she said.

It had been exactly 30 years since my first visit with Steffani to Australia and one of the most outstanding concerts which remained in my mind was the one arranged by Father Charles at the Sydney *Town Hall* in aid of funds for the erection of a Youth Centre in the city area. All of us artists gave our services for free and included Albert Fisher & the Tivoli Orchestra, John Coslanich, Angela Luppino, Arthur Bassett, Katherine McCormack, Elimar, Joseph Martinez, Clifford Guest, the Sydney Police Choir, Bill French, Vic Hyde, Mary Branagan, David Gray Buster Fiddess and me.

Immediately after the Sydney show we flew to New Zealand's capital, Wellington, where Roy had booked the *Town Hall* for my next show. I had a couple of very interesting days in the city. I was introduced to the inmates of Arohata Women's Prison, which turned out to be a very musical occasion as some brought their guitars and performed some beautiful Maori music for me and to say thank you for my taking time out to entertain them they had prepared a present in the form of greenstone cufflinks.

Another visit I made was to Kelburn School, where I met a group of blind children who, with the aid of their seeing hands, followed every movement of my fingers as I performed for them. One young boy, Gary Kreig, was particularly interested and asked if he could interview me at Wellington's *Radio Windy* station. I was fascinated by this youngster. They all knew him at the station and without further ado vacated one of the recording studios for his use. As we sat down to begin the taping of the interview he suddenly turned round in his chair and asked Roy Watterson, who had been standing silently behind him, to leave the room – he could handle the situation.

The next port of call was Christchurch. What a beautiful city. So very English with its amazing Botanical Gardens, its Cathedral and, of course, the Wizard giving his speeches in Cathedral Square. Again Roy Watterson had arranged for me to visit schools, the Coronation Hospital and radio stations. On one talkback programme, the call board lit up like a Christmas tree – I was told that I beat Cliff Richard – so many people wanted to speak to me. I saw the inside of every radio station between Christchurch and Dunedin, where I performed at the *Regent Theatre*. I also paid a visit to Dunedin's Police Station and their Men's Prison, entertaining the inmates. We had a great time and the only way the wardens could show their appreciation was to handcuff me and with much laughter put me behind bars. I suppose in a way they were already afraid of the practice whistling noises coming from the different cells after lights out.

On to Invercargill's *Civic Theatre*, then Christchurch *Town Hall* and Timaru *Theatre Royal,* award-winning 'Queen of the Banjo' Jenny Blackadder was one of the acts touring the South Island with us.

Every new place we saw in New Zealand, Rosemarie and I viewed with the eyes of a possible settler in that region, everywhere was so beautiful, we could not make up our minds.

We left New Zealand and flew to Brisbane, where my first Show was at *The Centre* on the Gold Coast and also featured Irish tenor Patrick O'Hagan. Then via Sydney to Melbourne's *Dallas Brooks Hall* and my last concert appearance was 13 March at the *Concert Hall* in Perth. Perth really brought back memories as I saw Phil Woods again, a dear, dear friend who was kind to me during my wartime stay in Peterborough's army quarters. I was thrilled to introduce her to my wife. We spent a glorious afternoon together with many of her family.

Immediately after my show finished and getting changed in my dressing room I heard a sudden commotion outside. Rosemarie opened the door to investigate only to be confronted by couple with the woman frantically waving what looked like a cutout newspaper article above her head. When she realised she was speaking to my wife her voice rose:

'You don't know how lucky you are!' And all the time she kept waving that piece of newspaper. Roy Watterson became a little perturbed and tried to close the dressing room. Eventually the purpose of her visit came to light. She was holding an English newspaper cutting from the 1950s, showing a photo of a bathing beauty being kissed by me, and this bathing beauty was none other than her.

At last a very successful tour had come to an end. I had made many new friends, in Australia and New Zealand, was interviewed right up to the last minute before my departure by Derryn Hinch and Bert Newton, and even managed to leave a few dollars behind in the Casino in Perth. I was eager to get back to the Isle of Man and see how the emigration visa to New Zealand had progressed. The moment we stepped off the plane, the family was all there, happy to see us again, but at the same time laughingly told us that we had to virtually turn round within a couple of days and fly off again, to Holland.

Jacqueline Sleeswijk, from *Joop van den Ende Productions*, wanted me to appear in the *De Henny Huisman Surprise Show*, filmed from the *Aalsmeer TV Studios*. The surprise was for a long-standing Dutch fan of mine, whose family had written in to the studios and told them of his once in a lifetime wish to whistle with me on stage. So Rosemarie and I were off again, to Amsterdam. We were asked to keep a low profile because of the surprise factor of the show. Very hush hush we were driven to the rehearsals, which were already in progress. A couple of the other entertainers had left their props on stage in readiness for the live evening's show. It was not long before I was called to have my run through with the music. The song requested was the 'Tritsch-Tratsch Polka' and to keep in time with my whistling to the fast moving music I was tapping with my foot on the wooden stage floor.

Alas my concentration was suddenly disrupted as my eyes fell on one of the so-called props. Lying on the floor next to a large wooden box, 'the prop' was opening and closing its eyes, looking at me, opening its mouth like a big yawn and showing all its teeth, then closing it again – help, this was a ginormous, live, fully grown, bloody crocodile!

Thank God my rehearsal was finished so without further ado I quickly walked off the stage and sat down next to the dance girls as the producer wanted to run through the animal act again.

This I just had to see.

They always say that elephants don't forget. Well, let me tell you, nor do crocodiles.

The animal trainer had taken the crocodile off its chain and commanded it to stay in the middle of the stage. Well the animal thought different; with one big swish of its tail it had turned, slid off the stage, across the rolling camera area and cables and heaved its heavy but agile body on to the steps that led to the auditorium where the girls and I were sitting. The girls exploded into what sounded like one big scream and tried to outrun each other to the exit doors. And me? At first I sat there mesmerised and then I did what I usually do in emergencies: think and think again, and then act. I was on my second 'think' when the crocodile reached my feet – that's when I fled. To this day I truly believe that the crocodile saw me as a juicy bit of bird while I was performing on stage and it didn't forget to go after its prey, again bringing back the meaning of whistling sensuality.

When we returned to the Isle of Man our long-awaited permission to emigrate to New Zealand had at last been granted and was duly celebrated.

It was then that I received a telephone call from Ada, Cyril's wife.

'Ronnie, you're one of the first to know, Cyril has died!'

My lifelong agent and friend had passed on.

Stage newspaper excerpts:

...Cyril Berlin born May 9 1906, died July 6 1988. On leaving school he entered showbusiness as a junior to the agent Manny Jay, progressing to become a road manager

to the late Sid Field and bandleader Jack Hylton. On declaration of war he joined the Royal Artillery... reaching the rank of Regimental Sergeant Major. On his demob he returned to Jack Hylton who gave him the sole booking of the 'Crazy Gang' shows... he formed an agency with Keith Devon, subsequently to join Hymie Zahl in April 1947. He formed his own agency Cyril Berlin (Associates) Ltd. and was asked to join the Grade Agency in April 1963... he was one of the founder members of London Management Ltd. He was responsible for guiding the careers of many talents including Arthur Askey, Jeannie Carson, Roy Castle, Lonnie Donegan, Diana Dors, Miki & Griff, Des O'Connor, Reg Varney, Ronnie Ronalde...

...His unique talents became a byword, 'Ask Cyril'...he was a gentle man, a true gentleman...'

I was shattered. A whole era of my life had gone. Rosemarie and I flew to London to attend Cyril's funeral and after the service, speaking with Des O'Connor I remembered when Cyril had taken me to *Shepherds Bush Empire* to see an up and coming star he had decided to add to his books, it was Des.

I stood there as one after the other, family, friends, agents and artistes left, until only Rosemarie and I remained. As I looked down at all the flowers and wreaths I felt as if Cyril was saying to me:

'Ronnie, there's nobody holding you here any more, go to New Zealand, go and be happy.'

The sun was shining brightly when I was greeted by Bob Kerridge at Auckland Airport; Bob first introduced me to New Zealand some years earlier. He gave my family and me so much help and guided us on our way. I quickly purchased a 12 acre property – so I don't annoy the neighbours with my daily whistling exercises – in Silverdale, north of Auckland and called it 'Whistler's Lodge' and of course we had to have a boat which I called 'Blackbird' and keep at nearby Gulf Harbour Marina on the Hibiscus Coast.

Our daughter Carolyn, who had married Lloyd Shipstone, a Yorkshireman has two sons, Samuel (13) and Nathan (11) stayed in the Isle of Man.

Our daughter Christina married a Guernseyman and they have three Kiwi born children, Stephanie (9), Richard (7) and Matthew (3) and our son Ronnie JR. married Therese Hookham from the Isle of Man who have a Kiwi born son, Christopher (2), live in New Zealand. Each one of the six grandchildren has its own joyous personality.

Since I have moved to New Zealand my theatrical life has been a constant juggle to find time from one event to the other.

It all started with the two sellout Aotea Centre concerts in Auckland, many newspaper and magazine interviews, (with Tony Potter statement: *'Ronnie Ronalde is the Pavarotti of Whistlers'*) radio and Television programmes, even from London. The BBC Radio 4 London's Fiona Cooper interviewed me via satellite for a whistling programme. Live radio call-ins from Sheffield, London and Great Yarmouth, Theatre engagements, concerts and tours in New Zealand and Australia.

The Prix de Monte Carlo – Roy Hudd's *Give a Little Whistle* programme brought forth the International jury comment of: *There has never been a programme in the history of Prix de Monte Carlo that has brought so much joy to the panel.* I was pleased that Roy Hudd let me be part of his success.

My latest Australian tour brought me again into the hands of theatrical accountant, whose name I will never forget, *Finikotis & Father Ltd.*

Robert Finikotis is a unique man, always trying to help and offering his guidance to the entertainment World fraternity. His friendship and advice I value greatly and it is always great fun to keep up with his whirlwind visits he periodically makes all over the world when he manages to fit in moments with his theatrical friends, accompanied by his wife Jenny and daughters Kirra and Tania.

It was also great to catch up with Johnny Lister again who came to visit me at Sydney's *Town Hall* dressingroom and we had a good laugh over past times in Great Yarmouth. Even the telephone kept ringing with calls from, Jack Neary, Mimi Law and Johnny Lockwood who is fully praised in Roy Hudd's recent book 'Cavalcade of Variety'. It was good to see that I was on the cover of his book together with Gracie fields, Joe Church, Frankie Vaughan and Max Miller.

One sunny Sunday morning Phil Warren, during his Radio Pacific *Open Country* announced, for all New Zealand to hear, that he is going to bring a surprise guest for lunch to my house that very day.

True to his word, in they drove, Mr. Showbiz, Philip Warren CBE with his wife Pat and with them, their surprise, was none other than Bill Roberton, UK Agent and Producer, brother of Jack Douglas who partnered Des O'Connor in his early successes. Bill had produced many shows I had been in and I had worked with Jack numerous times. Over lunch we reminisced and spoke with affection of one of UK's gentleman of showbusiness, his father, John D. Roberton. Phil and Bill hatched a plan to put me on the *Barrymore* show, which was filmed in the autumn of 1995 in London. It was fun reminiscing with Spike Milligan on the same show, we could go back 60 years. I also caught up with Norman Wisdom who had been a neighbour of mine in the Isle of Man for many years.

For two years I was seen in the New Zealand TV commercial produced by Saatchi & Saatchi for Huntley & Palmers Griffins Biscuits playing the whistling character of Sharpie Benz.

Then Reg Coles, a fellow whistler from Britain, visited me. Reg is also a member of the Magic Circle and he was most interested to hear my stories about magicians. I wish he could put some magic over the greyhound which a consortium has named after me, he might start to win some races!

Another regular visitor to my home is entertainer Billy Moore and his wife Ena during their yearly trips to New Zealand. That's when I catch up with all the latest news of the theatre world in Britain.

I was also invited to the Wellington *Town Hall* as a surprise guest star at the 75th Rotary Dinner arranged by radio personality Hewitt Humphrey, in attendance was Governor-General Sir Michael Hardie Boys and at the Sheraton Auckland I performed at the Humanitarian Awards Dinner given in honour of Sir Edmund Hillary during the 1997 International Variety Club Convention.

As members of the New Zealand Variety Club Rosemarie and I travelled to the Las Vegas – and the Toronto International Variety Club Conventions where I was proud to be called on stage by Tony Hatch, International Variety Club President, to accept on behalf of New Zealand's Tent the 'Sunshine Coach Award'. This trophy was most precious to me, as it brought back so many memories of one time Agent and friend Leslie Macdonnell CBE who had been a partner of my theatrical Agency in London, the Fosters Agency. He had taken great interest in my future and the deep thinker he was, gave me the advice not to sign any contract offered by the Syndicate who had signed up Sinatra.

His involvement with the British Variety Club and again, after visiting an eight year old incurably ill girl who had never been out of Queen Mary's Hospital in Surrey, his deep thinking of how to help brought forth this idea of specially designed and equipped coaches to carry these unfortunate youngsters out into some sunshine. He became quite obsessed with this idea and the 'Sunshine Coach Programme' was eventually born with the result that today over 8000 of these 'coaches' are now operated all over the world, allowing children with special needs to be conveyed to many places of interest and enjoyment, he had made 'Variety' work to lighten the burden of so much suffering.

Attending another Charity dinner I was speaking with Joan Collins and I reminded her that her late father agent Joe Collins once wrote to me, specifying:

'Anything I can do for you Ronnie, just say!'

So I asked her for her room number!!!

Louisburg North Carolina gave me the greatest satisfaction where Allen deHart had organised the presentation by Louisburg Mayor Lucy T. Allen of the *Whistlers Hall of Fame Award*, their highest to an Artiste of International Distinction and Merit, during their 22nd Whistlers' Convention to me. A replica of the award is kept in the 'Whistlers Hall of Fame Museum' in Louisburg North Carolina, USA.

Neil Finn wrote 'Try Whistling This' and as Neil can't whistle enterprising promoter Ian Magan booked me to whistle on stage while Neil sang. The date of this concert was the 29th of June, my 75th Birthday. It was great! And great to see the young audiences on their feet for my 'Tritsch Tratsch Polka'.

Nostalgia is also popular shown by 1998 *'Evergreen's* cassette called

Ronnie Ronalde: THE WHISTLING YODELLER

and the *EMI* release of a CD and cassette called:

Around The World On A Whistle

which has reached GOLD status and I received EMI's framed GOLD Disc.

1999 – EMI is compiling **'Around The World On A Whistle Vol 2'** featuring more of my past hits.

...*Ronnie Ronalde on National Radio with Brian Edwards was sheer delight...* and the *Listener* carried an article written by Steve Braunias:

...*Pass out the radio awards now. Jim Sutton's recent nostalgia show on Newstalk ZB featuring special guest Ronnie Ronalde, was an absolute classic. The legendary music-hall whistler was celebrating his 60th year in showbiz – and it felt as if the whole of old New Zealand called to say "I love you"...But it was the music of course, that came first... Panis Angelicus... an amazing piece of music – the whistling was so weird and haunting, so unnatural and beautiful, it sounded like that amazing instrument called the theremin. Pure sound. Great show.*

The GOLD Disc and Whistlers Award and trophy have pride of place in my home as it is an official acknowledgement of my art which I have been able to bring to people all over the world since my first professional engagement in the theatre 60 years ago and able to work every year without fail in my chosen profession and loved and still loving every minute of it.

I have already been invited to the Millennium Whistling Musical Championship at the Francis Winspear Centre, Edmonton, Alberta in Canada to whistle into the year of 2000.

Going... going... gone

Neill Finn gets his Gold

Roy Castle

With Phil Warren & theatrical agent
Bill Robertson (brother of Jack Douglas)

Tony Hatch

Joan Collins

'Mr Nasty' – Clifford Davis

Louisbourg Whistlers' Convention, 1996

Still 'in to' boats

Ooops!

With our children in Guernsey, 1985

*...and grandchildren
in New Zealand, 1998*

Nathan & Samuel

Stephanie & Richard

Matthew & Christopher

EPILOGE

George Bernard Shaw wrote in 1936 that if he could show his true feelings he would have cried *New Zealand, is the best country I have been in.*

'London Times' columnist Bernard Levin wrote that *'everytime I close my eyes I think of what I saw among the New Zealand Hills, I am overwhelmed by its beauty, the likes I have never seen before and will never see again unless I go back to New Zealand'*

British writer Rudyard Kipling and American writer James Michener wrote about the most beautiful country in the world.

Irish born, New Zealand citizen Sam McCready the creator of beautiful roses, said: *I can think of nothing worse than living in one country and having loyalties to another.*

Ronnie Ronalde and his Austrian born wife Rosemarie became naturalised New Zealanders in September 1995.

> *The flowers appear on the earth;*
> *The time of the singing of birds is come*
> *Song of Solomon 2:12*

Silver Songsters Names

Atkinson, Alexander, Arnott
Bryson, Bounds, Burze, Bohanna, Brown, Birch, Burnet, Banks, Burnett, Bramley, Biss, Bartholomew
Callaghan, Coles, Carroll, Chilcott Bros., Crosby, Conway, Cox Twins
Dockerty, Davies, Denton, Davis, Dennis, Dixon, Donnelly, Davey, Daubney, Dunn, Drewe, Doucas, Day, Dutton, Dennis
Evans, Emerson, Eldridge
Fenny, Fitzpatrick, Ford, Farrer, Forster, Fry, Fraser
Graham, Geraint, Geof, Gelder, Gower, Glan, Gutteridge, Gatt
Henshaw, Hargreaves, Hutin Bros., Higgans, Heansman, Helland, Hibbutt, Hyland, Harper, Humphries, Higgins, Hyland, Hagen, Hughes, Harrison, Haygreaves, Holliday, Humphys, Hassan, Haydn, Hopkins, Hill, Hope, Harvey
Illsley
Jennings, Jackson, Jenkins, Jones, James
Kelly, Kemp
Taylor, Tucker, Thomson, Thomas, Thompson
Laud, Leslie, Lewis
Marshall, Mills, Morton, Morrison, Moris, More, Maldwyn, Morris, Murphy
Newman
O'Hagan, O'Grady
Procter, Paton, Phillips, Purnell
Roulston
Reynolds, Ridding, Ramsell, Roy
Sewell, Smith, Sinnett, Spargo, Stanley, Shepherd, Scot, Sweeney, Stephens, Sinnott
Williams, Woods, Wingate, Ward, Whitehead, Wall, Walker, Watson, Wooding, Wingate, Wilson, Wakeley, Warren, Walsh, Wilkinson, Waters, Webb, Walton, Watkin
VivianYoung, Yarr, Yare

A RECORD ROMANCE

By Christine Eldrett, my personal Secretary. Based upon the first 44 Song Titles recorded by RONNIE RONALDE on 'Columbia', EMI.

When I was **SWEET SIXTEEN** I said to myself **I WANT TO MAKE MY MOTHER PROUD OF ME** but to achieve this I was obliged to **LEAVE MY HEART IN AN ENGLISH COUNTRY GARDEN**, where I always listened to the **SONG OF THE THRUSH** and the **NIGHTINGALE SONG** and where I dreamed my **DREAMS OF OLWEN**, the girl I thought one day to marry.

LO HEAR THE GENTLE LARK, it is time I was climbing **MOCKING BIRD HILL**, so off I went **ON WINGS OF SONG** thinking, how much quicker I could travel **IF I WERE A BALCKBIRD**, and in the distance I heard the **BELLS ACROSS THE MEADOW**. That day I travelled over the sea, walked **DOWN THE OLD ZYDER ZEE** where I found it was **CHRISTMAS IN THE VILLAGE** and where, to my surprise, the band was playing **THE SKATERS WALTZ** and not the **WINDMILL SONGS** as I had expected.

I continued my journey and whilst dancing the **TRITSCH TRATSCH POLKA**, I suddenly found **MY ROMANCE IN VIENNA,** for it was here that I met my **ROSE OF THE MOUNTAIN** and loved her **WITH ALL MY HEART**. At the end of the dance we sang **AULD LANG SYNE FOREVER**, she called me her **WHISTLING YODELLER** and I promised to **FORGET ME NOT**, but alas she left me a **LONELY LITTLE ROBIN**, whistling **IL BACIO, DOWN THE TRAIL OF ACHING HEARTS**. I went along sadly, past the **SOLDIERS IN THE PARK**, to a place **WHERE THE SWEETHEART ROSES GROW**, but all I could think of was how **I MISS MY SWISS MISS**. Still, it will soon be **SPRINGTIME** and I hope they'll **LET ME SING IN ECHO VALLEY** again **WHEN THE FIELDS ARE WHITE WITH DASIES**, **BECAUSE** then I will see **MARIANDL**, leaning on the arm of **GRANDFATHER KRINGLE**, wearing her **GRANDMOTHER'S WEDDING DRESS**, making their way to **THE LITTLE OLD CHURCH ON THE HILL.**

Spring fades… then summer… and now **AUTUMN EVENSONG**. I said a quiet **PRAYER IN THE TWILIGHT** and to the strains of **LARGO** I walked **IN A MONASTERY GARDEN** the very **SANCTUARY OF THE HEART. I BELIEVE** that the **STARS ARE THE WINDOWS OF HEAVEN** and maybe they will hear my **SONG OF THE MOUNTAINS** and guide my lover back to me.

Continued in New Zealand in 1996 by my wife Rosemarie, with more of my Decca and EMI recordings:

WHEN YOU ARE IN LOVE you feel you are **SOMEWHERE BEYOND THE STARS** and when you walk **DOWN THE FOREST** you can hear the **BIRDSONG AT EVENTIDE** and as the little **YODELLING BOY** hurried through the woods he heard **THE ANGELS SING** the **STARLIGHT LULLABYE** and **AVE MARIA** to guide him on his **HAPPY TRAILS**.

At last **SAFE IN THE HARBOUR** and ON THE QUARTER DECK he listened to the **MACNAMARA BAND** playing the **YARMOUTH SONG**. The little **HAPPY WHISTLER WE'LL ALWAYS REMEMBER** playing **ROBIN HOOD** and **DAVEY CROCKET** at school but since he met the **LADY FROM LUXEMBOURG** and **the LADY OF LUCERNE** on board his ship the **SKYEBOAT SONG** who taught him the **YODELLING WALTZ** he became **a BEAUTIFUL DREAMER** thinking, whilst he was listening to the **EVENING CHIMES** if he could fly this **CHRISTMAS TIDE** to his lost love **MIRABELLE**. Her **HAIR OF GOLD** she would wash in the **SWEETWATER MOUNTAIN** brook as **A BIRD SINGS** from the top of a tree with all the other little feathered **INNOCENT SINNERS** watching her dance to the **DANISH RHAPSODY** whilst the **BUCCANEERS** and **MOUNTAIN CLIMBERS** tried to have **CHRISTMAS AT HOME** so they could play their **PARTY RHYMES**.

Picking up the **YODELLING RAG** to wipe his tears, dreaming of **CHRISTMAS IN ENGLAND**, the young boy was told by the **PLEASANT PEASANT** the **STORY OF CHRISTMAS** and he remembered the **LITTLE SWISS MAID** when he was a **LONELY GOATHERD** picking **EDELWEISS** and dancing the **ALPINE POLKA** with her.

When **THE WORLD IS WAITING FOR THE SUNRISE** and the **MORNING STAR** is fading, **LOVES OLD SWEET SONG** of **IF YOU WERE THE ONLY GIRL IN THE WORLD** is not a **MISTAKE**. It would be **A SIN TO TELL A LIE** when one is asked **HAVE YOU EVER BEEN LONELY?**

WHO'S SORRY NOW when we walked **TIP TOE THROUGH THE TULIPS** and he was thinking of his new love **CHARMAINE** with **FASCINATION** and his heart was throbbing with the rhythm to the **BIRTH OF THE BLUES,** begging her to **HOLD ME IN YOUR ARMS.**

Every year **THE GOOD OLD CHRISTMAS DAY** with all its **JINGLE BELLS** and **LITTLE WHITE BERRY** soon succumbed to **WHEN ITS SPRINGTIME IN THE ROCKIES, RAMBLIN ROSES** grew **SOUTH OF THE BORDER, SEA SHELLS** were gathered on the shore and girls danced to the **CAN CAN** before **AUTUMN LEAVES** once again whispered **BYE BYE BLACKBIRD.**

IF THOSE LIPS COULD ONLY SPEAK of the **SILVER THREADS AMONG THE GOLD** as the by now grown up man looked up to the **WANDERING STAR** through the **UMBRELLA MAN'S** canopy of **GREENSLEEVES** while he was resting once again. He dreamed they were **ROMEO AND JULIET, SOMEWHERE MY LOVE, MY MEMORIES OF YOU** tell me in my **LIEBESTRAUM** that I am walking like **AIR ON A G STRING**, gentle breeze is full of **PLAISIER** D'AMOUR. YO-TE-AMO forever and ever **let PANIS ANGELICUS** always protect you.
He looked around his friends and bade them **GOD REST YE MERRY GENTLEMEN** as the **SILENT NIGHT** drew to its close. He knew that once in **ROYAL DAVID'S CITY BRAHMS LULLABYE** was sung by the angels. **SLEEP HOLY BABE** so far **AWAY IN THE MANGER**.

He had been told by the monks to **BRING IN THE HOLLY BROUGH** for his **FIRST NOEL**, a **WHITE CHRISTMAS** and doing so he quietly whistled **OH COME ALL YE FAITHFUL**. He hoped that God would **HEAR MY PRAYER**, which he sent to him **OH FOR THE WINGS OF DOVE** every night as his Mother had taught him to **NEVER BREAK A PROMIS**.

He had fought **A DAY IN THE NAVY** and after they came **ALL ASHORE** many **A DAY IN THE ARMY**, clad in armor like the tinman in **THE WIZARD OF OZ** which made him feel the size of the giant in **GULLIVER'S TRAVEL**, whistling the **PENNY SERENADE** during his many gallops on his horse, **RIDE TENDERFOOT RIDE**, hurry I want to find my **CINDERELLA**.

God **BLESS THIS HOUSE** and this wonderful world of ours.

Albert Burdon

Anne Shelton

Arthur Worsley

Variety Club breakfast

Enjoying a 'bash'

Bert Weedon

Beryl Reid

Robert Farnon

Charles Trenet

Charlie Kunz

The Idol of Radio Millions
HENRY HALL AND HIS ORCHESTRA
with
BETTY DRIVER

INTERVAL

LILIAN KEYES
Charming Singer of Charming Songs

Listen to the Lightning fingers of
REUB SILVER & MARION DAY

Britains Premier Light Comedian
RANDOLPH SUTTON
at the piano: Eric Fowler

GERALDINE O'BRIAN
Ballad Singer

STEFFANI and his 30 SILVER SONGSTERS
Variety's Greatest Emotional Experience
— ◇◇◇ —

Cliff Richard

Daisy May & Co

David Whitfield

Duggie Wakefield

Ernie & Marcheta

Edna Savage

Fan Virginia de Cruz

Ferry Forst, illusionist

Frank Formby

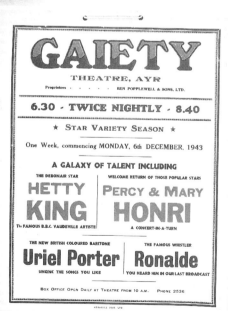

Frankie Laine

Hewitt Humphrey

Jimmie James

Jack Sherwin

Trumpeter John Lister

Variety Club Convention, Las Vegas, with Pam Fauvell, Philip Leishman, Joneen Smith and Wayne Adsett

Ken Dodd

Lester Ferguson

Lonnie Starr, Station WNEW, New York

I, the Lord Chamberlain of The Queen's Household for the time being, do by virtue of my Office and in pursuance of powers given to me by the Act of Parliament for regulating Theatres, 6 & 7 Victoria, Cap. 68, Section 12. Allow the Performance of a new Stage Play, of which a copy has been submitted to me by you, being a ~~revue~~ in 2 Acts, entitled

"The Ronnie Ronalde Show"

with the exception of all Words and Passages which are specified in the endorsement of this Licence and without any further variations whatsoever.

Given under my hand this 14th day of July 1959

Scarbrough

Lord Chamberlain.

To The Manager of the Garrick Theatre, Southport.

T38.

Mike Craig, producer & writer

Naughton & Gold (Crazy Gang)

Peter Sellers

Paul Kohler

ROYAL HIPPODROME

PHONE — 995   DOVER.   PHONE — 995

● — WEEK COMMENCING MONDAY, NOVEMBER 27th, 1939 — ●
CONTINUOUS from 6.0 to 9.55.

— COLOSSAL VARIETY ATTRACTION —

THOSE FAMOUS WELSH BOY SINGERS

STEFFANI
AND
HIS SILVE
SONGSTER

EDDIE BARTHOLOMEW
Cousin of FREDDIE BARTHOLOMEW
RON WARREN
The World's Greatest Boy Whist

WINSOR & WILTON
DON'T TAKE THEM SERIOUSLY.

| THE DEL RIOS | JACK NOLAN | HENRY D. ADA |
| WESTERN PASTIMES. | THE CHEERFUL JESTER. | THE JUGGLING FOOL |

THE HELENA TRIO
BEAUTY, GRACE and STRENGTH.

— Until Further Notice the Booking of Seats will be suspended —
PRICES: Box Seats 2/6; Stalls 2/-, 1/6, 1/3, 1/-; Circle 1/6, 1/3, 1/-; 9d.; Balcony 6d.

SHAKESPEARE
THEATRE OF
VARIETIES

6.0	Where the Best People see the Best Shows	8.0
	TWICE NIGHTLY	
	Week commencing MONDAY, NOV. 27th, 1944	

STEFFANI and HARRY DRURY present their Spectacular Revue Attraction

SHOWTIME
IN FIFTEEN GLORIOUS SCENES - With All Star Cast of Fifty Star Artistes

ROY LESTER   HI-YA, PALS!

Variety's Greatest Emotional Experience   THE "TANK" AND THE LITTLE "JEEP"

STEFFANI AND HIS   JONES & THOMAS
The World's Most Glamorous Whistling Personality

30 SILVER SONGSTERS   RONALDE
ALL THE "BIRDS" COME TO HEAR HIM

The Famous Radio, Recording and Film Stars
THE ACT WHICH GLORIFIES THIS STAGE

JACK CRANSTON	BERT COLLINS	HARRY MILLS
CHARLES FORD	GORDON LAUD	John JACKSON
		John CUMMINGS

| 10 TILLER GIRLS | THE VIVACIOUS PERSONALITY PEGGY STAMULA | THOSE THRILLING DANCERS PETRO AND PETROVA |

THE SHAKESPEARE GRAND ORCHESTRA under the direction of W. H. SYDNEY-JONES
FOR PRICES SEE DAYBILLS

BOX OFFICE OPEN   TELEPHONES: NORTH 0036 & 0037
at 10 a.m. to 11 p.m.

Sandy Powell

Teeth

... and the answer, my friend, is blowin' in the wind

Taking it to...
Variety Club
Breakfast

Celebs give schoolchildren in
Otara a great start to the day.
Glen Brown took the photos

Austin motorshow

COMPLETE CHANGE OF PROGRAMME EACH WEEK ! ! | SOME OF THE STARS AND SCENES IN THESE GREAT FAMILY PRODUCTIONS ::

BILLY WHITTAKER

THE TWO REXANOS

MIMI LAW

THE JACKDAW OF RHEIMS

RONNIE RONALDE

THE SWISS SCENE

BOB ANDREWS

BRANDON & HILLIARD

HELEN TURNER

● SEEN BY OVER 200,000 PEOPLE IN GREAT YARMOUTH ●

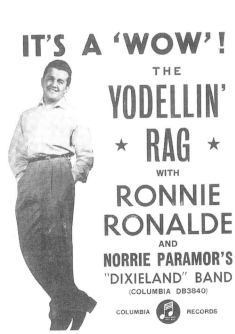

Cyril Berlin, Lawrence Wright, Ronnie & Steff

Radio City Music Hall, Rockefeller Centre, New York

Joy Turpin

Harry Secombe

Norrie Paramour

Edith Piaf

304